BRIDGE OF WAVES

Also by W. A. Mathieu

*Harmonic Experience: Tonal Harmony from Its
Natural Origins to Its Modern Expression*

The Listening Book: Discovering Your Own Music

The Musical Life: Reflections on What It Is and How to Live It

BRIDGE of WAVES

What Music Is
and
How Listening to It
Changes the World

W. A. MATHIEU

SHAMBHALA
Boulder
2010

Shambhala Publications, Inc.
4720 Walnut Street
Boulder, Colorado 80301
www.shambhala.com

9 8 7 6 5 4 3

Printed in the United States of America

♾ This edition is printed on acid-free paper that meets the
American National Standards Institute Z39.48 Standard.

♻ Shambhala Publications makes every effort to print on recycled paper.
For more information please visit www.shambhala.com.

Distributed in the United States by Penguin Random House LLC
and in Canada by Random House of Canada Ltd

Interior design and composition by Greta D. Sibley & Associates

Library of Congress Cataloging-in-Publication Data
Mathieu, W. A.
Bridge of waves: what music is and how listening to it
changes the world / W. A. Mathieu.—1st ed.
p.   cm.
Includes bibliographical references.
ISBN 978-1-59030-732-8 (pbk.: alk. paper)
1. Music—Philosophy and aesthetics. 2. Listening. I. Title.
ML3800.M2473 2010
781'.1—dc22
2010022473

Where there is listening there is love.

Contents

There is a musical dynamic between the cognitive and intuitive in music, intellect and intuition. The wordless language of music integrates the territories of the mind and the heart.

There are parallels between the rules of music and the codes of daily life. The give-and-take of music is a model of harmonious living.

Music can be heard as representing a story outside of the music, or as a listener's personal narrative, as a biography of the composer, or as ritual, as cultural history, as the story of humankind, of all life, or purely as the story of itself.

In revealing ways, music and life reflect one another in our minds, our behaviors, our evolution, and our cosmologies.

On the path toward wholeness, music transcends the paradoxes of the cognitive mind, facilitates the co-arising of the relative and absolute, and guides us toward our ideal.

9. *The Enlightened Listener*   *209*

As proactive listeners we can become more aware of the consumer's role, and reclaim music as personal core experience. Learning to practice and compose is a way of learning one's own self.

10. *Living the Waves*   *245*

The vibrational states of music connect a universe of waves and are ultimately a guide to being-in-itself. Some of the metaphors we have used for the connective and expansive powers of music are reexamined.

End Papers

One Hundred Ways to Listen to Music   *259*

Some of the practices and ideas discussed throughout the book are summarized and embellished.

BRIDGE OF WAVES

Introduction

A Report from the Piano Bench

Mid-concert. Small town, small hall, wood walls, two hundred listeners. The Steinway is old, trustworthy, very black. I'm about to improvise a piece—eight, maybe ten minutes long. I have to start someplace right now. In my head a note arrives and simultaneously I see it on the keyboard in front of me. It's the black one in the middle of a group of three black ones just even with my extended right arm. I reach out and press that one down. Instantly I feel the percussion of the hammer against the string. Then, as a familiar sky lights up in my skull, the tone extends into a gold ribbon leading to an inner horizon where an ocean of the waves called music begins to surge in all directions.

Where has that first note come from?

From childhood I've had a stubborn fascination with the ground of being, the perception of being-as-itself, the pure sensibility given to us prior to reason. I have memories of mere standing in a field or in a garden, silent in nameless being. From the height of a four-year-old eye I see patterns of dew on new grass, fluorescing moss spores, exotic-colored boots lined up in the nursery school cloakroom, a red-coated woman just beyond the window, sun through windless maple leaves. Various as these memories are, there is a constant sense of no beginning, no ending, only completion.

I grew to my majority learning to name everything in sight, like Adam at the Lord's bidding: *ox, field, thigh*. The mind does love to name, but as a boy I was never told, and I did not come to realize until much later, how names occlude direct experience in the act of describing it. I never knew I'd left the garden.

As a six-year-old musician, I learned *middle C, major triad*, and eventually *oblique motion, legato touch*. As I grew, I did fortunately begin to recognize that naming something is different from hearing it, just as surely as reading the menu is not eating the dinner. Though I wish I'd had more guidance, I did gradually learn that there is a time for the name and a time for the nameless. In my twenties I began to realize how deeply musicians train to keep nameless knowing paramount, while maintaining fidelity to the mind-play implicit in music making. Since I'm a teacher and a writer as well as a composer of written music, I have learned to name just about anything nameable in music; at the same time I've had to develop strategies for dwelling long and clear in the nameless intuitive.

Back to the concert. It turns out that first note I play (which is about to let loose thousands more) is named G-sharp, although I know this only later, in hindsight. At the moment I play the G-sharp, I know its name only in the way we know the spelling of words as we speak them.

Ultimately the named and the nameless co-arise; they are inseparably braided, not unlike speaking and writing. One learns devotion to a life of braiding the named and the nameless. The lessons I've learned in this braiding work hold true for music, and I've learned them first and foremost as a musician. And, as has become evident to me only over many decades, they hold true for daily life as well. The way music's lessons and life's lessons modulate one another have become the substance of my life, and the focus of this book.

So now back to the question. Where has this G-sharp come from? Somehow, even as I play the G-sharp, I know it has come from a hidden part of myself, the same part that has come from the very first sound ever made. My note is a direct descendent of The Word that In the Beginning There Was. My note is a remnant of the Big Bang, just as surely as the cosmic microwave background is its far earlier descendant. Every vibration that ever has existed has gone into producing my G-sharp, and my G-sharp is going to be part of every vibration that happens after I'm finished with it.

Another question, a most perplexing one: What is this tone that we are listening to? It is nothing. A musical tone has no substance. It is motion through time—but motion of what? The tone that began as a notion in my mind went through the muscles in my arm to a black key that operated a series of levers resulting in a felt hammer striking a taut string that agitated the room's air in a pattern of waves that found our eardrums and traveled thence through skin and bone to a hidden liquid which, rippling like a pond in rain, cajoled teeny hair cells growing like reeds in rivers to transform the sodium ions in their roots into a train of electrical pulses that split apart and regrouped like startled birds and became at last our consciousness of something we can call G-sharp, but which actually has no name complete enough to honor its power.

And the life of that G-sharp didn't stop after it was "over." It let loose a stream of notes that had been waiting impatiently for the sluices to open, a stream begun in past ideas and actions and now racing in a sudden flood toward future oceans. Maybe every action we make does that, but every action is not G-sharp—*this* G-sharp—that I can isolate in space and in time, a G-sharp that feels clear and right, and connects my inside self with yours, and with the other selves listening in the room, and with the selves we will touch when we leave the room.

We could ask more questions. Why am I doing such a thing as performing an improvisation on a piano? I have a quick answer. I need to know who I am, and this is my most complete way of knowing. And as for why are you listening? You need something as well, some connective beauty we all seem to be longing for.

Now the piece is over. In the quiet moment before applause, the sense of community is palpable. We've been connected, but not necessarily in the same ways to the same places. If there is anything we can hold onto in music it is perhaps this quiet, infinite instant when we can inhabit our collective body. In myriad ways, energies have been bridged. The waves have done their special work.

———

This book primarily is about open, intentional listening, how to practice it, and what to expect from it. Because music is both embodied and free-flowing energy, it has the capacity to connect thing to thing, body to body, mind to mind, heart to heart, and spirit to spirit. Neither heaven nor earth, it is the middle way, a wave bridge between nameable and nameless, between relative and absolute, thinking and feeling, the grammar of language and the cadences of the sea. It weaves the world together in an energetic web. You can be anywhere in the weave you want—all you have to do to get there is to listen for it.

I think a wave is what energy is made of and a bridge is where you stomp your feet. The music bridge is made of energy but it lives in the substance of my body and feels as substantial as anything in life ever feels. In *Bridge of Waves* I'd like you to appreciate energetic and corporeal terms at once, "with your head in the clouds and your feet on the ground," as the saying goes. I describe how this bridge made of waves behaves, where it goes, and how to use it to get where you're going.

Unfootnotes

Half my heart belongs in school, but I'm not an academic, and cannot speak or write academese except under duress. I know scholars who thrive on the ongoing nourishment of footnotes but, for me, the little numbers freeze my eyes and skid my mind. Usually I read all the footnotes first, but then again I'm the sort who begins to look at a book from back to front. Just in case there happens to come a time when I've forgotten that I'm the author of *Bridge of Waves,* and I pick it up thinking it might be an interesting read, I've got myself covered: I've tried to make the book just as interesting in either direction.

The other half of this is that, as an author, I often want to impart parenthetical commentary without unsettling the rhythm of the main text. Also, like most authors, I want to honor whenever possible the anecdotal, conversational, and printed sources of my ideas. So what to do? For this book, I've decided on the symbol ✒ in the margin of the text to guide the reader, at his or her discretion, to the appropriate pages in *Sources, Notes, and Commentary* at the end of the book, just in case he or she hasn't gotten there first.

PART ONE

~

The Music in Here . . .

I

Music as Body

It is probably impossible to say where music stops and the rest of the world begins, if there is a rest of the world. *Music* is a noun like *love* or *sanity*, with a hard core and fuzzy boundaries. Some people hear music in a waterfall, others tell their kids to turn down the noise. Yet whatever music is, most everyone has a personal, often intimate relationship with it.

This book, concerned primarily with wordless music, will define music broadly, freely including all styles, all cultures, all history, and go even beyond that by focusing on your own responses to what you hear *as* music. Let's say that you recognize music when you hear it precisely *because* you have a certain kind of response, the kind you might call a musical response. Your musical responses, not mine, not anyone else's, are the subject of this book.

There is no need right now — or maybe ever — to try to pin down and describe any particular response. The intention here is rather for you to grow to appreciate more deeply the qualities of your own responses, whatever they are and however you feel them. I want you to experience your responses fully and, through the process of sifting and sorting them, perhaps to savor them even more.

IN HERE

The place to start is your body. This is at once the simplest and most complex thing to do. You know you have one, but to appreciate that, especially while responding to music, is not always an obvious thing. People not musically trained only too easily assume that music is something going on *out there,* something that happens elsewhere and that others do, rather than something *in here* that I do. If I'm not a trained and gifted music maker, I had best leave the music making to the trained and gifted—it's something for them to do over *there* and a thing for me to consume over *here.* Not only to consume, but to own, just like I own all these silver discs, and this neat pod-thing in my hand. I can carry around thousands of things on my personal machine, but a thing on my machine is not a dimension of my body.

In closely knit tribal societies, music and dance were primary modes of social communion. Today we can listen to recordings of African forest villages still vibrantly alive with singing. Just as with the animal calls and natural sounds of the forest itself, there were, long ago, no musicians and no name for music, only the sound of daily life lived over lifetimes passing in that village in that forest. But in today's villages of the contemporary world, music has largely become, for most of us, a commodity made for mass consumption and manufactured by specialists. We don't make music, we buy it. Even the air guitar kids, who formed their own bands because everyone had a band, grew up to become old guys in the audience listening to The Stones and The Boss. When the resonances of music are experienced as traveling from *out there* to *in here,* we become estranged from the rhythmic and harmonic states that arise naturally from our own bodies. One of the hard truths of my own American life is

4

that it's been decades since I've heard "Happy Birthday" sung in a restaurant in tune. What has happened to us?

Not to paint too dark a canvas—in a great variety of ways, many people do participate in music making. And our culture still knows how to dance, which gets us closer in a certain way. But overall, we know better how to consume music than how to physically participate in the making of it, and the trend of specialization continues. So as an individual in a society remarkably cut off from its own music-making body, how does one go about making the body connection?

Gravity

Gravity is the first answer. Gravity is an attractive force; you are alive in a field of desire. The earth wants you, and you want it. But does a fish know it's in water? Weighty Reader, feel your weight right now, as you read. Pick up an arm an inch and let it fall deadweight: *womp*. The earth is pulling your arm and your arm is pulling the earth, that's the deal between mass and mass, a marriage contract. Try a leg: *womp*. Become aware of your whole body resting down like ocean water in its bed.

Your mass is innate to your being, and every aspect of your body's form has been shaped by the attractive force drawing your mass and the earth's mass toward one another—love in its simplest form. Yet as in any love relationship, one has to learn to be separate as well as conjoined, so you know also how to lift your arms and legs, to rise up against the pull of the earth. Your body rises up and falls down. When you pick up your arm and let it fall, you can sense how it has evolved to navigate the gravitational field, and thus to further life's purposes. This is the quintessential experience of walking. When you walk consciously in tune with gravity and your body's innate responses to it, you tend to walk most easily and efficiently, like a marriage going well.

Gravity is a plumb line between the center of the earth and

the center of your body, the two primary cardinal points of your spatial compass. Yet moving about in the gravitational field is such a common experience, it is easy to forget this. When you become deeply engaged with words, for instance, you forget that words don't weigh anything, they don't go *womp*. Ideas don't go *womp*. Athletes, however, can never for an instant forget about gravity, nor can dancers, nor can musicians. The moment a musician loses gravity, the music flies apart.

Music helps you realize gravity in a special way. Low-pitched music—basses, tubas, trombones, tympani—remind us of big, heavy things, which move more slowly than little, light things. A long, thick piano string vibrates more slowly than a short, thin one. We recognize slower vibration as lower and faster vibration as higher. Our experience further tells us that big things are heavy and small things are light. A big, low-sounding tuba weighs a lot more than a high-sounding piccolo. So when we hear a relatively slow-frequency sound (say 65 cycles per second, a tuba's nice fat low C), we *interpret* as low and *infer* big/heavy. When we hear a relatively fast-frequency sound (say a thousand cycles per second, near a flute's high C), we *interpret* as high and *infer* small/light. Although the neurons in your inner ear are indeed responding to the flute and the tuba by firing with relatively greater or lesser frequency, there is nothing *physical* in the act of hearing itself that is in a higher or lower location. So why do we interpret the location of the flute sound as high and the tuba sound as low?

The Mind Maps the Body

Low-big-heavy and *high-small-light* are metaphors for what we are hearing. Even though a low sound doesn't weigh more than a high one, our life experience as a body navigating within earth's gravitational field has given us an ability to construct this map of reality in our minds. No one knows completely how this works, although the fields of cognitive psychology, neurobiology, and psychoacoustics focus their research through their own particular lenses on aspects of the question. Bodily response to a certain quality of sound is called *embodied cognition*—a way of saying that our minds map what we hear onto our bodies in specific ways. This is a powerful idea, and the fact that music is an atlas of such maps makes music a primary area for research into how our minds and our bodies are hooked up.

When you recognize the bass as down and the treble as up you are doing your own research into music's mysterious power. You might not solve the mystery, but there will be more mystery to appreciate. When you feel your gut respond to a funky bass line, or you shape a lovely melody with your hands, or lift your eyes upward to a soaring violin, this is your private embodied-cognition research. When you notice how your feet seek the floor on the low drum sounds of downbeats (*boom*), and your body rises against gravity on the high cymbal sounds of upbeats (*chick*), you are doing *boom-chick* research—unfunded, perhaps, but no less authentic. How do music, gravity, and human body all become one fluid thing? You yourself are the researcher, and this is your noble science.

Occasionally music tries to cut itself loose from gravity by musical means: it rises and hovers, the strings and woodwinds soar, *womps* and *booms* disappear, no limbs fall, there is only angelic floating, then more rising until we are disoriented and, perhaps, exhilarated. But how long can we survive cut off from the forces that formed us? (Is this why we're fascinated by space travel?) Pretty soon we'll need to call home, and a deep drum and a lush cello and will bring us back to earth.

It is interesting to notice that Western music notation follows the high/low paradigm: treble is written above bass. The faster the frequency of the sound, the higher it is written on the page.

This spatial arrangement is accepted so unconsciously by most of us that piano teachers can't understand why a young child would be confused by the less intuitive arrangement of the keyboard, which translates low-high into left-right. I'm still confused, seventy years and ten billion notes later. (In a stunning reversal, accordions sound higher in pitch as the fingers of the right hand move downward.)

The low/down, high/up metaphor seems to be the most widely shared across cultures, but there are many other ways our minds have of mapping sounds onto our bodies and the spaces around them. Music is slow as a yawn or fast as a blink, and all of its time scales and periodicities are measured against the natural dimensions of the body. Music is languid or energetic, relaxed or tense; our bodies are the measure of these. Melodies *step* (two successive tones are neighbors in the scale, hence easy to sing) or *leap* (successive tones are far apart in the scale, less easy to sing). Music's sonorities are full or empty, its textures crowded or spacious; it sounds up close or far away. Notice that these are not emotional or psychological responses, even though they could easily lead to them (we will discuss those in chapter 3). These are cognitive perceptions that correlate musical sounds to your body in space.

WHERE'S THE MUSIC?

Here is a two-part research experiment. Sit in a quiet room, alone if possible, close your eyes and listen to any music without words (words would complicate the experiment for now). Let the music take over, and as you become immersed in it, *imagine* you are dancing, even though your body is relaxed and perfectly quiet. Imagine your dancing as if it were you yourself dancing, not watching yourself (or someone else) dancing.

Then, when the dance is over, turn off the music. For the second part of the experiment, again in a quiet environment, but this time with no music in the air, improvise an actual dance. This time, *imagine* the music as you dance. Any sort of music or quasi-music is OK: whatever comes to you. Trust that the very act of imagining the music is the music itself. Your dance does not have to be fancy or strenuous, just actually physical. Move fast or slow, a lot or a little.

This might take some getting used to, but it could result in a heightened feeling of your body in space. Inner music imbues your body with a new definition of itself. Notice the correlations between inner sounds and outer movements. Does a high sound mean an upward gesture? Or are the connections counterintuitive? Fast just could make you slow down. What *is* the relationship between musical space and physical space? You could be the music's literal puppet. Or not.

The primary question this experiment addresses is: Where is the music, out there or in here? If it is out there, how do you internalize it? And if it's in here, *where* is it, and how does it externalize into your dancing? It is most fruitful to consider these questions not as interesting ideas or as problems to be solved, but rather as conscious, intentional experiences that illumine your sensibilities.

Here is another, perhaps more subtle experiment. In a quiet, protected place, close your eyes. Without thinking about it, sing a sustained tone. You may need to try a few times to find a calm, even tone. Then, just before you sing the tone one last time, become aware of your in-breath, and what happens inside you the moment before your vocal chords become engaged. Then sing the tone.

Next, do the same thing in the same way, but this time don't actually sing the tone. In the precious split second before you *would* have sung the tone, you may find that you hear the tone, perhaps briefly and faintly, but the tone's pitch will register nonetheless. This is pitch memory, which musicians learn to develop with considerable discipline. When you sing a tone and then begin to sing it again, the memory of what you just sang guides the vocal apparatus with amazing accuracy to exactly the right tensions and resonances to produce the tone again. Singers need this faculty to sing in much the same way you need to call up the words you speak just before you speak them. The process is so fast and submerged beneath the mind's surface that it's difficult to bring it up to consciousness. You hear the pitch inside your head, but where is it? What is vibrating? What neurons are firing? Once he became stone-deaf, where were the string quartets Beethoven heard? Where is the music in your dreams?

Although current scientific research addresses inner hearing, and much is being learned, there is no clear description of how it works, at least not so far. But you can frame a subjective answer for yourself simply by noticing deeply your experience when you hear a musical tone—or phrase—in your head. No need to describe it, even to yourself, much less to quantify it with measurement. The *sine qua non* is to experience it.

Walking

A walking body makes whole-body music. Drummers sit in closed rooms practicing beats for years to perfect their representations of the metabolic and physical entrainment we get on the natch by striding long over level ground. Most people, while they are walking, think or daydream, or become absorbed in their surroundings. But it's wonderful to rediscover the pleasure of the natural swing of walking itself. First, there is the forever feel of it, the left-right duple truth of it. But the duple truth is deeper than just the one-two, left-right of the footfalls. Each leg in turn gives in to gravity, then rises up against it, giving a fall-rise cycle for the left foot followed by a fall-rise cycle for the right foot. From this arises the basic four-meter of music: LEFT-up RIGHT-up; or onomatopoeically and repetitively: BOOM-chick BAM-cheek, BOOM-chick BAM-cheek, BOOM-chick BAM cheek, and so on. The most basic metric structure of music is an embodied metaphor for the body's primary means of mobility.

Things become more complex when you add in the sound of your steps, the swing of your arms, and the intricate way the skeleton has of balancing a body being simultaneously pulled down and propelled forward. If you are moved to make rhythmic mouth sounds, or little syllabic riffs, or to sing anything at all, the polyphony of rhythms and sounds can be intricate and compelling. A few minutes of paying attention to your walking, with its mix of simple and complex swinging periodicities, will demonstrate like no other experience how our body is the original music that has never left us.

Breath

Since breathing is automatic, focusing consciousness on it has become a special skill, a central practice of meditation. The need for breath is so connected to each part of your organism that when you notice it, each part of your body seems more accessible to consciousness. You can feel all the places in your body holding tension and all the places in your mind whirring like toys. Pain and beauty seep in. And the mechanics of the breathing apparatus itself, suddenly onstage, become terrifying and miraculous. You feel your body's raw intention to live. You and survival are on the same wave. And you sense the complexity within the simplicity of *in* and *out*.

There is a moment at the top and a moment at the bottom of each breath when the polarity is reversing, where *in* becomes *out*. In this instant everything is balanced, and this vanishingly small slice of your life becomes an eternity. The cycle continues consciously or unconsciously as long as you live. "Timed breathing" sharpens the focus: five even counts in, five even counts out. This practice smoothes out the natural irregularities in breathing—in musical terms, it meters the natural rhythms of the breath. Then, when your breathing seems calm, you can stop the numbers, let go of the pulse, and just listen to the wave-music of the breath. There are small sounds inside the larger ones: vortices of air flowing over your lips and interior surfaces of your nostrils receding to inaudibility. It may stretch the definition of music past any functional limit to say that the breath *is* music. However, for all the ways the mind has of mapping the body, the basic in and out of breathing is the map that music uses most to understand itself.

The next time you listen to music, pretend it is an exotic living animal with its own way of breathing—that what you are hearing is the sound this animal makes as it breathes to stay alive. You will hear how music has both simple and elegant ways of breathing, how it is entwined through many simultaneous orders of duration and frequency. But the overall breath of the musical animal is what to listen for. You may find that the composer and the performers speed or slow the breath, or hyperventilate it, or even suck the breath out of the music in order, in various ways, to engage your empathy. The most difficult job for a composer is to make the overall breath of an entire piece feel organic. Among many masters, Mozart, especially in his later works, was the greatest—notably in the concerti, wherein the breath of the soloist and the breath of the orchestra braid together into one live being.

Body Rhythms

When you focus on your breathing and enter a deep meditative state, you may go through a stage when all of the waveforms associated with your metabolism seem individually sensible within the vibrational mix. One can't actually hear brain waves, of course, nor are any of the other periodic signals of the body normally audible, not even your heartbeat. But there can be a sense, nonetheless, that on some level you are a living symphony of pulsing blood, twanging electromagnetic signals, and limitless waveforms, alive and conscious of itself. This self-reflexive metaphor—that a symphony is alive and life is a symphony—is itself a musical kind of thinking.

Body rhythms can be direct experience; they are the facts of normal life. You shiver; you tremble; you knead dough and knock on doors. If you are quiet enough you can feel the beating of your heart and, if you are active enough, its pulse in your ears. We have cycles of energy and ennui, tension and relaxation; we are in turns hungry and sated, lustful and satisfied. The deepest mechanisms of our metabolism—sleep and fertility—have been shaped by the diurnal and lunar cycles, and we mark and renew our lives by the solar cycle. All of these simultaneous periodicities, from the smallest to the largest orders of magnitude, are mirrored in the periodicities of music's aliveness. From the blink of a triangle's *ting* to our sigh at the end of a symphony, your body recognizes itself in music's mirror.

Sex

Composers reference periodic cycles in the subject matter of their compositions. There is plenty of music about the planets, the seasons, dusk and dawn, sun and moon—naturally occurring cycles that through the agency of music are embodied in human form. Of all the cycles of living energy coursing through us, the one least talked about—at least in public—is the cycle of sexual arousal and release. Private discussion is a different story. The sexual metaphor of music is freely discussed among musicians of every stripe in sequestered conversations. It isn't all that far from being acknowledged outright in public discourse either, if one learns to read between the lines of music criticism and analysis. We talk of the slow buildup of music, its rushes of passion leading to its peaks and climaxes (of a new symphony, one tight-laced critic enjoyed its "forward thrusting mass") followed by its passages of ecstatic calm. Popular music, especially dance music, does indeed know how to be sexually explicit in both its music and its lyrics, often to the point of prurience, and quite joyfully so if one goes there joyfully. But we are not referring to music that is deliberately *about* lust or sexual passion. What we seem to look away from in public discussion is the innate sexuality of the elemental structures of music, plain old music: the gathering of energy and its release in a typical phrase, the vibrato and swell of a singer's sustained tone and its dying fall, the entreating climb of a melody to its high notes and the subsequent subsiding, the magnificent, prolonged moments of release and completion after a stormy passage.

In purely energetic terms, mutual human lovemaking has its own waveforms—complex as can be while at the same time primally simple. If you could hook up a mating couple to a machine that measured biorhythms, and could see a printout of the intricate curve of their flirting, arousal, orgasm, and subsequent relaxation, you might well be looking at the energy graph of a good concerto—or movie, or play, or ballet, or any kind of art that streams through time. Not to imply that all temporal art has the same curve—some art takes pains to avoid the climactic model. Nor to imply that all temporal art that contains climaxes necessarily references the sexual model: lots of climactic life experiences are not singularly sexual in origin. The climactic metaphor is, however, a highly accessible one, and its sexual aspect—hard to miss—is usually not far from consciousness.

Consider sexual acts themselves as having intrinsic musical energy: the come-hither and get-thee-away, the promising and withholding, the waxing and the waning, the emotional dramas, the chemical changes, the energies of two minds locked into mutually shared sensuality, the cross rhythms of two heartbeats, and the phasing in and out of entrainment of two muscular bodies. Mothers often report that the pain of childbirth is so intense that, years after the fact, it is forgotten. I wonder about the pleasures of orgasmic plateaus. Are they too intense to carry about in the quotidian world? Where do we keep them? Are the swirling climaxes of music a free pass to buried memories, a safe reliving of private ecstasies—sex *sans* sex? Even in public? Especially in public?

Not to forget the actual sounds: the little sighs and moans, the half-lies and throaty truths, the cries and pants, shrieks and moans of pleasures and pains so vivid and various, the rhythms of high passion and near exhaustion (or, in certain instances, the mutual suppression of the soundtrack so as not to be overheard). Not to mention the songs we sing in the spell of afterward, by which I mean every imaginable deep breath and sigh, often with little vocalizations hidden inside them, and even sometimes—most lovely of all—the actual singing of drawn-out tones or made-up tunes, eye to eye, breath to breath gliding in similar and oblique motions, sweeping apart in contrary motion then falling parallel together: after-love arias by grown children, quintessentially human music, ravishing as exotic birds.

I'm not sure what the difference between art and anything, especially sex, is, but in this case the difference may simply be one of intention: sex is usually meant to be private and personal, whereas art is meant to be shared. My purpose is not to fuzz the boundaries between the two but rather to encourage your free consideration of how deeply the metabolism of sex informs the dynamics of temporal art. Music does not come from sex, nor is sex music, but they do have the same ancestors. The protosexual dynamics of the first stuff of the universe created the galaxies that evolved into organisms, then humans, and then me, and now I make music that is an interface between me and the world that made me. Sex and music are family.

EMBODIED MUSIC

If you listen quietly to purely instrumental music, and imagine it to be shapes of air in deep, flowing courtship with one another, sharing and dispersing energies like shameless lovers, and *embody* that, you may be able to sense how musicians bring their full humanity, including the full range of biorhythms, into every phrase. Since music is perhaps of all languages the one most subject to individual interpretation, I encourage you to hear the connection directly in your own terms. Music is such a special category of experience — it can be so heady and so angelic — that it is sometimes easy to forget how rooted it is in the plain old everyday realities of gravity, motion through space, breath, and biological cycles. Sink toward the ground and rise up again and again; breathe in and breathe out; get hungry, eat your fill; go to sleep, get up; have a nice orgasm, then forget about it; dress warm in winter, soak up the rays in summer; be born, get high, and die: all protomusic.

Every soul who has ever made music has a body to experience it with, and every aspect of the music thus made is to some degree a mirror of that body. This is a lovely and effortless way to appreciate even the most challenging and unfamiliar music. Every person involved in the existence of a piece of music, from the person(s) who invented the sounds, through the person(s) who performed it, all the way through to your very ears listening to it — every jack one of them had limbs, lungs, stomachs, sexual organs (however active), and nervous systems, and it is somehow, while deep in the thrall of ecstatic musical experience, quite wonderful to realize that.

2

Music as Mind

ai d'ê
mean
mind *rais*
is to extra
act mean
mind is extra mean
Your mind's *raison d'être*
is act ing
Your mind's *raison d'être* is to extract meaning.

If you witness the working of your mind as you reread the words
above, you can catch it in the very act of trying to make sense of
what you're reading. As it is presented with streaming phenomena of every sort, your hungry intellect is searching for patterns
of meaning. Its hunger pangs light the inside of your skull as
you read, listen, and watch. The mind's primal need is to comprehend—and thus respond to—events. It wants to know that
everything is OK. It wants to know how to make things better. It
resists randomness because disorder can be dangerous.

The gradual unveiling of meaning is a dramatic technique commonly used for poems, stories, and movies. A typical movie, for instance, starts with a series of unrelated, even jarringly disparate scenes; only gradually do they come to make sense. In a good mystery, all the pieces fall into place only near the end. Poems often save the epiphany for the last few lines. The most mindful instrumental music—Beethoven symphonies, for instance—is a continual piecing together of musical ideas until, at the end, a single "piece" has emerged whole. Even a painting viewed over a span of time can take on more and more meaning before your eyes.

In temporal art, the dynamic of moving from a sequence of chaotic experiences toward a single coherent event is such a common practice that it is easy to overlook. Your need to grasp at and cling to meaning through a barrage of apparent chaos is the artist's best friend. As you are listening to an unfamiliar piece of music by a composer (especially one you've learned to trust), and at the same time are witnessing this gradual unveiling of meaning, you can feel your mind's need to know being *played* out. You are experiencing a musical aspect of your mind—your mind as music.

The composer relies on your mind's hunger. If you are listening with your mental hunger awake, music can lead you on intricately engaging journeys. The composer's (or improviser's) part of the deal is to hold your interest not only with compelling sequences of events but also with arresting sounds and unexpected surprises. A successful work of temporal art has to have enough sameness for patterns to emerge, and enough newness so you won't get bored.

In a movie, for instance, the plot has to be clear enough to follow and complex enough to engage you. Movies with lame plots typically seek to sate your senses and emotions so your mind, overwhelmed with sensations, will not notice how underwhelmingly the pieces fit together. Improbably, this often works—at least as long as we remain willing to sacrifice cogency for spell-binding visuals, brilliant acting, brutal violence, and believable sex. But even these won't save a movie when you wake up the next morning feeling robbed.

It's the same with music. When you listen fully to a piece of music and it rewards you for your attention, when you feel afterward that it was a meaningful experience well worth the effort—that piece endures.

In songs, much of the meaning is embedded in the words. But in purely instrumental music, meaning must arise from the intrinsic nature of the sounds themselves, and how they are ordered through time. Your mind's capacity to extract meaning depends on its ability—and willingness—to distinguish between similar and dissimilar events. Similarity, however, is hard to pin down. It depends on your frame of reference. For instance, if your frame of reference is instrumental timbre, anything whatsoever played on a flute is similar to anything else played on a flute: it is flute music. Likewise, any high music is similar to any other. High, fast music is similar to low, fast music because it's fast. Any familiar thing is familiar because it is in the same family as some other thing. Since there are an infinite number of families—"Music Performed on Sunday Afternoons" for example—the subject of similarity is infinitely complex. So how can you ever know how your mind sorts through the infinite families of events to find meaning?

We will approach this complex question from a simple musical perspective, beginning with the mind's perception of one thing at a time, and go on from there.

BOOM-BOOM MIND (ONE THING AT A TIME)
Pulse

Let's begin with the experience of periodicity. A periodic event is one that occurs at regular intervals of time—your birthday,

for instance (even if it occurs only in leap years), or the full
moon, or the swing of a pendulum, or the idle of a motorcycle.
The periodic events that occur in living things can be almost as
regular and simple as a pendulum swing: the drill of a woodpecker's beak, a dog's rapid scratch, the chattering of your teeth
from a chill, your footsteps as you run. But it is more likely for
organic events to be complex and tend toward aperiodicity. Even
when your breathing is regular, for instance, the in-breath takes
less long than the out-breath, and a deep breath (disturbing the
periodicity of the overall cycle) is never too far away. Likewise,
in an evenly beating heart the contraction phase is shorter than
the relaxation phase. Even if you are holding quite still, your
heart rate can change substantially over time through thought
alone, as in a nightmare, or a sexy dream, or both at once.

In music, the simplest periodicity is referred to as *pulse:* an
elemental signal repeated at a constant interval, like the evenly
spaced beats of a drum. In the purest case, there is no differ-
entiation in the signal from one point in time to the next. The
counting of such a pulse is properly *"one, one, one, one, one…"*
You can experience its effect by evenly clapping your hands at
the tempo of slow applause and saying *"one"* with each clap, or
"now, now, now, now…" with utmost concentration. How long
can you do this without dropping a stitch?

When a steady pulse occurs in the natural world it seems,
like the brief tattoo of a woodpecker, to be an automatic neural
release. But a prolonged, *intentionally* steady pulse seems char-
acteristically human. All it takes is four or five evenly spaced
knocks on your door to let you know there is someone human
on the other side. Left to its own devices, nature is not normally
static, so when a living being produces a nondynamic (non-
changing) signal it strikes us as a deliberate, consciously motivated act. When we produce such periodic pulses intentionally
over a long period of time, our intention even seems intensified,
as in a throbbing tympani part at the climax of a movie: *boom,*

boom, boom, boom, boom… or the crowd at a football game chanting: *go, go, go, go, go, go…*

Meter

As you may have already noticed, remaining completely attentive while clapping a steady pulse is not easy. A full minute of complete focus would be impressive. But release the insistence of *"one, one, one…"* into *"one,* two, *one,* two, *one,* two…" and, having invented meter, you can dance all night. You have metered out the undifferentiated universe into a world of possibility.

The pattern *"one,* two, *one,* two" is called duple meter, and it can consist of any contrasting elements: down-up, strong-weak, left-right, loud-soft. We have already mentioned the innate musicality of walking and its duple give-and-take with gravity — it is not surprising to find the bipedal simplicity of walking so embedded in our fundamental perception of musical time. What is remarkable is the extent to which duple meter has become so inescapably woven into our soundscape. Stopped at a stop sign, or walking through the mall, or simply surfing this modern life, you hear from all sides the ubiquitous, endlessly self-reaffirming mantra of the universal session drummer's backbeat going *-chick,* boom-*chick,* boom-*chick…* with the accent on the upbeat, spinning the Western prayer wheel into the night.

I think I know why boom-*chick* is the sound logo of our culture. We live in a cacophonous place. The air is filled with the work of millions of us ordering our lives, but these life-sounds easily become a threatening sort of babble to us, just as do the often chaotic thought forms of quotidian life. The simplest, most available, and evidently most effective ordering element — for the outer soundscape as well as the inner mindscape — is duple meter. For many folks, a stream of boom-*chicks* keeps the lid on disorder. This is what I tell myself when boom boxes are cruising my bucolic country road: I'd rather have a surfeit of duple meter if it means a little less insanity. Duple meter, godhead of all counterirritants, is better than berserk.

Triple meter goes "*down*-up-up, *down*-up-up..." Are there two kinds of "up"? Yes, that's what makes triple meter complex and engaging. Try conducting a waltz with a straight downward motion of your arm, then a motion up-to-the-left, then up-to-the-right, then start over again: two kinds of up. How are they different? Aha!—another private research project.

The moment I learned to keep time to music, a new world came into focus. When I was a young child, my parents would sometimes let me listen to the family Philco in the nursery before I dropped off to sleep. From the front of the bell-shaped wooden cabinet glowed a round glass dial, yellow-orange, with brown numbers around the edge. One night sometime in my third or fourth year, just before lights out, my mother sat down on the bed next to me and said, "Do you know what this music is on the radio? It's Brahms." When she turned off the light, the dial shone like the moon, and out of the moon poured Brahms. I didn't know Brahms was a person; Brahms was a yellow-orange river of sound. "Can you clap your hands to it?" asked Mom. I clapped my hands like applause. "No, I mean in time to it, like this," and she took my hands in hers and clapped in time to the music. I knew that the clapping belonged somewhere inside the sound, but I didn't know where it fit. She turned the radio low and snuggled me down in the sheets. "I'll show you tomorrow." I went to sleep under Brahmslight.

The next morning before anyone else was awake, I clicked on the radio: a popular song on *The Arthur Godfrey Show*. I knew immediately how to keep time to it, as easily as if I were bouncing a ball. So that's what she'd meant. What had been a river of sound last night was now a neat row of wavy shapes, one after the other. I lay in my cocoon tapping one finger.

What I learned then was that meter gives shape to the river of time, morphs it from a steady surge into segmented patterns. Music that is neither pulsed nor metered is temporally amorphous—although no less pleasing for that. Such music is airy and spacey, atmospheric as drifting clouds. But if you want to *build* something, musical architecture needs measure. Metric patterning gives meaning to the sound stream, saves it measure by measure from the chaos of unknowing, from the undifferentiated is-ness of infancy. Thus we march from Eden *via* the drumbeat of cognition: boom-chick all the way to church, school, and work. Welcome to the meaningful world.

It is astonishing how musical meaning is distorted when the metric message somehow goes awry. Once, back in the '60s, when I was a stoned passenger in a fast car, we were listening to the Beatles on the radio, some happy duple-metered song, the two's arranged in groups of two (making fours), which were themselves arranged in groups of two (making eights), and so on into duple eternity. The song ended, some talking came on, and the driver abruptly changed the station, breaking into the middle of the strangest thing I'd ever heard: music from Mars, ultramodern, wondrously incomprehensible. "Pop is getting *really* far out," I thought, as the music became increasingly meaningless. Even though I could recognize certain familiar sounds of singers, instruments, and harmonies, what I heard was exotic, almost threatening nonsense. And the language, though I recognized familiar syllables, was utterly foreign, definitely cosmic. Was this the work of an avant-garde movement that had passed me by? Some prank? An actual message from outer space?

Then, feeling suddenly foolish, I recognized the piece: a popular doo-wop song, in English, of course, in the characteristic meter of doo-wop, namely, three's arranged in groups of four:

Yah-de-dee
Yah-de-dee

Yah-de-dee
Yah-de-dee

Immediately I knew what had happened. My weed-tangled mind hadn't budged from the duple meter of the previous song, and was trying to hear a new song organized by triple meter with my old duple interpretation. What I heard was:

Yah-de *dee*-ya
De-dee *yah*-de
Dee-yah *de*-dee (Try this)

First nothing had made sense; then, when my cognition suddenly flipped into triple meter, everything made sense. If the metric message goes haywire, so does the meaning. Meter keeps meaning in line.

What is astonishing is that the music of the entire earth is almost exclusively either duple (as in a march) or triple (as in a waltz), or combinations of these. *Four* is substantially the same as two duple measures, one after the other, as is eight, and all other powers of two. *Five* is a march followed by a waltz, or a waltz followed by a march; far less commonly is it an elemental meter in its own right. *Six* is either triple twice or duple thrice. Likewise are all higher-numbered meters actually compounds of duple and triple meters. The reason for this appears to be related to the reason we find it difficult to count five pennies (much less six, or seven or more) without grouping them into sets of twos and threes. There is a limit to what we can *subitize*, which means to intuitively grasp a quantity without counting. Indigenous languages typically contain words for one, two, and three; higher than that is often called "several" or "many." Our strategy for making sense out of the undifferentiated river of time is primitive and universal.

Pulse Becomes Tone

In music, periodicity occurs at many orders of magnitude. The pulses that underlie metric time typically range from around one per second to about four per second, although you can track them at twelve or more times per second. If the pulses exceed this cognitive limit, your sense of pulse evaporates and a new dimension of meaning arises. You begin to hear not pulse but tone—at first eerily low, then gradually rising as the frequency of the pulse increases. Much the same thing happens in vision. If the frames of a "motion picture" are flickering by at ten images per second, the eye will register individual images; but at a certain point, starting at about fourteen frames per second, the flicker gives way to the illusion of continuous motion.

The lowest string on a bass guitar typically vibrates back and forth about 40 times (or cycles) per second, producing the same pitch as the lowest E on a piano. This is a low but quite sensible tone. If a tape recording of it is made and then slowed down to quarter-speed, the vibrations will play at 10 cycles per second. The sense of tone will be gone; in its place you will hear ten thuds per second. If you then speed up the tape gradually, at roughly 18 thuds per second you will begin to distinguish a very low tone. At about 27 cycles per second that tone will have risen to the lowest note on the piano. At normal speed, the original 40-cycle E appears again. No one has fully plumbed the magic of how the frequency of successive events—which we register in terms of slow and fast—transforms at a certain threshold into the "pitch" of tone—which we register terms of low and high. Notice that, just as in the case of jerky stills becoming a smooth movie, what changes is not the events themselves but only their frequency, a change that seems to open a new dimension of our perception.

So pulse and tone are the same, but differently perceived. You can't experience a tone's periodicity directly—the periods are generally too rapid to cognize individually. But the sensation of a pure, sustained musical tone is your mind's way of telling you that what you are hearing *is* perfectly periodic sound, that within this particular micro-universe a kind of fundamental, primitive perfection maintains. A sustained tone means: everything is in order, all is well. Remember the first note of my concert? The perfectly periodic sound of that pitch, that "familiar sky," was the little heaven where we can find a breath of refuge.

There is in fact a narrow overlapping zone in which both pulse and tone can be perceived at once. A motorcycle typically idles at about 10 putts per second, but as it revs up and roars off you can gradually detect a rising bass tone. If the motor revs fast enough, and recedes into the distance, the putts will turn into a kind of grainy texture as the bass tone climbs to a tenor whine. Similarly, when a slow-flying propeller airplane is nearby, even if the individual explosions in the engine are too fast to count, your body can still feel them while hearing the continuous drone hum across the sky.

HARMONIOUS MIND (TWO THINGS AT ONCE)
On Being Close: Two Kinds of Musical Space

If you are sitting next to a stranger in a crowded bus, the two of you are physically close, maybe even too close for comfort. Now if you think of a relative with whom you have a deep bond, yet who happens to be miles away, you experience another kind of closeness. We have more than one way of being "close" to each other. The closeness to the stranger can be gauged in one way, with your kin in another. Your closeness to the stranger is one inch, a linear measure we use for points along a line. The closeness with a loved one is multidimensional, involving shared experiences and psychological space—the two of you are "in synch" or "on the same wavelength." Musical tones provide a deep metaphor for each of these kinds of closeness.

Imagine two parallel ropes (like two clotheslines), each ten or so feet long, each tied to a hook in the wall at arm level. Grasp a rope in each hand, stand back, and pull the two ropes parallel and taut. Suppose that between the hooks and the wall there are oscillators that cause the ropes to gently vibrate independently at different frequencies. Now the oscillators are turned on. At first they are both at the same frequency, say 5 cycles per second. Because you're holding on to the ropes, your two arms are being vibrated like two strings of a cello tuned to the same pitch. (The ropes' vibrations, although big enough to be felt, are too slow to be heard.) The ropes have begun in synch, with no frequency difference between them. This feels like a good agreement in your arms, and throughout your whole body as well. The two ropes are "in tune," and their synchronicity allows you to feel in tune with them.

Remember that these oscillators are set up to operate independently and indeed, now the right rope begins to move just a little faster, say 5.2 cycles per second. Over the next five seconds, that will work out to 26 cycles of the right rope for every 25 cycles of the left rope. After only a couple of seconds, the two sides of your body are at odds with one another, discombobulated, turbulent, out of synch. But there is gradual reprieve—after the full five seconds, the ropes have come back in synch and the little drama is set to begin again. The right rope's *increase* in frequency has been only a *little* bit—after all, 5.2 is pretty *close* to 5, the frequency difference is only two-tenths of a cycle per second—but this little bit has resulted in an experience for you, the rope-grasper, very different from when both ropes were vibrating at the same frequency.

Now imagine that the right rope is suddenly increased to 10 cycles per second while the left rope continues at 5 cycles per second. As before, your right arm is vibrating faster than your left, but this time the sensation is not at all turbulent. The vibrations seem like they belong together again, they are in synch.

27

They are clearly not doing *exactly* the same thing but seem to have a *close* fit, such that the fast vibration of your right side fits quite snugly into the slow vibrations of your left side. They fit because the right rope is vibrating twice for each time the left rope vibrates once; it is vibrating at twice the speed. The relationship of frequencies between the right rope and the left is spoken of as "two to one" and written 2:1.

You have now experienced two kinds of change, each involving some dimension of "close"—a *little bit* faster and *twice* as fast. Clarifying the acoustic distinction between these two kinds of "close" is crucial to understanding how the mind and music meet.

In the first kind of closeness, the right rope gets a *little bit* faster (and could indeed continue to get gradually faster or slower). This kind of change is called a linear, or arithmetic, progression, much like simple counting. In music, the result of such change is the gradual rising (or falling) of pitch, either in a smooth curve, like a leaf rising and falling in the wind, or perhaps in small increments, as in climbing up and down a ladder. We identify this ladder-type rising and falling as a musical "scale." Typically, what we call a melody ascends or descends "stepwise," that is, ladder rung by ladder rung, or scale-step by scale-step. The path of these steps is called the *melodic line.* Sometimes the melodic line will take a leap upward and then descend by steps; sometimes it will leap downward and climb back up by steps. Essentially, a musical melody is like a kid playing on the stairs, mostly step-by-step, but with some jumps thrown in for variety.

In the second kind of closeness, the frequency of the rope was doubled. The number 10 is arithmetically far from 5, but in the realm of multiplication, 10 is the *closest* number to 5—it is 5 times 2, and 2 is the smallest possible whole-number multiplicand other than 1. These numbers are not about distance, but about proportion. In terms of a proportional relationship, one frequency is *twice* another (2:1) or *thrice* another (3:1) and so on. These numbers are ratios, proportional numbers. Generally speaking, the word *harmony* means agreement among things. In music, whenever we are able to appreciate the *proportionality* between the various tones, we call our sense of this "the harmony" of the music. Harmony is proportion in sound.

The harmonies easiest to understand and appreciate have the simplest proportions, which are expressed by the lowest-numbered ratios, like 2:1 or 3:1 or 3:2 or 4:3. Harmonies that are increasingly difficult to understand have numerical expressions that may be *arithmetically* close, but proportionally complex, like 9:8, or 16:15 — or, as in the case of the first experiment with the rope, 26:25, which made your two arms crazy. The simpler the numbers in the ratio, the more we tend to call the harmony "consonant"; the more complex the numbers, the more we term the harmony "dissonant." A violin and a viola playing a duet, weaving in and out of the intoxications of dissonance and consonance, are not unlike two noisy lovers agreeing and disagreeing, reveling in all the engaging stages in between, waking the neighbors with their discord, and merging unashamed in their unisons.

We have described how musical tones are "close" in two different ways: the linear gradations of a melodic line, and the sensible *proportions* of harmonic combinations. The mind tries to extract meaning from all tones in two distinct ways: it processes linear *melodic* information in one way, and processes proportional *harmonic* information another way. Only over tens of millennia — and especially during the past eight hundred years — has the human mind evolved to do both of these things at once. In order to most fully celebrate the blessed marriage of these two cognitive talents, we must scrutinize them separately, at least for a few more pages.

Linear Mind

There are two reasons why I'm being so cautious in separating out the mind's perception of melody from that of harmony. The first is that the more their autonomy is appreciated, the more delicious is their union. The second is that the true distinction between them is almost universally blurred, even in the most revered academic texts and teachings, even, as we shall see, in the core language used to describe them. So we resolve, in this particular university, to maintain the purity of our experiences as long as possible.

What is pure melody—pure in the sense of being relieved from all metric and harmonic characteristics? That is, what is a pure *line* of sound? Examples abound: the whistle of wind around corners, the fluctuating drones of bees, the treble whines of mosquitoes, the cries of animals (some musically gifted birds and whales excepted), the human moans of pain and ecstasy, the rising and falling cadences of speech. Of course, we normally experience the melodies of actual music with more transformative pleasure than that associated with the drones of bees or with the singsong of plain speech. So what *is* the difference between the whistle of the wind—random up-and-down motion—and a gorgeous melody? The difference is this: If the tones of a melodic line are related by proportional ratios simple enough for the mind to understand and appreciate, that melody will have harmonic (and thus transformative) musical power. But if the frequencies of those tones are not harmonic with their neighbors, the result will be more like a leaf on the wind than a beautiful tune. In general usage (and, alas, in the musical nomenclature as well), we typically conflate the linear rise and fall of melody with the intoxicating power of harmonic proportion. Each needs to be separately understood if we are to comprehend the difference between wind and tune.

That's not to say that the shape of the wind and what rides on it is not beautiful. In the movie *American Beauty,* the video of a plastic bag caught in a whirling wind, and the actors' response to it, creates one of the most affecting scenes in film history. The undulating sounds and shapes of ocean waves are entrancing, as are the contours of the hills and valleys we live in and travel through. In music, although *mere* rise and fall unconditioned by harmonic or metric factors can be beautiful, it usually doesn't *mean* enough to engage our minds for long. Our musical minds want more. Sooner or later, some kind of agreement we have grown accustomed to, some particular kind of love—the love of proportion—needs to arise.

Proportional Mind

Musical harmony refers generally to the proportional agreement of all the tones of a piece to one another, both simultaneously and sequentially. When music is "in a key," like Mozart's Jupiter Symphony "in C," it means that there is consensual agreement among listeners that the note C sounds like the "home note"—that the music arises from and ultimately needs to return to that note in order to sound complete. But why is there such agreement among listeners? Why don't half the listeners think the home note is B-flat, or F-sharp, or some other tone? The answer is not well understood, so to ask "How does it come to pass that is such a thing as a *home note* exists?" is not at all a naive question.

It is evident that when confronted with a set of pitches— whether it be the first few tones of a lullaby or the beginning of a symphony—your mind hungers to know how those pitches relate to one another. To stave off randomness, your hearing-mind actively seeks for a meaningful grammar, an orderly hierarchy of tones, just as your reading-mind is doing right now in sifting through the words of this sentence. In order to extract meaning from language, you need to know the subject of a sentence, especially a long sentence (in the previous sentence it was "hearing-mind"). What this means in the realm of musical harmony is that your mind eagerly seeks to discover the single tone that somehow accounts for the pitches of the other tones. Under certain *amazing conditions,* it can ferret out that tone, and recognize it as the organizing principle. Our minds have evolved the capacity, whenever these amazing conditions are met, to determine which tone gives functional meaning to each of the other individual tones in the population of tones swarming around it. Such harmony is called *tonal harmony,* which simply means that kind of agreement wherein the ear can locate one single tone—the so-called *generating tone*—that organizes the many.

What are the "amazing conditions" under which your mind can perform such a feat? After all, some music sounds as though it uses tonal harmony, some sounds like it *sort of* does, and some, like the music of flying geese, or wind-in-the-trees music, or atonal music, sounds like it doesn't. When you examine music that sounds tonal, or experiment with making your own, you gradually discover the way music needs to be constructed for tonal harmony to arise. Indeed, the greater part of the study of music consists in precisely this. The amazing conditions have a way of revealing themselves heuristically—that is, by trial and error—to the degree that you are paying attention to what you are hearing.

What is it about the wiring of your mind that allows it to know when the amazing conditions of tonal harmony are being met? Does it *count* something going on among the tones? Just what would it be counting, and how fast, after all, can it be expected to count? Or does it recognize some *quality* between the combinations of tones? And what could cause such qualities to arise?

Although a great deal is known about these questions, and the research is valid and exciting, the thorn in the side of such putatively scientific research is the subjective nature of the problem. In this it somewhat resembles the "problem" of consciousness itself: You think you know what I mean, and I think I know what you mean, but an objective description of either is elusive indeed. Most everyone *groks*, or *gets*, tonal harmony, but there are many views on how we do it. *Your* view is the focal point of this book. But I'll let you in on mine.

Ropes "R" Us: A Proportional Experiment

We'll proceed from where we left off with the ropes, but this time we need to graduate from the sensibly faster/slower pulses of ropes to the higher/lower pitches of audible tones. Your new ropes will be your vocal chords. What was exterior will now become interior. Scary? Perhaps. You will need a friend.

The first thing to do is to sing a sustained tone around the middle C of a piano, or a somewhat lower tone for men. Even if you think you are tone-deaf, which no one is, with a little patience you can sing a sustained tone. Now ask your friend to sing that same tone along with you. For some folks this is familiar territory, but if it isn't, this may be a chance for a friendship to flower. Two tones sounding at the same frequency—in *unison*—produce the closest, simplest harmony, the kind you can experience most directly.

Remember the good bodily feeling when the two ropes were vibrating at the same frequency? The vocal chords of two singers singing in true unison likewise can result in a whole-making experience. A sung unison is an embodied metaphor for the closeness of deep agreement. This closeness can be casual—as in a community choir—or as intimate as two hearts beating as one, but in every case, mutuality is the essence. This mutuality taps a deep source of power. When we sing in unison we define our human connection. The sound waves of a sung unison, braided and entrained, form a bridge of waves from heart to heart.

Although two singers singing the same tone in unison is not a difficult idea to grasp, it nonetheless contains a powerful cognitive tool: a certain number of *these* sound waves in the same time frame as a certain number of *those* sound waves; or the frequency of x to the frequency of y; or $x:y$. (In a musical unison, the frequency of x and the frequency of y will be identical, so in this unique case, $x = y$, which in proportional language will always reduce to "one to one," or 1:1.) This concept of proportional frequency—*these* in the same time frame as *those*—is the Rosetta Stone for understanding how musical harmony lives in your mind and, as we shall elaborate in the next chapter, in your heart.

Now ask your friend to vibrate his or her vocal chords twice as fast as yours. This seems like an impossible task unless he or she knows the secret, which is that doubling the frequency of a tone produces another tone sounding so similar to the original tone that it is universally called by the same letter name ("C" for instance) even though your mind interprets it as being substantially "higher." The intuitive ability to double the frequency of a given pitch, or series of pitches, is innate to humans past the age of two or three. Virtually all humans can do so and no other living creature ever has.

Without anyone thinking about it or particularly trying, these doublings resound whenever men and women sing together. I continually find it astonishing to be singing, for instance, "Take Me Out to the Ball Game" with a huge crowd recognizing that the vocal chords of all the women are moving (more or less) twice as fast as the vocal chords of all the men without a thought being given to it. The relationship of the women's voices to the men's voices, in terms of the frequencies of their sound waves, is "two to one" and is written 2:1. The resulting harmony sounds amazingly and universally *right*, as though it is simply part of the act of singing. We seem to accomplish this marvel because we *can*, because it *is* us. We are the species of 2:1 beings. It appears that 2:1 is the harmony our minds make, and when we sing together, we produce it spontaneously.

In Western culture we ordinarily fill up the space between a given tone and its doubling with seven other tones arranged like the steps of a ladder—that is, a seven-tone step-ladder we call a scale. We call the eighth tone, the tone that doubles the frequency of the generating tone, the *octave*. Even accomplished musicians do not realize that the term *octave* refers to *only* the scalar (i.e., linear) dimension of its sound, that is, the eighth scale-step from where you began—not very "close" at all—and does *not* take into account the proportional dimension between the two tones. Every blessed tone in tonal music possesses both linear (melodic) and proportional (harmonic) meaning *simultaneously*. The easier, lazier, more obvious *linear* name "interval" is universally used. The more subtle (yet more affective) dimension of *proportion* is not named. The proportional (harmonic) name of an "octave," regardless of how many rungs you choose to build into your ladder, is a "two-to-one," or a "doubling," or 2:1—which is, proportionally speaking, very "close" indeed. It is important to recognize the proportional truth of an "octave"—or any "interval"—because the mind's talent for interpreting the proportions among tones is the very reason tonal harmony arises, and it is a primary reason why music sounds good to us. If training in music began with both linear (melodic) and proportional (harmonic) concepts in place, and with that distinction reflected in the nomenclature, students would cognize the two kinds of "close" early on, and our culture would have a deeper musical savvy.

Unity Is Home

How exactly does your mind recognize the similarity between the upper and lower tones of an octave? Is it counting really fast, "OK, *two* of you guys to *one* of you guys?" Is it just a pure quality we recognize, like tranquility, or a flavor, like mango? Is it an innate sense of how waves are in- and out-of-step, their phase-relationships? We don't really know, not yet. What we do know is that in the big-body world of legs and arms we experience directly the groove of two-to-one. Even though we don't understand fully the micromechanisms of the mind, there is nonetheless a definite, recognizable state of being that comes with an octave, a 2:1, and we recognize it every time. This is the crux. If you can relate your experience to this cognitive idea — that sensible *ratio* results in a recognizable *state of being* — the seed of musical harmony opens into a meadow of possibilities.

The only thing that changes as you proceed through the varied beauty of the harmonic landscape is the numerical values of the ratios: they become more complex. But they complexify in a very simple way. If we simply count upward, after 2 comes 3. The tripling of the original frequency results in a ratio of "three-to-one," or 3:1, and that is the next-most complex feeling-state. In our scale system, it happens to sound twelve scale-steps above the starting tone. The *scalar* name is "a perfect twelfth" — "perfect" really does mean "relatively simple" here. If you started from your original C, this note would be the G twelve scale-tones higher. The frequency of that G sounding together with the C twelve scale-tones beneath it is 3:1. This proportion sounds extremely harmonious, and folks sing it spontaneously, but it doesn't have the quality of *sameness* with the generating tone that 2:1 does, and consequently two tones thus related will always bear different letter-names (for instance, G and C; or E and A; or E♭ and A♭; or F♯ and B).

Next in complexity is the ratio 3:2 — in this case, the high G we just discovered, in combination with the C an octave higher than the original tone. This is the seminal "perfect fifth" of music. It is slightly less simple than 3:1 — it sounds a tad grainier — but since it has a smaller compass (five scale steps instead of twelve) it has become the functional workhorse of tonal harmony. From here on, incidentally, we are able to give each harmonic combination two names: its harmonic proportional number (3:2 in this case) and its scalar, or "interval" name (a perfect fifth in this case). The simplicity of our complexification will now begin to be revealed.

At this point, if you want to skirt around some math, skip the next four paragraphs.

Consider the next highest number after 3. Although 4 is a higher number, harmonically speaking 4:1 is *not* more complex than 3:1 or 3:2. Notice that 4 is a *doubling* of 2. If 2:1 is an octave, then 4:1 is an octave of an octave. Indeed, such a "double octave" is heard with the same sense of sameness as an octave itself, and the letter name of its tone is the self-same C. What about 8:1? Harmonically speaking, 8 also is less complex than 3 because it is made up of twos, that is, $2 \times 2 \times 2$. Its pitch is a C sounding at the *next* octave above. And 16:1? Likewise, the C another octave higher. These numbers are getting higher, but they are increasing *exponentially*—they are all powers of 2. Since your mind grasps *all* duple proportionality with ease, it scarcely senses an increase in harmonic complexity.

OK, the next number up from 4 is 5. The number 5 is definitely more harmonically complex than anything before it because it is not made of anything prior to it—that is, it is a prime number. Quintupling the frequency of the generating C yields the note E, which happens to fall seventeen scale-tones higher. Its ratio with the generating tone is 5:1. Again, casting aside the intervening octaves for practical purposes, 5:1 can be thought of as 5:2, which in turn can be thought of as 5:4. This is now equivalent to the *scalar* distance of a "major third."

If perfect fifths (3:2) serve as the harmonic skeleton of music, major thirds (5:4) are its blood. More will be said about this in the next chapter, but the salient point here is that your mind has to work much harder to extract the meaning from 5:4 than it does from 3:2. (There are even some music systems that prefer not to employ 5:4 at all.) This cognitive jump from tripling to quintupling—from prime-three to prime-five—is an enormous feat for your mind, and when added to the harmonic landscape turns black-and-white into lush color.

By now the nature of harmonic complexification is becoming clear: in tonal harmony, the mind recognizes frequency proportions generated by prime numbers, at least if the primes are low enough. *The prime numbers 2, 3, 5 (and 7 in a few cases)—and the ways your mind knows how to combine those numbers—are at the root of tonal harmony.* That is the big secret: Your mind can extract meaning from the combined wave patterns of these prime ratios even (up to a certain limit) when they are multiplied times themselves or times each other. Or divided by themselves or each other (as we shall soon see).

When you hear tonal music, your mind makes sense of the tones by sorting out their frequencies into low-prime ratios in respect to the home note. Speaking mathematically, it listens to all the sound frequencies streaming through the air and factors down their proportions to the low-primes 1, 2, 3, and 5. Even though you are not conscious of the process, whenever your mind has success in doing this, it senses the existence of a generating tone, a numerical *one*, the *key* the music is in at that moment, and the harmonic meaning of the whole emerges as a sensible *gestalt*. If it can't manage to do this, the tones make as much harmonic sense as if you were trying to read a message in boiling alphabet soup. Jean-Philippe Rameau, a great eighteenth-century composer and theorist, knew about the ear's ability to locate its coordinates in harmonic space by finding the single tone that, by factoring down to unity, most simply accounted for all the others. He believed in the cosmic principle of unity, *le principe de tout est un* — it's all about the *one*, the mind's innate hunger for the source tone, for home, the *key*, which the *Oxford English Dictionary* defines as "a solution or explanation for what is unknown, mysterious, or obscure."

Upside-Down Harmony

We now understand something about the "amazing conditions" under which the mind can locate a generating tone: if your mind can factor the frequencies of the tones you are hearing into low-prime ratios, what you are hearing is tonal harmony. But we have not quite fully described all of these conditions; there is one more in particular I'd like to mention.

In all the harmonic listening experiments we've done so far, we have begun with a given tone and built additional, higher tones from its various multiples. There is a perfect model for such a thing in the everyday world: the overtone series. When a string (or any long, thin thing) is activated, it vibrates all-of-a-piece, but at the same time it also vibrates in halves at twice the frequency; in thirds at triple the frequency; in quarters at quadruple the frequency; in fifth-parts at quintuple the frequency, and so on. Heard all together, this produces the "overtone chord" at precisely the ratios we've been discussing, namely 1:2:3:4:5 and so forth. Many people assume we hear harmony the way we do *because* of the overtone series — that the overtone series is somehow causal. I don't think so. I think the way strings vibrate and the way our ears hear are branches of the same cosmic evolution. The overtones of strings and the way we understand harmony are siblings who share the same remote ancestor. In my earlier books, I have written enough about this subject to have earned my nickname, Doctor Overtone. In *The Musical Life*, the section called "Sound Is the Teacher" is devoted to an in-depth discussion of the overtone series, and it alone is well worth the price of the book — take it from Dr. Overtone.

One of the reasons why we can't ascribe the way we hear harmony to the overtone series is that about half of the harmony we comprehend never occurs in the overtone series—it corresponds to the overtone series as if it were positioned upside down. Mathematically, this means that all the proportions of these tones are literally inverted. The G above C (3:2) becomes the F below C (2:3). Even if you raise that F above the C as many octaves as you like, it will still make the same kind of affective sense to us. This means that in some fashion your mind knows how to divide as well as multiply.

A useful image is the reflection in a lake of a tree on the shore. On yonder bank stands a lovely willow, and that very same willow appears upside down in the water. Every tone produced by a low-prime ratio (as in the first few tones of the overtone series) has a complementary tone that is its musical reflection. The onshore tones are called *overtonal;* the refection-in-the-water tones are called *reciprocal.* (Some theorists call these tones "undertones," a name I eschew.)

Just as there is mathematical complementarity between multiplication and division, so there is an affective complementarity between overtonal and reciprocal harmony. Here is the interesting thing: Just as most of us have to exert a little more mental energy to do division than to do multiplication, the mind seems to burn an extra nano-calorie or so when it deciphers reciprocal tones. Generally speaking, overtonal harmony (the easy kind) accounts for the music we call the major mode—often heard as (but not restricted to) bright, perhaps buoyant music. Reciprocal harmony (the extra-effort kind) accounts for what we call the minor mode—it is typically heard as (but not restricted to) darker, heavier, more serious or even tragic moods. By whatever miracle your brain knows how to recognize low-prime *multiples* of a given tone, that miracle's sister is how it recognizes low-prime *reciprocals.* And by a perhaps even greater miracle, the difference we discern is psychologically important to us. A change of mode is a change of mood. The back-and-forth motion between overtonal and reciprocal harmony—major and minor—swings our moods, pushes our buttons, and pulls our strings as if feelings were the puppets of some vibrational intelligence. This will be the subject of chapter 3.

High Mind (Everything at Once)
In Time and in Tune

Musically speaking, being "in time" involves pulses on the time-scale of arms, legs and torsos. Being "in tune" involves periodic vibrations at the timescale of wee hair cells in the inner ear. What is the difference in feeling between being in time and being in tune? It is fascinating to directly compare the two effects: swaying in time and singing in tune. You have to go there, to experience each in turn, and feel their difference and their sameness. This is inner work, just you and your appreciation of these qualities. Some other person might try to tell you what it is *like*, but no one can tell you what it *is*. Sitting quite still, sing a song with a friend; try isolating the last note and sing that note together as one voice. Consider that experience. Then take a little walk "in step"—with your steps synchronized—without singing. There is the same togetherness but in a different dimension.

When you put together "in time" and "in tune," the experiences merge into swinging, harmonious music. Wouldn't it be just glorious to see a choir singing a rhythmically juicy Bach motet, moving not only their mouths but also their bodies from the neck down? Some string quartets do become very physical, swing like mad, play in tune, and sound wonderful. I heard the Italian string orchestra Il Giardino Armonico play Vivaldi and it felt as rhythmically visceral and vibrant as bebop. It also sounded, to me, precisely like Vivaldi. I'm not alone in thinking that pre-nineteenth century music originally had more rhythmic vitality, more entrainment, more groove, than typically allowed today. Indeed, many "early music" specialists recognize the kinship of early music—circa 1400, say, give or take a couple of centuries—with what is now called popular music, and, without sacrificing stylistic refinement or musical subtlety, are revitalizing the literature.

The Marriage of Melody and Harmony

I think by now we have a fair idea of why tunes can make such good sense. Not taking into account the association of a melody with its text or lyrics, or the way a melody can remind us of the particulars of our history ("Lucy in the Sky with Diamonds" is a whole novel for me), melodies grab hold of us for (at least) two reasons. First, a mere linear curve can be pleasing, as we have discussed. But the salient reason is this: What makes melodies sensible (and feelingful) is the marriage of the line's curve with its harmonic proportions. As far as tonal music goes, harmonic cognition—which is not necessarily conscious, of course—must be operative in your mind in order for a series of tones to make sense and give feeling. Our focus here is on how the mind organizes what it hears by tracking the harmony throughout the linear curve. Each tone in the melody is heard not only in linear terms—up or down on the melodic curve—but also in terms of its proportional tether to the home note, whether that note is sounding or is merely sensed. It's not so much the neighbors that generate meaning, but the source tone; not the linear curve but the harmonic proportion to "one." Even in the case of a simple melody hummed in the shower, *le principe de tout est un.*

We can use "Twinkle, Twinkle, Little Star" as a demonstration. Sing along with the tune as you read these words. The home note is posited right at the beginning, articulated twice by the two syllables of *Twin-kle*. Immediately the tune leaps upward by a leap of five scale-steps, which by scalar standards is a sizable distance. But the crucial aspect of the leap is that the second *twinkle* is absolutely and precisely fixed at a 3:2 proportion to the first *Twinkle*. This is not just a big leap, it's *this* big leap, landing on the most comprehensible of all the harmonic ratios, the proportion which more than any other defines and stabilizes the generating tone.

The truly astonishing thing here is that, while singing the second *twinkle*, even if we are not *hearing* the pitch of the first *twinkle* we are remembering it, and referring to it in our minds. If the second *twinkle* is a tad sharp or a tad flat, it sounds "off." It must make an actual 3:2 with the first tone or the second *twinkle* won't twinkle. Does this mean that when we sing a tune solo we are deriving the streaming melodic meaning from our *memory* of the source tone? Yes, absolutely. Furthermore, everyone can do it or can be trained to (some more readily than others); except for rare pathologies there are no exceptions. This talent for hearing each tone of a melody in proportion to its source tone—whether the source tone is in the air or being remembered—is a milestone in the evolution of high musical mind.

―

Again, if you want to detour some numbers, skip to the next heading, but honest to goodness you'll get the gist even if your eyes glaze over the numbers. Ever So Slightly Frowning Reader, read my lips: trust me.

Going on then. *Little* goes up a scale-tone (to the sixth degree), and its harmonic proportion is 5:3 in relationship to the source tone. This is a somewhat more complex proportion than 3:2, but the trade-off is that you didn't have to leap to get to it, you stepped into it from a neighboring rung. A general rule of music (and of life, to be discussed in some detail in chapter 8) is that you can leap into easy stuff but you need to step into the harder stuff. The way you step or leap on the melodic stairs is intimately connected with the simplicity or complexity of the harmony.

Going on: *star* returns to the safety of 3:2, but its single sylla-ble breaks the pattern of repeated tones that the first three words set up. That repeated-tone pattern is reinstituted at *How I,* then *won-der,* then *what you,* and then, just as *star* rhymes with *are,* we return to the security of the home note with a single syllable. The words in the last line climbed down the stairs of the scale step by step, forming the familiar sound (and well-understood harmonic ratios) of the major scale.

The ratios that each tone makes with the home note look like this:

Twin- kle twin- kle lit- tle star / How I won-der what you are
  1:1   1:1   3:2   3:2 5:3 5:3 3:2   4:3 4:3 5:4 5:4   9:8 9:8 1:1

If these ratios are not sung or played well in tune, the song might still be recognizable because it's so familiar, but it will have no magic. The magic is not so much in the contour of the melodic line as it is in the specific proportional states set up between each tone and the generating tone.

Melodies that are atonal (intentionally so, I mean) can have a certain power, but the effect is more akin to the gestures of a mime than to the magic of a conjuror. Ninety-nine percent of the music of the earth is tonal and derives its primary mean-ing from what happens in the mind as it seeks the harmonic relationship of each tone to its source tone. It is entirely pos-sible, incidentally, to construct melodies that are quite prop-erly proportional but with such a dull linear motion that they don't engage you. In an engaging melody, line and proportion are happily married, and we celebrate their union each time we hear a good tune.

NEAR NORMAL: PERFECTION AND THE REAL WORLD

We have discussed the mind's response to pulse, meter, tone, and harmony. We have a working definition of the "amazing conditions" under which tonality can be understood by the mind. Although we have an experiential sense of our responses to these basic elements, remember that we've been discussing idealized cases: perfectly realized periodic pulses and harmonic ratios. Life itself does not consist in realized ideals. Life is untidy, swimming in approximation and rife with compromise. Music is likewise. Are the periodic pulses and harmonic ratios we have been considering ever actually *precisely* realized? Do the perfect inner norms for periodicity and ratio that we hold within our human architecture ever see the light of day? How could their bells be rung in such a messy world?

As an experiment, consider the norm of verticality. There is a plumb line between our center and the center of the earth. Something in us knows what a right angle to the earth is—your inner ballerina can stand on point, if only for a moment. But a perfect perpendicular is impossible to maintain. Try as he may, the best-trained mime cannot freeze for long on one leg. We find our bearings, in fact, by circling around what we know to be the center. A perfect right angle to the earth is both a necessary idea and unattainable goal. We realize the ideal in our fashion: by continually passing *through* it while in the act of recognizing our deviation *from* it. Such is indeed the case in realizing the hard-wired inner norms of the musical mind.

Our minds seem to have a gift for recognizing deviation from musical norms and, like kids walking atop a narrow wall, we seem to derive pleasure from playing with our talent. Consider a jazz singer singing over a swinging rhythm section. She sings on the beat, then deliberately falls behind, then catches up, then lags behind. The vocal line is flirting with the time line. Singing "behind the beat" occurs liberally in jazz, as well as to some degree in most vocal and instrumental musics. Playing catch-up and then arriving exactly on time at a crucial moment imbues the music with a certain drama. But keep in mind that there would be no drama if body and mind weren't able to recognize the underlying template of an entrained pulse.

The same dramatic play takes place in the pitch realm. Musicians in many styles often scoop up to an intended pitch from below, attaining the mark either quickly and firmly, or just barely at the last possible millisecond (with all possible variations of this). Another kind of play is to slide smoothly from a higher tone to a lower one, spending most of the time arcing between, leaving the listener in suspense until the new tone is finally realized. Again, this requires more than the mere appreciation of the hard-wired norms. The shape of the deviation from the norm can be appreciated only by a clear sense of a fixed departure point, or a clear arrival point, or both. But while the ball is in the air, so to speak, we are in no-man's-land: we go from known to unknown to known, over and over again, and each time it happens we track it, and it draws us in. To witness these pitch variations as you hear them is to witness your high musical mind in action.

There are three ways a musical moment can relate to a musical norm: the music can be ON, that is, as exact a realization of a pulse or ratio as possible; or it can be APPROACHING ON, with the expectation that the norm will be realized some time in the future; or it can be OFF, simply out of tune or out of time. Back to the body-metaphor of balance: a dancer can be either as balanced as possible, or moving from off-balance toward balance, or off-balance. None of this would be possible without the dancer's sense of the center of gravity and her relationship to it; and without that same sensibility on the part of the viewer the dance would lose its primary meaning and pleasure.

Vibrato, a tremulous rising and falling from a central tone, is another strategy for deviation from pitch. There are usually between two and six squiggles per second, ranging from very shallow — scarcely any pitch deviation at all — to a whole step or more. Vibrato dresses a tone and, like tasteful clothes tastefully worn, can be very appealing. When you look at a sonogram of its pitch variation, you can tell that very little time is spent dead-on; mostly the pitch is above or below (usually leaning toward above), and you wonder how your mind could possibly sort out the intended pitch from the deviation surrounding it. Since there are so many variables of pitch through time, the answer is not only complicated but probably subjective as well. But the ear *does* sort things out; its ability to undress a tone beautifully dressed in vibrato is one of the enduring miracles of the cognitive mind.

It is equally impressive that I can walk across the room without falling down. Let it be known, however, that on occasion Dr. Overtone does fall down, just as musicians who use heavy vibrato can easily find themselves simply out of tune — they lose the center of pitch. This is especially true for opera singers who perforce must sing with great power, thereby physically unleashing cataclysms of vibrato-producing and, only too often, atonal results. It is likewise lamentably common for string players to disguise unreliable intonation with indiscriminate vibrato. Some music stylistically requires little or no vibrato: early European music (up until about Mozart), Indian, African, and Balkan choir music, to name a few. For me, vibrato is most pleasing when it is used with both intention and discrimination.

Our ability to appreciate slight deviation from a given pitch is a particularly musical dimension of our mind's ability to ferret out meaning. You can experience this directly. Sing a unison tone with a friend. Once the pitch has been established, each singer in turn holds the agreed-upon tone while the other scoops up slowly from a little bit below. You can try veering on either side of the pitch from above or below. Or both of you can try scooping up together, and see how well you end up on the original unison. You can do this with more accuracy (but less fun) using a fixed tone from a piano, guitar, or any instrument with a sustained tone.

There is another aspect of near-normal that is crucial in the Western world: How do we tolerate pitches and pulses when they are only a *little* bit off, and never *quite* on? In terms of pulse and rhythm, I think the answer is — not very well. Rushing and dragging drummers get fired fast. But in one very special case of pitch tuning, a certain kind of tolerance for deviations from the inner norms of low-prime harmonic proportions is common to our experience. I'm referring to how we tune our keyboards, and our orchestras, and in some cases even, our ears.

All the 3:2 ratios (the scalar name is "perfect fifths") on a modern keyboard are almost indistinguishably flat — too narrow — but there's a good reason for this. If you stack up actual 3:2 distances on top of one another they will never repeat to some doubling ("octave") of your starting tone. Mathematically this is the very definition of a prime number: no multiplying by itself will ever equal another prime — so stacking triples will never line up with stacking doubles. That is, you can multiply $3 \times 3 \times 3 \times 3$ forever and never result in a number divisible by 2; no prime number times itself will ever equal another prime times itself. But if you "temper" (in this case, flatten, or lessen) the ratio by a teeny amount, twelve stacked fifths *will* add up to some duple (i.e., "octave") ratio, generating what is called a "circle of fifths" but in actuality is a circle of *almost*-fifths. This means that you can play the same piece starting on any of the twelve available tones and the tuning (that is, the out-of-tuning) will remain the same — none of the harmonic agreements, such as they are, will need to be renegotiated. The tuning that allows us to navigate equally well among twelve keys is called *twelve-*

tone equal temperament, a method of tuning that has received only gradual and grudging acceptance over the past four centuries. Ultimately, however, the beast was discovered to possess a beauty so great that it gave rise to musical forms of monumental dramatic scope, and has served as an enormous coevolutionary force in our culture.

If the cost of such tempering would be only the wee stunting of the 3:2, we would scarcely notice or care. But we need not only prime-two and prime-three for our music, we need prime-five as well. A functional 5:4 is crucial to our culture's ear, and on the equal-tempered keyboard, the 5:4 (the scalar name is "a major third") is considerably sharp (too wide). So all the "major thirds" on the keyboard are about as mellow as a rusty razor. We tolerate this because of the rewards of navigating, or *modulating,* through all twelve keys. Thanks to tonal modulation we get Beethoven and Stravinsky and Miles Davis, to begin a long list. But the cost is real. Four hundred years ago, Western musicians, natural and trained alike, were in tune and in touch with their low-prime gifts. Not so today—it is rare to find Western musicians who are deeply in tune, though country fiddlers and singers are often a welcome exception.

So why does a symphony orchestra with eighty players playing Mozart or Mahler sound so good? Well, first of all, it often doesn't. Also, remember that fifteen violinists playing the same note slightly fuzz the unison and hence allow the ear more easily to tolerate the deviations from pure harmonic ratios needed for modulation through keys. But wind sections with only one or two players on a part, for instance, often have a hard time navigating the temperament. Even excellent players from excellent orchestras, inured as they are to the contingencies of orchestral tuning, often aren't as sensitive to pure tuning as are, for example, jazz soloists, or lieder singers, who have more latitude to adjust to the pure norms. Orchestral brass players have trouble also, although a little less so, due to the tuning flexibility inherent in their instruments. And when you take away the army of string players from a string section and are left with only a string quartet, faulty intonation is extremely common. To be trapped in a concert played by an inexpert string quartet is to experience the full cost of our culture's marriage to equal-tempered tuning.

But when intonation is optimal, that is, when all the compromises that need to be made on the fly to produce the most harmonious result are being met, the sound of instrumental music played in equal temperament can be wondrous indeed. It is the best of both worlds: *nearly* pure harmonic ratio and unlimited modulation from key to key. It's a little like observing a master negotiator cajoling opposing factions into agreement. The factions are pure tuning versus tempered tuning, the agreement is called harmony, and the master negotiator is the high musical mind in action.

Another Near Miss: Loose Brains in Bali

In 1989, my wife, Devi, and I spent several weeks in Bali, high up in the rice terraces north of Ubud, observing the plant-to-harvest cycle of a rice crop. The sounds of ducks, chickens, water buffalo, and human labor with its singing and laughing were everywhere mixed. I was writing *The Listening Book* at the time, so my ears were particularly attuned to the life around me. The sounds that drew me most came from the village gamelan orchestras. I spent hours hanging around listening to them while the long, episodic compositions were being remembered, reconsidered, taught by rote, and performed by the villagers.

After a few weeks in Bali, one's brains get loosened up. As time expands, the local sounds flow into a seamless symphony of place. The human condition begins to feel open and endless.

The light of the island becomes clear but not harsh. You can feel wet, dry, warm, and cool all at the same time. You can feel other people's energy, and your own heart opening.

One day I came across a village blacksmith hammering rectangular metal objects in the heat of a red-orange, bellows-driven forge, and soon realized he was tuning gamelan bars. Nearby there was a control gamelan, the agreed-upon standard of tuning for that particular village, which he referred to from time to time. Tuning gamelan bars is not like tuning piano strings. The tone of a piano string is relatively pure, which is to say that its overtones can be expressed (more or less) in whole-number ratios, and one string can be tuned in unison to another with very high accuracy. That's because a piano string is long and thin and its metal is highly refined. A gamelan bar, however, is rectangular and thick, thinning toward the edges. When you strike it, it sounds more like a bell. Bells do not produce whole-number overtones. Their overtones are the formulae of madmen, including bell makers and Balinese blacksmiths. These tones rattle your mind and wake up your ears.

A few hours after leaving the blacksmith's compound, I realized something about my Balinese state of mind: it's the gamelan tuning. Each gamelan bar has, in fact, a fundamental tone that is quite soft, easily buried by the zoo of metallic harmonics above it. To increase its volume, a resonator is placed under the bar (as is done with marimbas) so when it's struck, the now audible fundamental tone is surrounded by a bright, starry sky of half-crazed overtones. Multiply this by the dozens and dozens of bars in the large gamelan array of a typical village orchestra. The fundamentals, taken together, form a loosely structured pentatonic scale—five tones to the octave—with a tuning that changes slightly from gamelan to gamelan. The music itself has a rhythmic structure and a polyrhythmic weave that make it one of the most complex, intelligent, surprising, and stimulating of all musics on the planet. The wisdom of the gamelan music itself, incidentally, is shared by many members of a community. Few if any individuals know an entire composition, but the village as a whole stores the entire repertoire in its collective memory. The standard of musicianship is typically quite high, which means accurate playing and ensemble discipline.

When you hear, from near and far, many hours of this music scattered throughout your day, your mind becomes oddly clear and addled at the same time. I think I know why. Taken together, the intense rhythms, the fine structure of the melodies, and the interlocking among the players are as precise and dense as the music of Bach. But the pitches themselves are a model of "near harmony"—approximate pentatonic tunings surrounded by a patina of overtonal inharmonicity. To understand the tonality of the gamelan, your mind has to peer through a fog so dense it finally stops squinting, and accepts the emerging shapes without trying to reconcile them with familiar inner norms. This could be irritating (it is to some Westerners), but when you live in it you become charmed, fascinated, and finally hooked. It is an addictive and quite musical state of high mind.

Polyrhythmic Mind

I was four years old in 1941, a good year for Brahms and Arthur Godfrey to assure us war-rattled Americans that there was a good life worth preserving. I turned nine in the summer of 1946, at the height of the postwar boom, when sanguine landowners were selling virgin real estate to build houses for returning veterans of a war hard-won. To my deep sadness, the twenty acres of sycamores and maples behind our family home were sold off by our neighbor for just this purpose. I'd always thought those dappled woods were my personal space, but my childhood came to an abrupt halt when I saw a sign posted on one of my trees that said (and this is true fact):

HOLSIER & RAPE
Real Estate
SOLD

A subdivision of tiny, modest, look-alike houses began to rise almost immediately, and all through that summer the din of sawing and hammering disturbed my lazy days, especially the hot August afternoons reserved for lying around. Things were different on one of those afternoons, though. I was lying on the back porch, just four cherry trees and a wire fence removed from the construction site, moping over loss as only a nine-year-old can, when I found myself, instead of blocking out the sound of the hammering carpenters, tracking it in a new way. Some of the five or six men on the job were nearer than others; some of the hammering was faster, some slower. In some cases the sound of a nail being driven into new, soft wood had a clear ring to it, its pitch rising as the nail was driven home. In other cases, the sound was less a pitch than a violent *thwack*. The din came into focus as a stream of individual pulses that were crossing and recrossing one another. The slightly differing speeds and varying distances of the men let my ear track each man's contribution to the hammering symphony. Their occasional calls, the intermittent sawing and the drones of the biplanes overhead fleshed out the scene. I was hearing something I'd never heard before, and suddenly I wasn't so sad.

The lazy afternoon experience of tracking several things simultaneously was sharply stimulating to my young mind. The cross-pulses of the hammerers, like friends with different strides walking together, gradually drifting out of phase, then back in again, were mesmerizing. The randomness of the entrances engaged me fully. But it wasn't just the hammering I heard. As I listened I realized that the carpenter's hammering was part and parcel of the act of building, the sound of real men working in the real world. Maybe, after all, our brave soldiers needed new houses for their new wives and babies. From the polyphony of house-raising, my mind extrapolated a more meaningful social order.

Polyphonic Mind

You sing a song and it is a perfectly good song. I sing a different song, also a perfectly good one. Polyphony is what happens when we sing our songs together and the relationship between them is more rich and pleasing than either song by itself. If we were to choose a single emblem of Western culture as it has developed over the last millennium, a motet by Machaut, or a mass by Josquin, or a fugue by Bach — all models of polyphony at its finest — would serve well.

When we began our consideration of tonal harmony, we looked at the relationship of various tones to a single given tone. Speaking both globally and historically, that is how the notion of harmony has risen: many tones against one. There is much music sung or played against a drone still extant today, notably North Indian music, wherein the generating tone is always present in an instrument called a tamboura that is dedicated to that purpose. In the teaching of North Indian music, the meaning and quality of each tone in respect to the generating tone is honored as a sacred transmission. The proportional harmony of each tone is held as a personal, direct tether to the divine.

Beginning in early medieval times, the chanting of Christian texts became common practice in churches across Europe. Gradually among the leading cathedral singers there arose the practice of improvising an embellished version of the chant, called *descant,* as an accompaniment to the given chant. By the twelfth century, the given chant was often deliberately slowed down, thereby accommodating the freely flowing, improvisatory, melismatic flourishes of the cantor singing descant. (Melisma is the singing of many tones to one syllable of text.)

In the late twelfth century, a perhaps mythical but certainly legendary musician named Léonin began to codify the relationships between the relatively sustained tones of the chant and the melisma of the descant. In a historical process especially familiar to Western music, what began as improvisational practices among singers eventually became codified into complex compositional styles.

By around 1350, two centuries later, the expressive, melodically brilliant, and harmonically plangent four-part polyphony of Guillaume de Machaut set a high-water mark for Western civilization. There followed four more centuries of truly glorious polyphonic composition featuring composers like Josquin Desprez, Orlande de Lassus, and Palestrina (among hundreds of others) and culminating in the huge oeuvre of Sebastian Bach. Bach's death in 1750 marked the close of the polyphonic era, but in the ensuing generations, polyphony wasn't dead, merely snoozing, only to awaken wide-eyed in inspired passages of Mozart and Beethoven. It slept more soundly in the nineteenth century, reviving somewhat in various inventive forms during the twentieth century.

Most music has conspicuously moving parts, but real polyphony requires melodic autonomy of each part and total interdependence among the parts. In other words, each melody will be complete in itself, and the whole will be greater than the parts. When you listen to true polyphony, your meaning-seeking mind is engaged at the highest level. I can't say for sure, but I suspect that more neurons are firing in more parts of the brain when you're playing a Bach fugue than at any other time. What I can say for sure is how it feels: it feels mighty good. Part of the reason is that there is a *surfeit* of meaningful content in such music. We *sense* an ocean of meaningful relationships that we can't directly track. Few can truly follow a dense polyphonic piece in real time, not even some of the composers who compose them. What is the mind's polyphonic limit?

Whatever one's capacity for hearing polyphony, you can get close to it by dedicated listening, closer still by singing in a choir, and closest by playing polyphony at the keyboard. For about fifty years I've been holding a few dozen pieces by Bach in my memory. Some, especially the ones I've played for thirty years or so, I know pretty well—I almost could play them in my sleep. Indeed, some nights when I can't sleep I lie awake hearing thick contrapuntal textures in slow motion, sixteenth note by sixteenth note, making sure I register the full meaning of each tone's relationship to all the others before my mind mercifully gives up. Do I really hear four parts at once?

Yes and no. For the hour or so every day or so when I play Bach at the piano, I listen to him like a fiend and love him like a big old dog. I do so honor him, and have spent years of conscious growth inside his mind and heart. I hear him clearly enough to play his music convincingly, every phrase tucked in and turned out. But what I don't hear (except in rare flashes) is all four parts with the same clarity that I would if I were singing each one in tune and with controlled, expressive nuance. Did Herr Bach? I've concluded after our many decades of intimate conversation that he, most rare among men, could hear in real time with utter clarity what he wrote. The kind of hearing I mean is rare because it requires the mind to separate out and then reassemble not only four linear tracks, but also all the harmonic relationships that are taking place among them—all this with total cognition. That means, among other things, being able to visualize the score as you hear the piece. Many musicians can do that with simpler music. I can hear an unfamiliar piece by, say Vivaldi, or Joni Mitchell (I love them both) and see as well as name all the notes in my mind. But I can't do that with a richly polyphonic piece by old Bach. The only music I know to match such polyphony in density is the highly developed polymetric tradition in certain parts of Africa—Ghana and Zimbabwe, to name two.

Much deference must be paid to Bach and his predecessors in the golden age of polyphonic composition. If you open your ears to their dense polyphony, it will light up your mind. And the more times you hear a piece, the more there is to hear inside it. I wish for you, Gentle Listener, that in your listening to Bach or Josquin or Machaut, you can allow your mind to be taken apart and put back together by the many seductive ways of polyphony. Each time your mind is fragmented and reassembled by a fugue it becomes a more musical mind. Polyphony is the most intimate and comforting way I have of being with my own high mind, and I wish it for you and everyone alive.

CROSS-TALK: MUSIC AS MEME

When you examine the kinds of things music does and the kinds of things your mind does, the complementarity is compelling. Periodicity is potentially present throughout the natural world — the musical mind refines this into pulse and meter. Rising and falling pitches are plentiful in nature — the human mind refines these into melodies we learn and sing repeatedly. Whole-number proportion is a universal structural principle — the human mind refines it into a micro-universe of musical harmony. Music is the sound our minds make as we evolve, a way we have of talking to ourselves individually and collectively, of becoming more and more human.

Vibrational signals from the world stream into our senses, our senses impart to them an aural code our minds can read, a human shape, and we exteriorize those signals in our own image. When you are making music you are coding experience, and when you are listening to it you are cracking the code. You know how to decode the message because you are the code-maker. Music is your mind having a coded conversation with itself. Human music is the cross-talk of humans. A village gamelan is a village newspaper. Popular music is a continuous musical referendum: *yes* to this, *no* to that, then yes to this *other,* a never-ending search for what is true for most of us right now. Garage-band subculture hears itself saying, We don't need no friggin' *studio,* then the mainstream begins to talk that way, then we have GarageBand running on our Macs.

Music is our precious aural meme—a deep aspect of our collective selves that we continually receive, shape, and give out again. It is our universal currency, the gossip of our minds, the ultimate confession. Music bridges mind to mind to mind, and finally bridges minds to Mind.

Imagine human music as a collective meme in the form of a living, glowing sphere encircling the planet. The notion of an all-encompassing, gigantic Mind where all the music in the world lives has cropped up long before the present era of satellites, but now, if you think about all the electromagnetic energy around us in the vibratory shapes of Machaut, Mozart, Mendelssohn, Messiaen, Madonna, Miles, and every Muslim muezzin, it's quite possible that a global meme of the musical mind is fully alive and well. And I say yes! Music, with its powers of clarity and transformation, puts our best Mind out there where it belongs.

3

Music as Heart

The first time I heard a North Indian flute I was in my early twenties, steeped in the traditions of American jazz and European classical music. Someone had given me an LP of North Indian ragas. When I took it home and dropped the stylus onto it, the first sound I heard was the background drone: *It's an E, something reedy, also some twangy thing.* Then immediately over that, a brush stroke of liquid silver. *What is that? Wood? Maybe bamboo?* My eyes widened and my heart warmed. Some new ray was traveling through me. By the time the flutist had taken his next breath, my sensible life had been changed. In the space of a single tone I had moved from sense (I hear something) to sensibility (I feel something). What had begun as the perception of a tone on a wooden flute became in that moment a new way of feeling the world.

THE LIFE OF A TONE

The flute tone wasn't straight like a ruled line. It began with a grace note from below, evened itself out, and ended with a most gentle undulation. The sound was like a bright, translucent stream and yet it was also dense as mercury. Inside it was the hollow feeling of breath. I heard the player's concentration and felt his devotion. I felt the warmth of the air column inside the flute's wooden body and the warm column of my own body. Then, just at the end of the breath, the patina around the tone seemed to enlarge and brighten, and the core glowed deeper and warmer, giving me a little rush of pleasure.

I had heard sounds similar in their startling presence played by jazz musicians of great refinement (Lester Young and Miles Davis, to name two), but there was something about the ancientness of the discipline—and where this episode fit into the story of my life—that woke me up. It was the first time I fully realized the affective power of a single tone of music.

Musical *affect* refers to the feeling, emotion, mood, or mental disposition that music imparts. In *The Republic,* Plato famously prohibits soldiers from listening to certain combinations of tones (called modes) because such music promotes cowardice and thwarts courage. All through the Middle Ages, various affective theories emerged assigning to specific musical elements specific emotional or psychological results: a certain melodic motion would promote a certain kind of passion, a certain combination of tones would produce despair. Not surprisingly, such ideas never codified into a useful Theory of Affects. I can think of several reasons why.

First, just as in spoken language, context is everything, and contexts abound infinitely. "No" can mean "yes" and "free" can mean "trapped." Another reason is that (again referring to spoken language), although we have identifiable categories of intention, like sarcasm, irony, kidding around, and so forth, subtexts are extremely subtle, various, and ambiguous—difficult if not impossible to pin down. From a psychological view, the reason there is no Law of Affects is because one man's happy can be another's sad. Like most art, music is highly subjective. A Law of Affects would, after all, require Affect Police to remind me that my joy in a "Crucifixus" or grief in a *gigue* is illegal. Your emotional responses to music are neither legal nor illegal, neither wrong nor right. They are simply yours. You have one hundred percent ownership of your responses to music; what is valid for you is valid, period. "A thing is not true unless it is true for you," says Kabir. In approaching the affective power of music in this way we go beyond the mere act of listening into the process of recognizing *ourselves* in the act of hearing. The greatest music lesson you can ever have is to realize that the most authentic response is the one you are having now.

Even a single tone can be such an epiphany, though this is less surprising the more you consider its many dimensions waiting to be discovered. The deeper the listening, the greater the discovery. Consider the very first moment of the sound, its *onset characteristics*, to use the acoustical term. Does the sound start suddenly or gently? Does the flutist "tongue" a tone by beginning the breath with *ta*, or is the note begun gently, like a breathy *ah*? Does the violinist lightly swipe the string with the bow, or awaken it with a heavy, resiny caress? Does the singer begin with a consonant like *k* or *ch*, or *mm*? Or *wh*, forming an open-throated vowel? At the end does the pitch simply stop or does it close off with a final *t* or with, perhaps, a half-aspirated vowel as in *leave*?

A sustained tone by definition has a certain constancy—it's the sound of a specific pitch. But it has variation as well. In fixed-pitch instruments like a piano or organ, the pitch of a single tone will remain relatively steady, but for instruments with variable pitch, like the violin, saxophone, or voice, a specific pitch may include subtly changing shapes. It might scoop up from below and level off (as did my Indian flutist); it might drop in from above; at the end it might taper downward or even occasionally scoop upward. The pitch may bend slightly—typically down, then up, but sometimes the reverse. It might be rendered sensuous and alive by vibrato of all kinds: slow, fast, fast, then gradually slower. The vibrato can be present from the beginning and then disappear into a straight line, or the line may start straight and wiggle at the end, a typical vocal model. A tone's pitch can gently vary in as many ways as you can imagine one could decorate the straightness of a line. Such lines are fun to draw, and such tones are deeply satisfying to sing.

But this is just the beginning of what a tone has to teach. A tone has a dynamic of soft and loud, just as a drawn line can have thickness or thinness. A piano tone has an initial spike in amplitude, a sudden loudness that drops rapidly in intensity; its gradual decay can last a minute or more. In strings, winds, and voice, the dialectic between louder and softer can tell an entire story, as does the changing thickness of a line drawn with a calligrapher's ink brush.

Then there is the timbre of the sound to consider, the palette of overtones that allows us to distinguish between a flute and an oboe. In addition, a flutist has dozens of different ways of sounding like a flute: by turning his breath more or less into the lip of the instrument, by subtle changes of embouchure, by various kinds of breath control. A bowed string can be sand or velvet, a trombone can jeer or cajole, and you can call up an encyclopedia of vocal timbres by singing gibberish on one tone. There is sweet gibberish, seductive gibberish, angry-as-hell gibberish, hungry gibberish. Try it. Pick a tone. Begin it some which way, wiggle the pitch, control the vibrato, experiment with soft and loud, invent a language. Try anything. Each tone is a whole life.

Finally, there is the most important dimension of all: the feeling of the person producing the tone. This is the core mystery of music, the open secret of its power. When you sing a tone, you put into it some immeasurable dimension of yourself that is the primary agent of the tone's affect. Listeners pick it up immediately. A sad singer sounds sad, a cocky singer "comes across" that way, and a joyous one lifts us up. Of course there is a certain degree of artifice in this, just as there is for an actor. A stage direction says *gently* and the actor has the craft to portray gentleness. Likewise, in his sheet music a musician reads *dolce* and plays sweetly, or reads *doloroso* and becomes dolorous, and has the inner satisfaction of being able to navigate such dramatic waters. Yet for actors and musicians alike, we the audience can sense something deeper: the innermost state of a musician's heart. It cannot be hidden. Nor does a musician want to hide it—not really. Deep down, everyone needs to be recognized, even in the act of hiding.

When you sing a tone there is no hiding. In song, the heart is naked as a jaybird even if it's got up in the costume of a jungle bird. We like it that way. We like to have safe psychic codes—music, for instance—that everyone can read. Music is a safe haven, a pool you can jump into with complete abandon and trust that you are at the same time naked and invisible. You're naked because you uncover yourself. You're invisible because you and the listener are two ends of the same bridge, an invisible bridge of audible waves.

Can you hear all this in a single tone? Yes indeed. Have a friend sing tones to you. Then sing tones for your friend. Don't talk about it *too* much, just listen, hearing what you hear and feeling what you feel. If you enter the experience, the streaming world of a sung tone has no edges.

Tones against Drones

A drone is a continuous tone, typically in the lower region of the soundscape, against which melodies rise and fall. It is heard by the ear as the home note, the keynote, the generating tone; it sounds the unity the mind seeks. The drone is a grounding reference for everything happening around it. Consequently, the harmonic values of tones sung against a drone are the most readily sensible. Such tones make a sequence of relationships with their parental drone, a sequence that functions as a harmonic—and thus affective—narrative. Tone by tone, you are bathed in a series of affective states: it feels *this* way, now *this* way, now *this,* now *this.*

Remember in science lab, playing with iron filings on a sheet of paper held over a magnet, how the filings formed into a pattern representing the "lines of force" in the magnetic field? Now imagine that the pattern of those iron filings is arrayed in three dimensions, not two, and that it is changing from moment to moment. Now imagine further that the pattern is—*you*—taking the form of a living, resonant mandala by virtue of sound in the air. It is true that you are following a melody as it rises and falls, tracking its curve it as it moves up and down the tones of the scale. But at the same time, a chariot is pulling you from one harmonic quality to another through a rainbow of affective states. This is not simply the kind of proportional cognition we discussed in the previous chapter. The subject here is how harmony *feels,* and how that feeling is braided into the melodic line. Each tone in every tune is not only a point on a curve, but also a vibrational resonance in a moving constellation of feelings. The two simultaneous dimensions of closeness, scalar and proportional, are imbued with feeling. This is true for every note of tonal music. One can know this consciously in the way composers may need to know it in the act of composition, but most of us simply "get" the streaming feelings of melody and harmony mixed.

I wasn't around at the time, but I imagine that when the ancient Greeks were giving homage to their panoply of gods and goddesses, each deity in turn had its own psychological quality associated with it. Apart from the everyday stuff one prays for, I'll wager there was a personal connection with each god and goddess. So imagine that Ancient You are walking through the Athenian countryside and here on your left is a little temple to Artemis; the feeling of the place is the feeling of the goddess. A little farther down the road is Athena's altar, permeated with her essence as you sense it; then a modest temple to Zeus, fearfully grand in its way; then later an altar to Dionysus, where you linger. These responses are not so removed from our own times. A prayer to Mary has a different quality than a prayer to Jesus. There are five Buddhist Families, each with its own quality. Allah has ninety-nine Holy Names, each a well of feeling states as active and entire as a gathering of trusted friends. Every ray of connection to the sacred is authentic.

I experience the pantheon of tones against a drone much in this way. If you play or sing a scale against a drone, drawing out each tone for a full breath so as to enter into the harmonic resonance, the tones will teach you over time how to fully open to them. Then you can learn to move around inside a scale of tones, dancing on the ladder, evoking temple after grotto after altar of connective harmonic states. And oh yes, that will make a tune, like "Twinkle, Twinkle, Little Star," for instance; but remember that the tune is the outer shell. The heart—what you feel inside—is the harmony.

Gentle Reader of Music Books, my ink is mixed with tears because I am not in your company now, singing along with you. You must sing for yourself. Play a drone on any instrument (piano, electronic keyboard, guitar, cello, dial tone, anything) and proceed slowly, slowly, maybe with the help of a musically trained friend, maybe not. If you actually *do* this, the pantheon of harmonic gods and goddesses will sing back to you in person.

I can't tell you what you feel when you feel the harmonies produced by scale-tones against a drone, but I can say that there is a sensible relationship between number and feeling. In musical harmony, we experience the numbers *as* feeling, and the numbers feel good. As we've mentioned, you do not have to cognize the specifics of these correspondences to experience the affective power of a melody moving through you. But you can indeed realize, in the act of listening, that you innately recognize real proportional relationships as they stream *via* sound waves into your ear, and into your mind's light, and that these real proportions result in real feelings. I'm saying (and I know it can't be said) that there is a mandala of feeling for you to discover in the harmonies of a scale, and that its power is innately yours in your wiring and in your nature.

The Dronal Truth

In order to carry affective meaning, do tones have to be heard against a sounding drone?

Yes and no. A tonal melody by definition *refers* to a home tone (or *tonic*) of the tune but that tone, as we have discussed, need not be sounding in air. If you sing "Twinkle, Twinkle, Little Star" *a cappella,* the tonic is the first note, but from then on it is remembered in the mind's ear (until "are," when it is reiterated). Your *memory* of the drone can serve the same function as the drone sounding in air. Somehow we have evolved to learn to keep the tonic alive in our minds, at least for long moments. Remember that the mind is hungry for meaning—it *needs* to know how tones are organized. It actively seeks the drone tone, sounding or not. In the scramble to find meaningful organization, it will even attempt to posit a new drone when the old one doesn't work. But a drone in the mind's ear is fainter, less assertive, less sensible than a drone sounding in air. As it fades in the memory, it fails to guide the singer. When the mind-drone fades entirely, the singer has no anchor. The singer then tries to find the tones' true proportions among *themselves,* which is vastly more subtle and, since errors tend to compound, much less reliable. Sooner than later, the singer begins to sing out of tune, usually flat, thanks to entropy. When the home tone is lost, even experienced *a cappella* choirs will typically drift lower in pitch. To a large degree, musical training consists in learning to "hold" the pitch, that is, to sustain the memory of the home tone, against which the other tones can be tuned. The collective impulse to value and nurture this innate ability seems to be fading in our culture. One of the reasons for writing this book is to encourage its re-emergence.

Modes

Each tone sung against a drone produces some feeling state or other. How many such tones, considered within the compass of a single octave, exist in the world's music? Not counting the deliberate mistuning of equal temperament or the quasi-randomized tuning of bells or ballophones, gamelans, steel drums (and other instruments with high inharmonicity as we discussed in the last chapter), there are at least thirty (or as many as forty plus) available tones within an octave, depending on the global scope of your listening and the acuity of your ear. I can sing about twenty-five. The dozen or so having the simplest ratios are the most common worldwide.

From a menu of thirty-odd tones within an octave, musicians choose five tones (a pentatonic mode), or maybe seven tones (a heptatonic mode), and occasionally eight or nine tones to fashion a mode. A few favorite pentatonic modes and a few favorite heptatonic modes account for most of the music in the planet's air at any given time. From a single mode a musician can fashion an entire piece, perhaps an entire evening. An Indian raga comprises just such a chosen collection of five, six, or seven tones, occasionally involving quite complex harmonic ratios. The first section of a forty-five-minute raga, called the *alap*, may typically spend fifteen or twenty minutes revealing the chosen tones one by one, combination by combination. At its best, this is done with utmost patience and devotion, as if praying to hidden deities.

The most flavorful choices from the menu of tones are not necessarily the simplest. Many Asian and Arabian modes involve complex ratios that sound and feel exotic to us. Like anything unfamiliar, they have to be met halfway. Open-minded listening pays off, though. The way to understand a culture is to understand its modal harmony, an understanding that leads to empathy and human bonding. When a strange mode from a strange people resonates with a familiar and perhaps forgotten place in your heart, you come to recognize that you are hearing the music of your own kin.

DEATH CHORDS, LIFE CHORDS

One winter morning I had to have my arthritic, fifteen-year-old golden retriever put down. That afternoon, Jack, a longtime student, trusted friend, and gifted pianist came for a lesson. I sat in the teacher's rocking chair, he sat at the keyboard. He asked how I was. I sighed, "Had to put my dog down."

An empathetic man, Jack. He shook his head, "Very bad." Then he turned to the piano and, with his foot on the sustain pedal, gently struck down the lowest seven or eight keys of the keyboard. He intended to console me, but the rumble of the strings struck me like a death knell, a chamber of black horrors, and there was no escaping its reverberating emptiness. I couldn't not listen; I was being siphoned into the night of it, sucked into grief and guilt.

One doesn't ordinarily listen carefully to a low chord like that—it's just a piece of thunder, nothing to hear, really, except lowness. But this time the dark was already upon me, and each vibration led to more blackness. The nothing of death opened inside me. For an instant I was really scared. I hadn't realized I'd taken the loss of my dog so to heart, and I was blindsided into suddenly feeling the fullness of loss. And all this thanks to the sympathetic gesture of a musical friend. Well, I got over it. But I'll never forget the *tragedy* of that low chord.

A chord is the simultaneous sounding of three tones or more. The chords used in everyday music are not in the thunderous bass, of course, but settle into clear tone combinations in mid-range. In tonal harmony, not only does each individual tone of a chord retain its affective relationship with the tonic, but the relationships among the tones themselves also become important. The mind scrambles to find the hierarchical meaning inside these clusters of sound. This is not even a little bit simple. Since we live in a world where our ears are continually bombarded with chordal harmonies, we take chords and chains of chords — called chord progressions — for granted. Yet historically these stacks of tones, these vertical affective packages, are quite new.

The first serious complexification of Western music came not in the form of chords, but in the simultaneously sounding melodies of twelfth-century polyphony. Only gradually, over many generations, did musicians become aware of the possibilities of vertical harmony. The everyday chordal vamps of our pop music were, in 1300, nascent mysteries.

Certain three-tone combinations were the first to be recognized as functionally affective units of sound. The simplest of these combinations all have one thing in common: they comprise every *other* degree of the seven-tone scale, for instance the tonic, the third and the fifth; or the second, the fourth and the sixth, or the third, the fifth and the seventh and so on. Three such tones taken together are called a *triad*. The most recognizable triads contain a 3:2 proportion — a scalar *perfect fifth* — between the outer tones. For instance, in a C major triad, which comprises C, E, and G, there is a 3:2 proportion from the upper note G down to the C below it.

The middle tone of the triad, called its *third*, splits the distance between the outer tones unevenly. If the distance is greater on the bottom, the chord is called a *major triad;* if the lesser distance is on the bottom, the triad is called *minor triad.* Any of the three tones in a triad can be played in *any* configuration in *any* octave, and the ear will still recognize it, and the heart will respond to its nature.

The affective nature of major and minor triads, so familiar to us in daily life, has taken many centuries to appreciate. It is an evolution that is Western in character, a passion of the Western mind, and largely confined to cultures influenced by our music (which thanks to Western pop and rock means, by now, almost but not quite everyone). Here is what has taken us so long to learn: Just as each *tone* has its own characteristic affective power in respect to the tonic, so does each *packet* of tones—each triad—built on that tone. Affectively speaking, what is true for tones is also true in the expanded dimension of triads. We now have a succession of affective packets of sound. Just as successive tones in a melody produce a succession of harmonic experiences, successive triads built on such tones result in similarly characteristic responses.

The difference between the succession of tones in a melody and the succession of chords in a chord progression is this: In a melody, the melodic *line* is what is perceived at the surface of the sound, and the harmony is operating undercover. In a chord progression, the *harmonic* narrative is the surface of the sound and the melody lies hidden, waiting to be brought forward.

With all these tones swirling around us, this might be a good time to ask the question: What is the status of the indispensable drone we began with? Has it disappeared? It hasn't disappeared, exactly, but it has become to an amazing extent internalized by the listener. By this I mean that over the centuries, our ears have learned to hear the home tone sustaining the architecture of the music even though that tone is not sounding in air. At least for a while, we *remember* the tonic, even amid the flux of a great multiplicity of tones. This astonishing capacity of the mind is one of the truly serendipitous products of human evolution. The gradual internalization of tonic has allowed a special kind of dramatic narrative to arise and develop in increasingly long, increasingly intricate musical forms, culminating in the colossal symphonies of composers from Mozart to Beethoven to Brahms to Mahler.

Back to triads and their progressions. In conventional harmonic analysis, triads based on the various scale degrees are designated by Roman numerals. For instance, a triad based on the first degree of a major scale is designated by the Roman numeral "I"; one on the fifth degree, "V". Uppercase numerals stand for major triads; lowercase numerals stand for minor triads. The most common triadic progression, and perhaps the most readily sensible, consists of a major triad based on the scalar fifth (V) moving to a major triad based on the tonic (I). We will notate it V→I. (In the key of C, this would mean a G major triad followed by a C major triad. In the key of C minor, this would be notated V→i, and would mean a G major triad followed by a C minor triad.) From the late sixteenth century on, this progression has been the harmonic engine for returning the music to home; it is the "x marks the spot" of harmony. To the ear it sounds as if the music says "right *here*." Positioned at the end of a phrase it says "*The End* (for now)."

In Latin, *cadere* means "to fall." A musical *cadence* can be understood as a release from a condition of relative complexity into a condition of relative simplicity or certainty, a stilling of restless waters. The motion from the V triad, which is relatively complex because it's *not-home,* to the I (tonic) triad, which is relatively simple (because it's *home*) can be understood as a falling into simplicity. The V→I cadence, the most readily recognized triadic progression in Western music, has been given the respectful name *perfect cadence* (or sometimes *authentic cadence*). Its reciprocal (upside down) twin, IV→I is called a *plagal cadence.* Reciprocal cadences seems to have a kind of rising energy, the kind you hear in church at the final *Amen,* or in the first three *Hallelujahs* of Handel's "Hallelujah Chorus," and are featured extensively in blues and gospel music.

Strung together, these two kinds of cadence—plagal and perfect—hone in on the tonic, first rising up from the reciprocal branch of the tonal family and then falling from the overtonal branch. The progression rises to home, then falls to home; the complete progression is called a *full cadence*. If there is such a thing as a Western mantra, it is this full cadence. Using Roman numeral notation, and beginning on the tonic triad, the major mode version of this mantra looks like this: $I \rightarrow IV \rightarrow I \rightarrow V \rightarrow I$. In the key of C major, it looks like this: $C \rightarrow F \rightarrow C \rightarrow G \rightarrow C$. Played over and over again, with equal duration for each chord, the mantric effect becomes increasingly compelling. We are being swung from side to side on the inners, two complementary ways of being away from, and returning to, our center. Remember, this is not necessarily a *scalar* rising and falling, in the sense of low pitches rising and high pitches falling. Rather, this is the truly mysterious harmonic affect that distinguishes upside-down harmony from right-side-up harmony. Although every listener under the sun is affected quite naturally by the qualities of harmonic cadences, musicians study deeply and at length to master their subtle voodoo.

The ubiquity of this tonal pattern and its characteristic affect in Western—and now virtually global—experience cannot be overestimated. Perfect cadences and endless variations of them have sounded in your ears from birth and will likely be sounding at your eulogy. But why are they so ubiquitous? Do they sound the same and feel the same for everyone? Remember that although I talk of characteristic affects and feeling states, ascribing various responses to you the respondee, I'm describing as infrequently and as minimally as possible the feelings themselves. No one can tell you what you should feel, or describe what you actually do feel. BUT—what we have been considering is the most commonly reiterated chord progression worldwide, and there seems to be consensual agreement as to its place and function in the affective grammar of Western harmony. So even if I don't want to tell you how to feel, I can nevertheless report what seems to be the *general* agreement in a world of listeners. We all seem to be nodding our heads and saying, "Yes, it goes like *this*."

Cadential progressions have many variations. A particular variation in the basic cadential model can define a musical style. European-influenced music spends more cadential time falling $V \rightarrow I$ (in C that is $G \rightarrow C$) than rising $IV \rightarrow I$ ($F \rightarrow C$). A favored European legacy is falling from *two* fifths above, which in the key of C corresponds to $D \rightarrow G \rightarrow C$. This progression, standard in Baroque and Classical music, sounds absolutely correct, old-fashioned and even good-timey to us now. Blues and gospel music, on the other hand, spends more time rising than falling. Merely vamping $C \rightarrow F \rightarrow C \rightarrow F \rightarrow C \rightarrow F \rightarrow C$ suggests to us a sacred cast. When the tone of a minor seventh above the root is added (building up from C that results in C, E, G, B♭; building up from F gives F, A, C, E♭), the progression is written $C^7 \rightarrow F^7 \rightarrow C^7 \rightarrow F^7$, and so on. The alternation between these two chords sounds bluesy to us and indeed, these are the characteristic chords of the blues. The blues raises you up for lots of reasons, not the least of which is the affect of its definitively chord progression.

One afternoon in the early 60s, while enjoying my morning French toast at the corner greasy spoon, I was astonished to hear from the juke box a popular hit song whose harmony rose up from *two* fifths below the tonic: $B♭ \rightarrow F \rightarrow C$. The last time that sound was around was in Renaissance madrigals, but by the mid-'60s it had become the harmonic signature of *rock 'n' roll*, and was seeping into all forms of popular and folk music. (In the key of A major, an easy key for the guitar, the progression goes $G \rightarrow D \rightarrow A$; ask any kid with a guitar.) So had we supplanted the iconic falling cadence of our Baroque grandfathers with the rising icon of the New Age? Had the polarity of the culture shifted? And had that shift been reflected in the elemental harmonic grammar? In hindsight, I think that is indeed what happened. It was an ancient affect for a new time, and it stoned everybody with ears. And in the unconscious way we have of hearing our music, I think, half a century later and counting, it still does. But this is only one example of a chord progression clarifying a culture's mood. As long as music is in the air, its chord progressions function as an affective grammar, a subtle syntax for socially shared feelings, casual or deep, an aural poetry floating above and beneath the surface of the times.

Many musicians call chord progressions "changes," and indeed it is the change in feeling, the slight change in the mood's light, from one little packet of sound to the next little packet that surprisingly and miraculously modulates the qualities of our inner lives. Some progressions are so well known that everyone responds to them reflexively, and many can play them almost unconsciously, like the $I \rightarrow vi \rightarrow IV \rightarrow V$ changes of the "Heart and Soul" ditty that someone at a party always plays on the piano. (In the key of C that would be: C major $\rightarrow$ A minor $\rightarrow$ F major $\rightarrow$ G major.) Other, more sophisticated progressions are the provenance of experienced musicians, many of whom have a personal relationship with their favorite changes. Remember the old monks who are so familiar with the jokes they tell and re-tell each other that they refer to them by number only? One monk shouts out, "Number 37!" and everyone else hoots and guffaws. Well, musicians gather in groups and tell their favorite chord changes:

—Ooh, I *love* that G seven flat thirteen in the middle of "Stella"!

— How 'bout the C nine flat thirteen at the end of the bridge of "All the Things You Are"?

—I'm down with Hindemith's quartal flat-two cadences, like *Mathis,* man!

For all musicians who improvise, the internalization of harmonic progressions—"knowing the changes"—is a primary musical protocol. What these musicians know is how melodies spontaneously arise from harmony. As the changes become second nature, melodies gradually and gently become audible, they simply *happen*, one begins to "sing the changes." In "Sing the Changes" (on his 2008 *Electric Arguments*), Paul McCartney points out that this is akin to "a sense of childlike wonder." And the more you do it, the more compelling and enduring seems the wonder.

For me, certain chord progressions are a matter of personal history. Like people who remember their first kiss, or their baby's first step, or where they were when men landed on the moon, or when Obama won, I remember the details of my life when I first internalized this or that chord change. I first truly *heard* V → i when I was eight, practicing a piece called "Knight Rupert" by Robert Schumann. The progression was in the key of the piece, A minor (so it was E^7 → Ami), and I began to play it over and over my own way, probably the first time I improvised anything at all. I vividly remember the moment of recognition: Oh, I can play that lots of ways, like this, like this, maybe like *this*. I didn't hear the progression as *beautiful*, really, that would have come later — primarily I heard it as *active*, something that moved me to engage in its energy. Then my mom called in from the kitchen, "What's that nice song, Honey?" and that sealed the deal.

Cut ahead fifteen years and I'm studying harmonic progressions (with strict polyphonic voice-leading) under Easley Blackwood, my mentor at the time. Waves of beauty are washing over me as I practice harmonic models cycling through the twelve keys. One especially complex sequence catches me broadside. I hear it suddenly; my heart is on fire. I hear myself saying, "This entire subject is actually *knowable*, and I can know it." At that moment, the afternoon winter light in my Chicago basement apartment seems epochal.

Cut ahead another forty years. I am writing *Harmonic Experience*, a book about tonal harmony. I have a big idea about how things work. It comes down to the wire: if I can compose an exhaustive set of musical examples that validates a certain idea, I can finish my book with confidence. I stop writing words for two weeks and compose a musical demonstration that is completely true *and* has never before been fully laid out (there it is on page 282). It's just a page full of cadential models configured in a particular way—a pedagogical bunch of chord changes—but because I hear it to my very core it is just about the most beautiful music I've ever heard. I feel like I felt when I was a kid hearing the harmony of "Knight Rupert" for the first time and I'm very grateful to be alive.

What is most amazing to me is the universality of response to our common chordal language. Indeed, the historical study of the rise of tonal harmony is a clear window into the evolution of the modern mind and heart. Yet as ever-present as it is, we still can't describe in words just how our responses feel. I cannot tell you how the changes of "Heart and Soul" sound, or even what they sound *like*, or if I feel the same way when I hear them as everyone else does, or *anyone* else. Tonal harmony is the language of our hearts, not our tongues. It is the secret code of our affections. Although its prevalence and utility are generally taken for granted, it is everywhere precious and irreplaceable.

As/Is

I hear something. It makes a certain kind of sense: it's high, say, and it's fast. My body responds: some high-up part of my body is moving very rapidly. We have used the term *embodied cognition*, the body's way of knowing. Then the sound makes another kind of sense: I recognize it as a high note on a violin, played with a fast vibrato. What was out there is cognized and now recognized—I've heard this violin sound before. Then presto!—I am overcome with feeling, a longing I didn't expect to be part of this day in my life. My heart floods, and I have *become* longing itself. First there was a sound in the air, I recognized it, and now I have become pure feeling. I *became* what I heard!

I can't say we are any closer now than we ever were to knowing exactly what happens inside us when we respond to music. Psycho-neuro-acoustic research can show that there is more blood in this part of the brain when this happens, and more in that part when that happens. From studying myriad pathologies we can schematize what the brain does and does not do. There is a rash of recent books espousing some empirical, objective version of what seems to go on. But you don't need science to know how you *feel* when you listen to music. My intention is to point out something quite specific to you: I want you to pay attention to the very moment when you are flooded with feeling, that long sweep of response when music becomes your own fullness. I want you to really *consider* this, if only once. It is your personal science, a mystery only you can know and embrace. You could come to know yourself in a new way—one little corner of one little flap lifted up to reveal a tendency or a capacity you hadn't quite realized to be your own. As a seasoned and compulsive music teacher, I feel much like a circus clown pointing to the aerialists—to all phenomena—with astonishment, all the more to encourage your own. Those flying, weightless bodies—how do they *do* that? How do *you* do that?

Composer John Adams tells a moving story about the affect of tonal harmony in his biography, *Hallelujah Junction*. In 1976, after a decade or so of experimental search for an expressive, personal style of composition, he was driving alone high along a ridge of the Sierra foothills in northern California listening to an opera by Wagner—a composer not typically on his playlist. As he drove along the sharp curves, and "looked out on mist lingering in the narrow ravines and riverbeds," he was suddenly and unexpectedly transported by the music, its beautiful harmonies and gracefully leaping melodies. It was a revelatory moment of discovery. "This was not just music about desire," he wrote later. "It was desire itself."

In the early 1970s, John and I were both teaching at the San Francisco Conservatory of Music. He taught composition and analysis, among other things. He also led the Conservatory's chamber orchestra devoted to contemporary scores. I taught keyboard harmony, counterpoint, and improvisation, and a course called "From Mode to Modulation" about the acoustic sources of tonal harmony. We were casual friends; he showed up in my Mode to Modulation classes and I hung out at his rehearsals. I admired his restive intelligence and his almost desperate experimentation with new forms and techniques, but secretly I thought he was barking up the wrong musical tree. In the '70s I lost track of John Adams, but sometime in the mid-'80s I heard his large orchestra piece *Harmonielehre*. Oddly enough I also was driving through the California hills when I heard it on my car radio, and I was so moved I had to park the car, close my eyes, and take in the musical miracle my old pal had come up with. *What beautiful thing has happened to John?* I wondered, but I didn't know the story until he told it in his book.

The beautiful thing that happened to John is this: An experimental composer, thanks in part to the music of his aesthetic forebears, allowed himself to appreciate, in an especially receptive moment, that music doesn't *stand for* something, it *is* something. Music at its zenith is not metaphor, not *like* this, not *as* the blooming rose, but substantive, direct experience: *my* blooming. The revelation that music is "desire itself" transformed the process of composition from something out-there-to-be-found to a realized experience of inner life.

It is not surprising that John's epiphany was connected to the transformative harmonies of the late nineteenth century. Adams (as part of that same story) quotes conductor-composer Esa-Pekka Salonen as saying that nine out of the ten moments in music that had affected him most "had to do with a change of harmony." Nor is it surprising that in discussing the heart aspect of music in this chapter we have talked mostly about tonal harmony (which just happens to be my area of study and delight). Yet to be fair, there are other primary affective elements in music, and books could be written about each of them. One could certainly write a lovely book about emotional and psychological responses to pulses and rhythms of every sort: "The Book of Groove." "Tempo, Trance, and Blood Pressure" could correlate various musical pulses with human biorhythms. "Timbre Poetry," a bestseller, could encourage readers to enter directly into the wordless auras of musical sounds, plunge into their light, color, and grain, feeling their hearts the while. The bonding of communal music would be the subject of "The Jam Book." For a thousand pages, "Gardens of Formal Delight" could demonstrate the uplifting, holistic affect of extended musical structures. Yet were we to read those books (as well as any of the many others that actually do exist), I think we would learn that what holds true for tonal harmony holds true as well for the other dimensions of music, namely that deep, focused listening allows us to proceed from the *as* of metaphor to the *is* of direct experience.

4

Feeling Mind, Thinking Heart

The first words my first music teacher said to me branded me forever.

When I was five, my nine-year-old sister, Sue, had already been studying piano for two years and was getting some good strokes for it.

—What a perfect darling she is!

—Play it again, honey.

I couldn't help but notice.

My parents weren't especially musical. My sister took her lessons at school. Except for the radio and the occasional record, there wasn't much music in the air. Although I liked music when I heard it, I never thought to be a musician. But I wanted strokes and I liked the shiny sounds, so I began to stand at the piano and touch the keys. I soon discovered that by playing the instrument myself, the sound went through my body as if it were my body itself. I wasn't a pounder; I liked to press down the key nearest to my nose and listen to the light as it peaked and dimmed—thick white lines with shimmering blue and muddy yellow stripes waving through them.

So I asked for lessons and sure enough, one Tuesday after school, my sister's music teacher, Mr. Keener, came to our house, sat me down with my belly button centered at the middle of the keyboard, and put my thumb on a key under my nose. I pressed it down and the familiar lighted waves sprang up. Mr. Keener said, "That is middle C," and instead of wavy light in the middle of my head, there was a bright neon "C." I think I became a composer in that instant.

I'm sure it works differently for different folks but for me, looking back, I was blessed in one way and doomed in another. The fact that a specific kind of sound and light had a specific name opened a new chamber in my mind. I wasn't ecstatic, but I do remember feeling very positive. I was a believer: the nameless now had a name, "C," and its scale-mates were soon imprinted forever. (Alas, that particular piano was a quarter-tone flat. We got a new one shortly thereafter, but as far as perfect pitch goes it was too late for me. I developed it only unreliably decades later.)

The name "C" felt right. It was something I could move around and play with, like a comeback or a stick. That I became a composer seems like a good thing, but from day one of lessons, music had lost its infancy and its innocence. The moment Adam said "You ox. Me Adam," he and ox were no longer one but two. My first moment with Mr. Keener showed me that music and I were now separate beings. I was me; music was notes with names. I decided to explore this further. The "me" named "Bill" asked Mr. Keener, where is "B"? He showed me and I pressed it down. It sounded like a slightly different shade of light, not Bill, not me but something named "B." Odd. "Where's "M?" asked the "me" named "Mathieu." With the kind of mock shock reserved for cute kids asking dumb questions, Mr. Keener said, "Oh! There is no 'M,' young man." For the first of many times, names betrayed me. I was ready to quit right then, two minutes into the first lesson.

Instead, following my newly lit musical intellect, I became not only a composer but—worse—a music theorist. Not that I harbor regrets, but these things come with a cost, as Adam found out. Names prove expensive. The names for the elements of music, and what happens among them, I integrated quickly and eagerly. Everyone—family, teachers, peers—was impressed at the precocity of my musical mind, but no one around me knew to protect the purity of naked, unnamed musical sound. I learned to manipulate sounds primarily by naming them and identifying their laws of behavior. I did hear the sound music makes, but not as deeply as in the good old days innocent of musical names. My brain simply got ahead of my ear, and who was to know the danger in that? I had to wait a quarter century before I knew once again how to enter the musical realm of the nameless.

Within two decades I had become an improviser, composer, and musical-theater director, but the price of my cleverness was that my hearing developed unevenly. I couldn't sing in tune. I had taken up the trumpet but couldn't play in tune. I simply didn't hear what others naturally seemed to hear. I was too busy building, making songs and orchestral pieces, and improvising my way through sophisticated harmonic progressions. I even learned to improvise using twelve-tone rows. But I couldn't learn or remember—internalize—a simple tune to save my soul unless I saw the notation on the page or somehow in the eye of my intellect.

Other people have other experiences. Most of the musicians on the planet, in fact, can scarcely name what they beautifully play or sing—they hear by ear. This is especially true of singers, who do not have to locate their pitches on a keyboard, finger-board, or fretboard. They experience the music they produce in the most direct possible way. On the other hand, many fortunate folks have an innate sense of balance between what is named and what is beyond name. Maybe they have had careful teachers who understand what is at stake. I was lucky, if tardy, to recognize my own imbalance, and I did start to learn, in my thirties, while studying North Indian raga, to sing in tune. This made all the difference. It made possible a deeply satisfying musical life. Now in my seventies, and having written hundreds of compositions and taught hundreds of composition students, I am realizing how the great valley that separates intellectual cognition from direct experience—name from sound—can be inhabited peacefully, with no feuding factions in the surrounding hills. But before discussing how name and sound can be brought together onto common ground, let's observe proper analytical protocol by separating them into their respective corners.

How Many Brains Did You Say?

Like an infant who has just discovered his fingers and made them his area of contemporary research, his newest object of play, modern man has discovered his brain. Psychologically and anatomically the brain—or to use the more expanded term, the mind—is our scientific passion, our most intriguing new toy. The many descriptions of what lives inside our skulls generally follow two basic morphological models, one about mapped space, the other about change over time.

The older model considers the brain as mapped territory. Freud's map (he actually drew it) famously includes the psychoactive domains of id, ego, and superego, a schema that has become more and more elaborated over the last century. Twentieth-century anatomical discoveries show the hemispheric structure of the brain, which resulted in the "dual brain" model. Subsequent evidence suggests that our brain has evolved outward from a central, ancient core, much like the growth of a tree's rings. In 1970, Paul MacLean presented a "triune brain" theory, which posits that there are three distinct structures: a *really old* (protoreptilian) central brain, basically the knee-jerk part of us; an *old* (paleomammalian) midbrain, from which arises self-awareness; and a *relatively new* (neo-mammalian) outer brain (the neocortex), which is what humans use to solve problems.

Recent science has presented a newer model of synthesis, suggesting that instead of structures evolving as add-ons, original structures became increasingly modified, resulting in an organ wherein everything has learned to be connected to everything else, a kind of global festival of lights, not entirely unlike the World Wide Web. Triune brain theory, scarcely four decades old at this writing, is no longer part of contemporary neuroscience, though it still seems useful to many psychotherapists.

Although no one knows just what does go on in our skulls, it seems clear that the connective, gradually morphing model is becoming reconciled with the territorial idea. Neuroscience is a growing, exciting field, mapping the mind with ever more precision, understanding ever more about the elaborate strategies of connectivity the mind has evolved, and learning ever more about how we retrieve data from the vast cache of interlocking maps in the mind's atlas. Connectivity is the key. In *The Body Has a Mind of Its Own,* Sandra and Matthew Blakeslee write that the core self is "an orchestra without a conductor or a fixed score, but whose players are so good at collaborative improv that wonderful music keeps flowing out of it. . . . And you, thankfully, have the irreducible illusion of being the conductor."

So where does that leave the popularly prevalent notion that we have a dual brain, "left" (for logic) and "right" (for emotion)? The left/right brain map, although not very functional scientifically, is nevertheless a useful paradigm in the cultural lexicon. To make it even more useful, however, we need to consider it alongside another dual concept, the inner/outer brain. In this simplified map, the inner, primitive brain is called reptilian. That brain, which matures in childhood, can be considered a magnificently complex gland. The outer brain, the neocortex, is where the more recent—in other words, the human—stuff is. (The Blakeslees point out that this new instrument is a thin sheet elaborately folded around the older structures, and is the size of a dinner napkin.) It reaches maturity with adulthood and arose as a biochemical tool to advance the survival agendas of the primitive brain. This is no doubt reductionist thinking, a simplified model of a very complex phenomenon. But I think it's a culturally useful simplification—useful because it resonates with how we feel. On a moment-to-moment basis we feel the tensions between the light of the mind and the passions of the heart. We want to *listen to our head*, but we also need to *follow our heart*. We need to *think before we act*, yet we need to *be in touch with our feelings*.

Everyone thinks about this, of course; much of what we collectively know about human being comes from our desire to modulate and resolve what seem to be the imbalances and tensions between various aspects of our nature. We want wholeness. The purpose of this chapter is to try to frame the role of music as a diplomat and arbiter in the ongoing negotiations among our faculties. Let's begin by comparing various words we use to talk about this apparent dichotomy, and thus come to some sort of collective description of the dual brain model as it plays out in everyday experience.

The list of terms on the following page is surely incomplete, and such distinctions may be at least somewhat specious, but they represent a common, even stylish way we have of defining complementary aspects of our nature. I do believe that terms contain their opposites, that every piece cut from a cloth is defined by the hole in the whole it was cut from. The intention here is to show how heart and mind need not live on opposite sides of a wall, and how music can serve to arbitrate their creative coexistence. But first we will view heart and mind as separate organelles of our parent-body, each with its own hungers and survival strategies.

Old Brain	New Brain
reptilian	neo-mammalian
ancient, archaic, primitive	modern
deep brain	neocortex, prefrontal cortex
gut	head
heart	mind
passion, emotion	reason, logic
thinking	feeling
direct experience	cognition, language
intuition	intellect
sexual aggression	sexual inhibition
feminine, *yin*	masculine, *yang*
hidden, inward	exposed, outward
mutable	fixed
cooperative	competitive
possibilities	strategies
nature and its bounty	civilization and its discontents
wholeness, synthesis	thesis and antithesis
art, inspiration	science, calculation
faith, religion	proof, empiricism
process	product
meditation	cogitation
unity	duality
union	self-recognition
merging	identifying
boundlessness	bounded space
eternal moment	arrow of time
eternity, no fear of death	life span, fear of death

Add some of your own.

Consider the ancient brain first. Everyone has stories, for better or worse, of intuitive, spontaneous reactions: avoiding a freeway crash, saying "no" for no reason, acting "from the gut." But we often seem to forget the white heat of these episodes, or at least to bury them in a shallow grave. Our most passionate memories generally live embedded just below the lid of consciousness. Headlong rushes, impassioned pleadings, adult tantrums, sexual whiteouts—all these are embers smoldering beneath the surface. The ancient brain, however, maintains secret archives of when and how it got stirred up.

This is especially true in respect to sexuality. For instance, we are equipped with hormones that lead us to the conviction, during high sexual arousal, that our bond with our partner is a bond for life. How accessible (or secret) is that memory after the act? For some, sexual union seems so cosmically complete that as it is taking place every other aspect of life vanishes: morality, humor, fear, distinctions sacred and arcane, past and future—there are no names, just the most ancient light of lights. Where do *those* memories get stashed? For others, sexual memories are painful, and receive a deep-six burial. (Alas, the deeper we bury them, the deeper they operate.)

Glancing down the "Old Brain" column may remind you of how much pure feeling you carry, a live mosaic of your heart connection. I'm not asking you to revel or writhe in your emotional memories, but only to recognize how continuously we carry our deep pools of emotion around with us dreaming or waking, like it or not. They serve as our wordless lexicon, a personal encyclopedia of feeling.

In contrast, certain moments of intuitive wholeness are pervasive, and can stay close to the surface. I remember, as a boy of eight on my walk to school, standing still in the middle of the huge lawn of Saint Theresa's Home for the Aged, transfixed between the morning dew and the blue-white sky. I could see and hear the world as if for the first time, the droplets quivering on

87

the well-trimmed grasses, the old folks in the distance like quiz-
zical statues, the playground calls and taunts a quarter-mile away
making kid siren music in my ears. These were not plural impressions, but one nameless impression, a single world entire. Empty
of thought, I was aware of the merge of viewer and view, listener
and sound. These moments diminished toward pre-adolescence,
and vanished by a pubescence obsessed with scheming for what
I wanted. They didn't reappear until fifteen years later, unbidden
at first, then eventually, through meditation, more reliably, then
more frequently in my forties. There is a gently sloping open field
between my music studio and my house; some of my most peace-
ful moments in recent decades have occurred when I was (literally) out standing in my field.

Once (in 1959) I saw Lenny Bruce do an especially off-the-
cuff improv based on a character he named The Great Stander.
"Man, could this guy ever *stand*. People would come from everywhere just to watch. They'd feel *good*. They'd nudge each other,
'Lookit, it's The Great Stander. Lookit 'im stand, Man, Lookit
'im *stand*.'" Then, after a brief pause: *"I wanna be that guy!"*

There's a wonderful set of ten Zen pictures and poems called
The Ten Bulls about stages of enlightenment. The last picture
shows an old Buddha-like fellow walking down the road. Over
his shoulder he carries a stick from which dangle his few pos-
sessions tied up in a cloth. He peers out genially at the reader.
The commentary beneath reads (in part) ". . . and everyone
who looks upon me is enlightened." I think that's the guy Lenny
meant.

Freud calls experiences of wholeness "oceanic" experiences.
They can sneak up on you, and are not easy to talk about — one
doesn't really want to mess with them, much less convince others. But people do talk about them. Teachers say, "When you are
in a state of unity...," and heads nod knowingly *as if*. Writers
write about them. In *A Soft Spring Night in Shillington* (1984),
John Updike recalls that in his childhood he loved to stand in

doorways during summer showers. He writes of "the intima-
tions of deep cosmic joy brought on by being "out of the rain,
but *just* out...."

Updike's little boy resonates with mine, but ultimately one's
experiences are one's own. My stories and cues may or may not
resonate with your experiences, so allow me once more to hand
this book over to you, Patient Reader, and ask you to scan for
those moments in your life when (without the aid of an artistic medium like music or the movies) the seams vanished, when
the world (with you in it) presented itself seamlessly whole.

—

Now for the new brain, the upstart, the stripling. Since we live
in a visually sophisticated culture (you *are* reading, I imagine),
it is probably not difficult to recall episodes when you were
utterly absorbed in your naming, controlling, calculating, ana-
lyzing, and otherwise brilliant mind. Maybe you even forgot
to drink water or breathe. Rationality seduces us. Every name
is a snare, an old lover you need to forget. Every thought is a
link in the heavy chain of reason, every concept a prison. Brain-
storms are life sentences. Searching for certainty, we identify
with our bright ideas and, in our rectitude, disdain or vanquish
our neighbors when they disagree. The modern brain, the tool
we use to construct a modern world replete with reliable com-
forts and outrageous pleasures, is also the source of its superego
doppelgänger, the directive from our otherness. We can thank it
for our inhibitions, our chivalry, and our remorse. The new kid
in the class invents the arrow of time and the doom of death. In
short, it thinks.

Yet is there, after all, anything in this world more stimulating
than good discourse with friends, the intense engagement of
shining minds? What better way to pass time than to take your
place in the Great Conversation, silver ideas streaking across the

bright screen of your mind well into the small hours? What better way to be human?

It is safe to say that identifying with the old brain is a palpably different experience from identifying with the new brain. Let me encourage you to experiment with teasing apart these complementary experiential qualities. That is one way of understanding how we get caught in the crossfire between them.

THE UNWINNABLE WAR

The job of the mystic is to guard sacred knowledge from its myriad names. The mystic knows that sacred is *secret*. In this context, secret means nameless and unnameable. To name it is to lose it. Some Jews are forbidden to utter the sacred name *Yahweh,* substituting the written *YHWH* or a spoken alternative (*Adonoi*), or writing *G-d* instead of *God.* At the mystical core of most religions is the teaching that the primary nature of existence is boundless, timeless, and nameless. It is not that a name for God is wrong, it's that by definition it is incomplete. Any name of God is a placeholder for what cannot be named. From the Dominican mystic Meister Eckhart:

> Enough talk for the night....
> I need to be silent for a while—
> worlds are forming in my heart.

One justification for such caution in describing direct experience in language is how easily words can be taken for experiences, a prime example of the uppity new brain in action. A nameless perception says to the neocortex, "*Stay away from me or I'll disappear.*" The neocortex says. "*You need me! Without names you can't* **do** *anything, you can't* **use** *your experience.*" But the gut knows that named experience—concepts, ideas, descriptions—are afterthoughts at best. It wants the real thing.

It wants what happens when lovers' glances meet, not "I love you." It wants the feeling of praise, not the congregation reading from the prayer book. It wants the music, not the score.

Our shiny, modern minds are ravenous dogs, hungry for the meat of meaning. Language is the drooling stalker we can't seem to ditch. Except for a few cool drops of grace, I can't stop talking, reading, and writing. I say to everyone I meet, *Listen! Listen NAMELESSLY to the music of this world!* Yet since I'm a music theorist I can, and do, name everything nameable in music. Poets are the same: their poems, "palpable and mute," lead you metaphor by metaphor into the zone of speechlessness, which lasts until the beginning of the next poem. The admonitions of poets and mystics are the same: *Hush! Enter the silence!* until the next cautionary tale, inventive and exhilarating, spills from their mouths.

There is a precious, vanishingly small moment before words have a chance to form themselves in the mind, when our experience is direct. Then, in flashes of recognition, linguistic synapses flood the mind, and words and names appear. With any luck that moment is not so very brief, and the precognitive mind is thus exposed to the light. This can happen when you walk into a beautiful, lofty church, or meet an extraordinary person, or suddenly, coming up over a rise, see the sun-drenched valley beneath. "I was at a loss for words." Indeed. Word loss gives access to direct, unmediated knowing. When language does come, sometimes so quickly that there is no sensation of ever having been without it, the quality of direct experience is inexorably altered. To *gain* words is to lose the pristine ancient mind. So wedded are we to language that it seems only in extreme times of danger, or passion, or aesthetic transport—times when we need something more comprehensive than language—only then does the ancient mind show itself. So expertly have we learned to verbalize our experience that this moment can vanish merely by looking at it.

This need not be. We can employ many strategies for fair and equal access to all parts of ourselves, meditation being foremost, and music being—at least in my book—high on the list. I want to focus on precisely that split second: the instant during which language can veil or paralyze direct knowing, the lightning strike of original sin, the single heartbeat between Eve's taste buds swimming in moist delight and her tongue speaking her new mode of knowing: "APPLE!"

In learning music, the parable of the snake and the apple has an eloquent manifestation: the fear of learning names. I teach music to adults at all levels, beginners as well as seasoned professionals, and about one-third of my students do not seem to be in the least troubled with naming anything their ears can hear. But most do have some difficulty, and more than a few have an active resistance to labeling even the most elemental sounds, like the tone "A-flat," or the chord "B diminished seventh," or the key "C minor," or the meter "12/8." One student in ten is so upset by the process of developing a musical lexicon that he or she feels resentful, depressed, discouraged, and defective. Some look down and bite their lips. Some weep.

I was recently teaching a seminar of about twenty-five students at various stages of musical development. To begin, I asked each person to define his or her musical wish list by completing the sentence, "How can I...?" in twenty-five words or less. One tall, thin, strong guy, very quiet, asked in a hushed tremble, "How can I get over my fear of music theory?" The room came alive. People nodded and sighed and made sounds empathetic with the intensity and sincerity of the questioner. Here is my answer to him then and to you now:

"Your fear of theory is a good thing. It shows that you have something to protect that is still intact. Your fear is a functional, positive part of your immune system, and you should honor it, but you need to know what it is protecting. Fear protects love, in this case your love of music as a sacred part of yourself. For you and many lucky people, music comes from an innocent place. The altar inside you where pure music lives must not be defiled by names, analyses, and rules of right and wrong. Conventionally, music theory is taught didactically, often aggressively, and sometimes with more than a hint of arrogance: if you aren't musically literate, you aren't a good musician. There's not much validation of subjective response in such teaching. Its underlying agenda seems to be to keep the likes of you out of school. To the extent that music theory is set up as the antagonist of your own pure, direct experience, you *should* fear it."

Fear can go hand in hand with guilt. Some years ago, I gave one of my students, an excellent Celtic harpist named Julia, the assignment of composing and notating a song. When she came for her next lesson, she felt good about the song, which she sang and played beautifully for me, but when I asked to see the score, she stammered excuses, blushed, and then tears came. She had successfully resisted notating the song, and that made her feel incomplete and guilty, but it was more than simply not doing her assignment. The emotion ran deep. She revealed her phobia about notation, the fear that notating the music would freeze it and thus kill it. Her guilt lay in having pieced the song together aurally and intuitively without resorting to the cognitive techniques she had been convinced (or had convinced herself) that she needed to learn.

There followed a long conversation, THE conversation, about the legitimacy of one's feelings and the various strategies for integrating musical experience so that the altar of the heart is not raped and pillaged by the hungers of the mind. What came out of this conversation was a clearer understanding (for both of us) of the nature of the conflict between heart and mind, especially as far as music is concerned. We agreed that although we use such terms as *feminine* and *masculine,* we are definitely not talking about girls and boys, but the mix of feminine and masculine qualities that are aspects of us all. We talked about how musical notation packages and crystallizes ideas, thereby turning flowing process into congealed product. I asked, "What would be the opposite of a musical *composition*?" She replied, "A heightened sensitivity to nature, and music like rivers flowing and clouds billowing, never contained or permanently bounded." I brought up how our culture's paradigms of music were historically focused on maestro and masterpiece, and asked her what the flip side of that was. She said, "Shaman and healing."

It occurred to me then that for the artist, works of art arrive stillborn — their birth is their end. Once a work is hatched, the artist is pretty much finished, he wants to hurl it into the bin of the world, leave it for others to deal with, and move on to the next work (as opposed to a real live baby, whose parents are just beginning the long road of nurture). Julia pointed out that ritual, arising from human needs, flows continually through daily life. So progressing from Julia's feelings of being defective and incomplete, we were now absorbed in the question of how art generally and music particularly can find a modicum of balance between these seeming opposites, and how the artist can dance with their forces and revel in their play.

What we came to by the end of our exchange was the necessity of the new brain to honor the primacy and privacy of the old. The modern mind has to learn to remember the sanctity of the ancient heart. I do believe that as a culture we've made a brave beginning of this. We've begun to learn how to train the mind to be the *willing* slave of the heart. The full integration will come when the mind learns to see itself as sacred also. The armored heart can then soften.

We also agreed that there was no reason for her to notate her song unless she felt the impulse to pass it along in that particular form to others. The singing of the song was its reality, the notation merely a tool of choice.

THE SUSTAINABLE PEACE

It was easy for the boy Bill to learn to identify middle C by name, and it was not so easy for him to learn to sing in tune. It was a long and slow road, but he did finally (and gratefully) learn. It was easy for the woman Julia to learn to play harp and sing songs with beauty and accuracy, but difficult for her to learn notation well enough to write down and complexify her compositions. But she did eventually, and (willingly) learn to notate her compositions without compromising the grace and ease of her music.

As in any love relationship, learning to listen to music — even music you love — takes practice. Partners learn to compromise, negotiate, take turns and, eventually, cohabit in peace. Same with the partnering of intellect and intuition in every listener. Your mind and heart learn to be a nice old married couple, completing each other's sentences and clipping each other's toenails.

I suppose if the linguistic centers of my new-fangled brain can find a way to be married to my ancient brain, anything can happen. Robert Bly has a good metaphor for this: *leaping poetry*. Poetry leaps when its metaphors zig and zag you from one part of yourself to another, perhaps fraying but never severing the connective thread. Leaps are work. Leaping poetry makes the mind work so hard to discover meaning that, *in the act* of giving up, new meaning arises — thanks not to the usual suspects, but to the exertion of leaping from a known place to a place it didn't know it knew. Such leaps light up new paths from words to pure feeling and back again. In the poetic leap, the mind and the heart are, if only in midair, fused.

Dr. Michel Odent, the great pioneer in natural birthing, points out the ways the new mind, through the agency of various artistic media, learns to be *in the service* of the old. "In any artistic activity, a technique (which is governed by the specifically human neocortex) puts itself in the service of a function governed by older structures.... There is no physiological function that cannot be the basis for artistic activity." Thus the techniques learned in the new brains of painters evoke emotional responses *via* the eyes; of musicians, the ears; of dancers, their bodies; of the perfumer, the sense of smell; of the chef, the gustatory function. "Art," he says in a clear formulation, "is an artifice used by humans to harmonize their two brains."

I think this is true for sports also—but with a telling difference. The skills of the athlete are commensurate in difficulty with the techniques of the artist, and the involvement of the neocortex in learning those skills and techniques can be equivalently strenuous. But in most sports, the intention is to win, or at least to attain or surpass some objective standard. Since the intended outcome is so clearly defined, the athlete is either on or off his game. When an athlete is on his game, "in the zone," the learned techniques and the gut responses are indeed "harmonized." The zone is elusive, but the outcome is obvious: you win or lose.

For art, the intended outcome is harder to pin down. Artists go for beauty and meaning where they can find it and, with any luck, gain their own integration in the process. I'll try to describe how, as a performing musician, I experience this integration. First, of course, there is grace: sometimes everything simply clicks. But when it doesn't, I can feel myself toggling back and forth between my two brains. There will be moments of cognition: *Where am I?...What's next?...What key is this?...Here's the tricky part...This is in A Lydian going to D Phrygian* NOW.... These alternate with moments of pure feeling, nameless clarity. The harmonization of thinking and feeling seems to come and go in cycles, unpredictable ones — but that seems to be the nature of the process.

Of course it's not only athletes and artists who have learned specialized techniques for navigating the streaming phenomena of this world. As civilized persons, we each have personal agendas for finding balance between the teeter and the totter of our minds. Perhaps that's why we are held in such thrall by daredevils, like tightrope walkers working without a net: out of the zone and you're dead. And why also the bottom-of-the-ninth, score-tied, two-out, bases-loaded, three-two pitch captivates an entire country: Which guy, the pitcher or the batter, will be able, in the last split second, to attain the greatest integration? There is a similar suspense when a concert pianist fearlessly emotes thunder and lightning during the most difficult passages of Rachmaninoff. We are fascinated with Jackson Pollack, whose enduring masterpieces are records of a succession of split seconds during which paint was arcing through space. (Talk about stillborn: he said the painting was alive for him only while the paint was in the air.)

Our strategies for integration are not confined to art streaming through time. Our biology helps us. Typically, we each spend sixteen waking hours naming and cognizing our world, our neocortex lit up like a mall at Christmas — then eight sleeping hours communing with our ancient parent brain, singing the old primal songs, revisiting the oldies and the goodies. The long arc of learning is a narrative of development and regression, two steps forward and one step back, sampling every tasty apple the civilized world has in store, then becoming sufficiently stupid (neocortically speaking) to regain our authentic, ancient bearings.

Another strategy for integration is zooming in and out. Long ago, the enduring book *Powers of Ten* taught us to zoom in to the smallest dimensions and out into the largest by flicking pages. Now, thanks to Google Earth (among many other demonstrations of the wonders of scale), the pages have technologically morphed into mouse clicks to both ends of infinity, zoom-in — zoom-out. The small is what we squint at: a concrete grain of sand, *this* dust mote, *this* atomic nucleus, *this* quark, this *string* not made of anything but itself! Zoom out to the universe, the cosmos, the *omni*verse . . . and then, for a moment, our cognitive mind turns off and our direct knowing of vastness comes in.

Dear friends, would it be so very difficult to give up The Masterpiece once and for all? To dwell in earnest in Julia's billowing clouds and flowing rivers? To join hands in circles around timeless trees, dancing conjoined to the moon? To let the *Grosse Fugue* and *Starry Night* languish without our ears and eyes? My answer is that civilization is doom, but doom ain't so bad. Yes we have our discontents, but we also have our skills; we can toggle between opposites and seesaw our way to the momentary balance point often *enough*.

Recently, I went to the north coast of Maui to write this chapter. One afternoon found me perched on a cliff three hundred feet above the Pacific looking out at half the world and studying the reflection of blue-white sky in green-blue water. I computed that my view took in a thousand square miles of ocean. After a lovely interval of not writing, I began to spot individual white caps about a mile out and track them in to shore. Then I began to notice the synchrony among the whitecaps, soon recognizing that they were all moving shoreward at the same speed. And then, *Eureka*! They were all the same wave! By some reframing of cognition, instead of dwelling on a particular event I was experiencing the wholeness of the scene. I was swept into a direct experience of unity, yet I could still single out each wave. I could seesaw between discriminating with my cognitive mind and the unity of land, sea, and sky. Could I learn to do both at once?

Mental connectivity is an active subject of scientific inquiry. On the physiological level, recent research has examined the interaction of individual neurons with their immediate neighbors, who seem to offer themselves up for help in storing information, thus clustering cells into socially supportive communities, called neural neighborhoods. These synaptic neighborhoods remain sensitive for about ten minutes, about long enough to think through a problem, or take in a movement of a classical concerto.

An expansion of the idea of the neural neighborhood is the "global workspace" theory of consciousness: Information becomes conscious when "workspace" neurons broadcast it to many areas of the brain at once, making it simultaneously available for language, memory, and the organization of perception. In this model, "more global" becomes "more conscious." Consciousness thereby becomes a kind of cerebral celebrity or, as the American philosopher Daniel Dennett describes it, "fame in the brain."

The more the connectivity, the greater the insight. In a 2008 article in the *New Yorker* titled "The Eureka Hunt," insight is described as a balancing act between the prefrontal cortex, which controls cognition and logic, and the deeper, older parts of the brain responsible for intuition. The deeper parts, which reach out with longer dendrites and axons, tune more broadly for data. They scan for information while the prefrontal cortex focuses and organizes. As musicians know, it doesn't take much to shift from scanning to focusing. Your deep brain is working all the time. When its long-stored information undergoes sudden restructuring by the prefrontal cortex, the result can be a *Eureka* moment. A concrete insight thus offers a fleeting glimpse of your huge store of deep knowledge.

Certain bodily states can induce balance. Some of our best thinking is done half asleep, warm showers are good for insight, and meditators intentionally develop the capacity for mental equilibrium. Decreased activity in the prefrontal cortex can contribute to original thinking. Even a wandering mind can be considered a type of scanning, a kind of peripheral vision of the mind, and can aid insight. According to the

Harvard psychology researcher Shelley Carson, distractibility can even increase the amount of information available to the conscious mind. The prolific American author Dawna Markova says she can't write without staring out a window. Grandmas and grandpas have a wider span of attention, can scan more broadly, have a reduced filter, and are hence both more absentminded (can't recall specifics) and wiser (possess a wider field of understanding).

The various strategies the mind has used to integrate itself over eons of evolution remind us of how the many parts of complex organisms were once autonomous in themselves. Mitochondria, for instance, who used to be happy campers on their own, are now a crucial component of each mammalian cell. In the same way, cells once autonomous are now parts of entire minds attached to entire humans. This leads to the connections among humans, to aggregations of states and nations, to global ecology, and finally to global mind, where, thanks to the World Wide Web, many millions of ideas can be simultaneously operative. In "open-source science" (similar to open-source software), ideas are allowed to arrive from any point of a vast network of minds. Sometimes the best ideas come from outside the disciplines they address. It's been found that not uncommonly, the further the problem is from a solver's expertise, the more likely he is to solve it, often by applying expertise developed for a different purpose. The scanning is thus worldwide. Humanity has, perhaps dangerously, connected itself into a collective, modern version of its ancient brain.

We have been talking as though the feelings of the heart are located in the mind, or at least as if they originate there. This is dangerous talk. We know that mind stuff is located not only in the cerebellum, the optic nerve, and the gut but, in some sense, could be considered to exist everywhere in the body. We speak to locating our feelings in the chest cavity, where the physical heart is. We place our hand over our heart to show sincerity. Common language bears this out: you're in my heart; I sing my heart out; I wear my heart on my sleeve; I hear your cry from the heart; in love my heart is aflame, broken, or foolish. We even send symmetric little representations of the ruddy organ itself as a symbol of affection. In the Hindu yogic system, emotions are centered in the heart chakra, which can be imaged as a warm, hollow chamber below the Adam's apple and above the sternum. A primary yogic discipline is to calm your breath, then focus your attention on the heart chakra. When you breathe into and out of your heart, you can feel the glow in it.

For me, the glow of the heart is not distinct from the light in the mind. It is our connection to the light of the very oldest Mind, far older than the human heart. The glow of the heart is the sign of desire *and* aversion at every scale, from the forces and oscillations of subatomic particles to the gravitational gyrations of the cosmos. Scientists have been trying to understand and integrate this desire/aversion field, the "forces of nature," ever since there has been science, and if they succeed we'll have a splendid Unified Field Theory of Everything. Meanwhile, we have to look for this integration in ourselves, perhaps most usefully by sitting still. From this position you simply have a view; the more still your conscious mind, the more comprehensive the view. The view has a *sensible* quality, the feeling of experiencing your whole, integrated self (at least as integrated as it can be right now). The broad subject of self-integration can be approached from this quality of feeling, from the top down, so to speak. From this vantage point, the connections between the parts seem mere happenstance inside the single experience of being present.

Music as Mediator

I am not a mathematician, but I do arithmetic quickly, and have learned the simple algebraic maneuvers necessary to name by ratio whatever happens in tonal harmony. Since I've had to become sufficiently agile in this to explain it harmlessly (I hope) to others, I've had to do a lot of thinking about numbers and what they really are. What numbers are is creepy. They magnificently describe reality in quite useful ways but nonetheless never quite get it right. A mathematician friend tells me that mathematicians have fifty different ways of saying *is*. But to me they all seem to be the same weird mirror with hidden warps. For one thing, math is always looking for answers, whatever *they* are, and for another it measures *dimensions,* and dimensions are creepy.

In my world everything is always morphing, and since nothing like a line or an area can be pinned down *exactly,* wouldn't the discrete numbers representing them always be at least a weeny bit off? There's no such thing as a line anyway, because a line has a single discrete dimension and no real thing can exist in only one discrete dimension. Everything that exists exists always in all dimensions—you can't separate the dimensions out without warping the mirror. And as far as the reality of a *point* is concerned, I give up. When you look closely enough, every boundary is permeable, so there isn't even anything sufficiently discrete to count as "1." And 1 = 1 bothers me even more, because by the time you clamber all the way across to the other side of the equal sign, the universe has changed.

Math is all abstractions, figments of the mind, which is fine, but in my own education I didn't recognize that for the longest time. My teachers told me that math was truth and they had proof. I recognized only gradually the great danger in mistaking a mathematical description of the world for the world it describes, and came to realize that my problem wasn't so much with mathematics as with the way it is conventionally presented.

Such discontents led me to muse about a different kind of math, a description of the world that is *feeling*-based rather than number-based. Instead of *commutative* and *exhaustive* and *exclusive*, I wanted *cooperative* and *nested*, and *merged*. Rumi says, "Why are you so busy with this or that? Pay attention to how things blend." Could there be a description of the world that proceeds from the sensibility of union, a language of integration that *derives* duality, rather than a language like ours that begins with "terms" and tries to resolve them? I thought and thought about this, perhaps none too clearly. I did my best to explain it to yet another mathematician friend, who said the only reason he wasn't insulted was that what I was saying was utter nonsense. I thought some more. I kept coming back to the fact that the ratios of tonal harmony *feel* so whole-making. I knew I felt the numbers and the numbers felt good. And I realized that historically the rise of proportional relationship in music predates algebra, math, and, probably, counting. Then I had a *Eureka* moment. "I've invented music!" I exclaimed in the shower.

Feeling-based math is the music I do day in and day out. It starts in unity and never leaves. This and that happen, but always from a sense of the whole. Music is everywhere, nowhere, and right here. It's a piece of what never began and will never be over. It's a description of my reality that integrates mind and heart, just what I was looking for all along.

———

Music is surely not our only medium of integration, but it is an old, close, and true friend. Although music lives in the body, the gate to the body is the ear. The ear hears waves that vibrate us from head to toe to eardrum to neuron to electron to energies so refined that we see the play of light in our minds. The waves have physical immediacy. They range in frequency from walking to trembling to the sensual periodicities of tone—thousands of streaming bits-per-second of news from the splendid world. Through music, we immerse our grossly physical selves in the most refined vibrational realm we know of. The ecstatic labors of decoding proportional harmony take us apart and put us back together again. Musical waves are harmonious at many orders of magnitude, and as their energies are transformed and retransformed in our bodies, they harmonize us. Music survives as high church for human beings, because when we absorb it we become more whole in body, mind, heart, and spirit.

One aspect that affects us most is the wordlessness of music's grammar. The *sound* of music, like the cry of an animal, goes directly to the oldest brain. It immediately swamps the ancient circuits, *then* the neocortex tells us what we hear. Nowhere is this more evident than in chord changes, the progression of (usually) triad-based harmonies that lead us on coherent journeys. Tonal harmony is linguistic in that it makes syntactical sense: a series of chords can thwart, fulfill, or even exceed expectations, can be heard in syntax as wrong, right, or a surprise, and thus behave more or less grammatically. What harmonic grammar organizes, however, is not the abstractions of words, but the directly experienced vibratory sensations of periodicity and the proportionality of wave frequencies to one another. The response to these proportions, the harmonic ratios and their many combinations, light up great swaths of the old and new real estate of the mind.

Diane, a psychologist learning to compose, is unusually bright, verbally concise, and retains conceptual information astonishingly well—I know because of how thoroughly she answers my questions about psychology. At the beginning of her studies with me, however, she was not so swift in learning to hear the intrinsic logic of chordal harmony. Identifying and learning to use certain harmonic progressions is part of every musician's training, and for serious composers there is a sacred collection of them to internalize (called harmonic cadences and sequences). I knew she could learn to hear this stuff given enough space and time—everyone who tries succeeds sooner or later. When it began to happen she was genuinely amazed—not primarily by the beauty or the logic of the music, but by the fact that there could be such a part of her mind so sensually experienced. She said, "This uses a part of my brain that has no words in it. It's a *tangible* feeling. Weird." But after a while it didn't feel weird at all, it felt like music, which she began to produce with considerable enthusiasm. "It takes me to wordlessness," she says of her work.

In music, the best way to bridge the gap between sound and name is to *first* hear and *then* to name. That's somewhat saner than trying to squeeze experience out of what you've already given a name to, which is the more conventional method. In either case, the road can feel treacherous, especially at first, as the tremble in my seminar student's voice can attest. The subject is addressed head-on in the basic act of naming the tones of a scale. When you name a tone it turns into a note. I heard the *tone* of middle C first; then learned the *note*. This is reflected in the etymology of the terms: I *sound* a tone (Latin *tonus*, to stretch, as in strings); I *mark* a note (Latin *nota*, as in "notate"). Although common usage frequently conflates these terms, and English and American usage differs, let's preserve the original distinction for now.

During the very moment you give an unnamed tone a note-name, you can teach yourself to palpably feel the separation of your intuitive, direct experience from your cognizing self. This transfer of dominance from one kind of knowing to the other need not be permanent, nor involve any kind of loss. We learn to juggle these two modes of knowing in much the same way that when we are speaking clearly we can be aware of our feelings and still frame our sentences. To assist us in this, our new brains come with a marvelous tool (sometimes called the pre-conscious) that allows us to access needed information immediately. So smooth and rapid is the transfer from storage to usage that you can talk, write, and play music without naming what you are doing unless you need to.

Early training does help. From a very young age, North Indian musicians are taught note-names as a mantric, intuitive aspect of the tones themselves. They learn to name the tones they are singing as rapidly and as easily as we can spell what we are writing. Yet anyone can do this to some degree. Even if you have never studied music, music does much of the work for you; intrinsically it is a teacher of integration between the cognitive and the intuitive. For instance, when you are listening to a piece of music, you can concentrate either on your intuitive responses to sheer sound—your bodily responses to the pulses and rhythms—or you can concentrate on the "what happens next" aspect of the music, its narrative. In the first way of hearing, your ancient brain is listening innocently, so to speak, with its eyes wide; it is drinking in the vibrations. In the second way, you are constantly storing, remembering, and comparing numerous events, just as you would with any story, extracting coherent meaning. If you find a piece of music you enjoy, and practice listening to it first one way, then the other, you'll find that with amazing ease you can toggle between the two: pure *sound*, then meaningful *events*, then back to pure sound again, and so on, until *Eureka!*—the two ways become one way and the full globe is lit. By its own nature, music teaches us the integration of heart and mind. It knows how to be feelingful sounds, and how to be pure architecture, and how to be the sublime marriage of the two.

PART TWO

...Out There...

5

Music as Life

Since we are the very humans who make human music, it is not surprising to recognize many things that happen in music as reflections of things that happen in our daily lives—lives of rushing, pausing, drawing folks in, pushing folks away, repeating ourselves, or looking for something new. These happenings are not stories, exactly, but protostories that arise from our embodied cognition of music as we listen to it. We put our human ways into music, and music is a metaphor for our human ways. In this chapter we'll consider how music and daily life reflect and illuminate one another.

THE RULES OF MUSIC AND LIFE

In music as in life there is scarcely a rule that cannot be broken for some reason or other. Experience teaches continuously that the commission of a lesser evil can result in a greater good. Never jaywalk—unless you are whisking an old woman out of the path of a speeding car. Never tell a lie—unless to conceal from frail old Uncle Henry how troublesome he actually is. Never kill—unless you want to eat. Yes, we need rules, but too much inflexibility in our codes of behavior produces boring, or worse, destructive, despotic lives.

Is there an unbreakable rule in life? Maybe to be kind, although I can think of a scenario where a mean man might still be a valuable man, if only inadvertently. Much more commonly, being kind to one person may involve the appearance of meanness to others. Is there an unbreakable rule in music?

If It Sounds Good

In music I can think of one maybe unbreakable rule: If it sounds good, it is good. The rule applies generally to composers and improvisers, and is meant to encourage free, creative play—intuitive choice balanced by subsequent reflection and discernment. The enemy is self-censure: *Well, it sounds good, but you're not supposed to do it that way.* The "rule" addresses that voice. I do believe that if you are the only one listening, and the music sounds good to you, then it is good music. If others happen to be listening, however, they had best be consulted. "Good" in the arts can be taken to mean "beneficial," and what is beneficial sorts itself out over many years and souls. A musician acting alone has only himself or herself as arbiter of "good." When the music is let loose upon the world, the "goodness" of the music becomes as complex as the world.

The commensurate rule in real life would be: If it feels good, it is good. "Feels good" is broader than "sounds good" and that much harder to come to terms with. Let's say that "feels" requires a scan of one's whole being, so that smoking might feel good to part of yourself but the whole self knows it's bad. "If it sounds good, it is good" has proved liberating for me as a composer, and for my composition students as I have been able to guide them to it. There's a trick in these rules though. "Sounds good" changes over time as one's skills and tastes develop. The rule works only if you factor in your potential for technical mastery and aesthetic growth, as well as your compassionate connection to the ear of the world. The real-life version, "if it feels good it is good," is even more sensitively modulated by one's growth. Not only your aesthetic sensibilities grow, but also your morals. Your awareness expands outward from mother's breast to self to family to others to the cosmos, and one's sense of what "feels good to the whole being" expands along with it.

Over the decades I've gained confidence in my compositional choices, my ability to zero in on the best available choice for the moment, and this has guided me in understanding that in real life there is always a best choice also: right action. The musical world has given me confidence in the larger world. This can be true not only for musicians but for any listener as well. Good-sounding music is a microworld where all the choices sound right. A good piece is a skein of right actions, a consensual utopia. The enduring music of all cultures seems to provide this model of rightness and goodness. The "standards," the oldies-but-goodies, the tribal elegies of the African village *griot*, all are like our ancestors carved into totem poles in our backyards watching over us and reassuring us that we can always have a taste of the good and the true. Mozart's Clarinet Concerto, The Beatles' "Here Comes the Sun," a raga by Ram Naryam, a middle-period Miles solo, Guillaume Machaut *complet*—these are the totems on my pole, all reminders of a greater good. An iPod is a portable totem pole: lots of wise friends and guides to help you through the day. Will the music you've chosen for your iPod still sound good to you in twenty years? Send me a postcard.

Only Three Things

In life as in music, there are only three things you can do: what you just did, what you just did but differently, or something else.

I first heard this *zeitgeist* articulated *via* Ruth Zaporah, a brilliant teacher of theater improvisation. The concept, useful for all temporal phenomena in art and life, seems to cut through complexities and lead to a general organizational framework for experience. "What you just did," though strictly speaking is impossible (because you can't step into the same river twice), becomes more meaningful when it refers to your intention: "I mean to repeat my action." Think of how important this is in life: the creative or destructive potential of routine. In music, repetition is the *Ur*-pattern, the clearest path to meaning. Too much repetition is boring, not enough results in chaos. Let's briefly revisit "Twinkle, Twinkle, Little Star." It begins with a tone that is immediately repeated (*Twin-kle*); then proceeds to another tone, and *that* one is immediately repeated (*twin-kle*, then *another*, likewise repeated (*lit-tle*); then the previous tone is sounded but it is *not* repeated (*star*). Stop for a moment and hear this. Children grok this straightforward repetition, and so do we.

In classical music, especially around the turn of the eighteenth century, entire chunks of pieces—sometimes four or six minutes' worth—were repeated note for note, and such is the complexity of the style that we welcome the chance to hear long passages once again before proceeding further. In contemporary "minimal" music the far briefer repetitions sometimes seem designed to drive the listener past rage into a submissive trance. Too much of this is boring; just the right amount—an *efficient* substrate of repetition (listen to the composers Terry Riley, John Adams, and Steve Reich, for instance)—can focus the listener's musical concentration in compelling ways. Likewise, one seeks a life organized but not tyrannized by routine. Just enough routine liberates our creative juices; too much is deadly.

⁓

The most fascinating and complex of the three things is "you can do what you just did but differently." This goes to the very core of the way music plays out. There are many dimensions of music, and most can be easily isolated and examined. The rise and fall of tones (melody), the relative duration of tones (rhythm), the hierarchy of tone combinations (harmony), and the color of a tone that distinguishes a violin from an oboe (timbre)—any of these elements could change and any stay the same. The mind takes delight in sorting out the similarities and differences. Most of the music you listen to involves this process of teasing apart what is the same and what is different within the stream of musical information.

Think of the tune of the Christmas carol "Joy to the World." It begins with an easily recognizable melodic device: a descending major scale. If you keep the familiar rhythm but change the tune (for instance by beginning on the lowest tone of the scale and ascending rather than descending), you have done something the same but different. To get the point, Gentle Reader, you need to pause and hear in your head (or on an instrument, but that's not necessary) what it sounds like—or more accurately, what it feels like—to sing the first line of "Joy to the World" ascending rather than descending. I will not promise this is life-changing, but it could be. By "feels" I mean how your mind feels in recognizing, literally re-cognizing, the old tune in a new form. Part of your brain says *I know you* while another part asks *Who are you?* How exactly do you experience the way your mind resolves these two parallel strands of experience? However it feels to you subjectively (there's no way your personal experience can be precisely objectified), it's safe to say that something creative happens in the instant of realizing that old wine is in a new bottle, the precise moment *old/new* turns into *now*. The brain must supply something to the mix; it has to burn energy to make sense of its environment. For me, it's a tiny *aha* experience, the kind that happens over and over continuously when we listen—actually listen—to music, resulting in a kind of rolling, contagious glee.

Alternatively, we could keep the original tune, but change the rhythm, say by prolonging the prepositions and articles: *Joy to-o-o-o-o the-e-e-e-e world, The-e-e-e-e Lord-has-come.* That sounds plain wrong to us, but if you take away the words, the music alone is a decent enough variation of the original. Or we could slow the tune way down and give it to the trombones; or we could speed it up and give it to a flute; or we could sing it in Latin, or pig Latin, or scat syllables, or adorn it with outrageous trills. We could do two (or more) of the above simultaneously—for instance, a highly ornamented, slowed-down version in Persian. As long as the ear/brain is able to recognize the original source, it will have done its same-but-different work. What if we sang it without the words, rendered the first note five times instead of once, changed the rhythm drastically, and left out the last note? Then we'd have "Lucy in the Sky with Diamonds," but would the brain make the connection? Mine didn't until just now.

On the level of common knowledge, old wine in new bottles is old hat. We have many phrasings for the same thing, many microroutes down to the corner and back, many ways to skin a cat. Music brings a special value to this general understanding, because the elements of music—like the rhythm of a tune, or its up-and-down contour—are easy to isolate and understand even for ears untrained in music. The elements of musical narrative are sensible to any listener who chooses to become aware of them. A simple, concentrated moment of listening does for hearing music what an X-ray does for seeing the body. As one becomes more aware of the process of changing-and-keeping-the-same in music, the bewildering fabric of change and stasis in quotidian life becomes illuminated as well. Music abstracts life's stasis/change flux into an accessible, understandable, often even predictable weave of streaming patterns. While we are truly paying attention to well-woven music, everything inside it makes sense. And when the music is over, the streaming events of noisy life can be informed by music's lessons. What is at the core of music is at the core of life as well. Music comes from life, but it also pays life forward, like children teaching their grandparents a thing or two.

If you were to study musical composition in school, the subject of same-but-different would be called *variation* or *development*, usually with a codifier: *harmonic* variation, *thematic* variation, or *motific* development. A musical *motif* is a brief thematic fragment the ear can recognize, like the dot-dot-dot-dash that begins Beethoven's Fifth Symphony; the playing out of that particular motif becomes arguably the most severe essay on rational beauty of all time.

—

The third thing of "only three things" is: "you can do something else," that is, something that hasn't been done before, something novel. You might say that the first thing ("do what you just did") and the third thing are the extremes of the middle "same-but-different" thing. The first and third things operate like terms, that is, terminals: end points along a continuum of experience. As we mentioned, since nothing can be exactly repeated, there can be no absolute realization of the first term. Similarly there is no absolute realization of the third term, since nothing is ever really completely, entirely new. Something about the new is historically old, if only the identity of the observer. Nevertheless, things that happen in life can seem relatively new, even bizarrely alien, and we do pursue novelty even when it's frightening.

All three "things" happen in "Frère Jacques." As you sing the tune to yourself, you will find that the opening phrase has four tones (*Frè-re Jac-ques*), the fourth of which (*-ques*) is the same as the first (*Frè-*). We start off from somewhere; we go up a stair; then we go up another stair (that's what-we-just-did-but-different); then we finish where we started, thereby reminding us of the first thing we did. So there were two kinds of same-but-different experiences: the rise to the third tone resembled the rise to the second tone, but ended higher, as stairs will; and the sudden return to the starting point placed us where we began, but later. These four tones seem like a single gesture until you recognize all the work the mind has done, consciously or not, in making sense of them. Sing the phrase to yourself tracking these events. Then sing it one more time without particularly thinking about it. One can appreciate why simple phrases hang on in the collective ear for so many generations: they actually have an enduring wisdom inside them, or more accurately, inside our cognition of them.

The next phrase of "Frère Jacques" repeats the first phrase, of course, fulfilling as much as possible the definition of the first "thing," that is, "do what you just did." It's as if there is enough information packed inside those four tones to warrant the mind's wanting to hear them again. In fact, it seems downright *pleased* to hear them again. Then it's time to go on. *Dormez-vous* begins on the highest step of the first phrase, and proceeds, as before, to the next step, and then the next—so business as usual, but this time we are higher up the stairs. Now comes another kind of difference: *vous* hangs on, it doesn't return to a lower position. That held-on tone leaves you literally stranded on the stairs. So now what?

What happens next is very interesting because it hardly seems interesting at all: *Dormez-vous* is repeated verbatim. Not only is the phrase repeated, but seeing as the opening phrase of the song was also repeated verbatim, the entire narrative strategy has been predictably repeated to the point of boredom. We have been led to the point of fish-or-cut-bait. If something doesn't happen soon, I'm going home. Great tunes, compositions, plays, and movies share this in common. The master temporal artist knows just when to jump-cut into the payoff. "Frère Jacques" pays off with a flourish. *Sonnez les ma-* is the flourish: these four quick notes are substantially different from what has gone before to qualify for the third "thing," something different. And if you let yourself feel it as if hearing the song for the first time, you can feel the excitement brought on by that admirable quickening. Until I began writing this analysis, however, I hadn't realized that the final two tones of that phrase (*-tines*) are in fact the same two tones in the same position as those at the end of the opening phrase (*Jac-ques*). Now, since I've cognized that, I admire the song even more. The something-different has been followed by a just-did, but the sneaky part is the "just:" ten musical beats of dense musical organization have intervened between the second *Jac-ques* and the first *-tines*, resulting in a subtle sonic weave. *Sonnez les matin-es* is then repeated, a repetition that has been musically earned.

The last phrase is old because the duration of the tones (the rhythm) is identical to the second phrase (*Din, dan, don* equals *Dormez-vous*); but it is new because of the location of the pitches; *dan* drops several tones below *Din* to deepen the compass and add a fillip to an already rich piece of music.

Where has all this analysis gotten us? Let's go back to the discussion about the meaning of the three "things" in real life, which we could call routine (same), variation (sort of different), and novelty (new). The representation of these three principles of temporal organization in a simple folk tune gives us a glimpse of how musical events are compact, powerful sonic icons. When the ear/brain is presented with these icons, there is a resonance with the real-life unfoldings the icons are a code for. If you have the time and the inclination, sing through "Frère Jacques" again, and see if your newly acquired recognition of the "three things" heightens your experience of what music is and what it does.

Either Coming or Going

An even more enigmatic formulation can be made about temporal art, particularly music: Music is either coming or going.

I'm not sure I know what this means, but it works when I listen for it in music, and it works when I look for it in the thick of real life events. One senses that something's either beginning or it's finishing, that the energy is either gathering or dispersing, inhaling or exhaling. The enigma is that we can spend a lot of time in between, feeling both energies at once—most famously when affairs of the heart have become reticent to reveal if they have a future or if they are history. Expressed sexual energy comes and then goes more or less definitively; but here too, there can be those long (and no less engaging) moments when the subtext is: are we done, or is there more? Some music, like trance music, or certain dance music, like disco, intends to suspend you in a state between coming and going, just like deep meditation will transcend such dualistic terms. But then, after returning to earth, we do recognize that on some level we came and we went.

If you listen to a piece of music, continually asking the question, "Are we coming or going," you can hear how carefully the composer and the performers have spaced and sculpted the gatherings and dispersings. Quite often, pieces of music are true to the idealized sexual model, a series of climaxes that plateau and leave off gently with an afterglow. Some pieces end at their highest point (like Ravel's *Bolero*), leaving the listener invigorated—but where is the loving gaze and harmonious embrace after the fireworks? That happens after the piece is over, mixed with deafening applause and considerable hollering.

Over and again we see how the little bubble that music lives in models the globe of our lives. Music is a way of experiencing the whole of life in a little piece of sound.

Steps Easy, Leaps Hard

Here is how to compose a pretty good melody rather casually. Stand at the piano and locate middle C. Extend your index finger, and with that finger alone, starting with middle C, press down only white keys that are neighbors to one another. After the first note, C, you may either repeat C, play D (directly to the right of it) or play B (directly to the left). Say you choose B; your next note will be either B (again) or (back to) C, or (down to) A. Such neighborly progression from tone to tone is called stepwise motion. Keep playing stepwise, passing through middle C every now and again. You may hurry or linger, but never leap. End on C. You have composed a workable melody at least, and a masterpiece at best. Why?

Since the white notes centered on C produce our most familiar mode (major) and since scale-tones adjacent to one another—that is, steps—are most easily cognized (as we have briefly discussed in chapter 2), your melody is relatively easy to hear and easy to sing. Our ability to sing a melody is probably closely related to how clearly we cognize it, and it is easier to aim and find your mark on something near than on something far. Additionally, stepwise melodies do not tax or challenge vocal mechanics. You burn more calories singing leaps (less so for professional singers, but still true) and hence, both for singing and for hearing, "steps easy, leaps hard."

To verify this by the one-finger method, play another melody, again on white notes only, again starting and ending on C, but this time leap about, perhaps wildly. Clearly, your tune is harder to sing and harder to hear. That is not to say that it is necessarily any less beautiful—just more difficult, less "accessible."

Some leaps are easier than others. From a given note, say middle C, to an octave above it is quite a leap for the voice, but it is easy to hear because of its harmonic closeness to the lower tone (2:1). From C up to G is quite a bit less of a leap, and only slightly more harmonically complex (3:2). I will point out that Cole Porter's song "I Love You," one of the most beautiful (and popular) melodies of all time, begins with the *downward* leap of a major seventh, both distant and complex but, in this context, gorgeous and, evidently, just accessible enough.

In daily life, the equivalent of "steps easy, leaps hard" becomes, let's say: conservative moves are safer than daring ones. The vocal and aural stretch of a melodic leap is embodied as the risk and uncertainty of a daring move. There is nothing wrong with a leap, of course — the right leap at the right time is a good move. However, in both music and real life, there is a codicil to "steps easy, leaps hard": leaps are dramatic events, leaving gaps that want to be filled in. For instance, in the case of "Twinkle, Twinkle, Little Star," the initial bold leap gets filled in stepwise during the remainder of the phrase. "Somewhere Over the Rainbow" begins with an octave leap; continues by backing, filling, and expanding (downward); and finishes the stanza with all of its leapt-over material finally filled in. Those of us who have run away from home know how, over the course of our lives, we keeping looking over our shoulders at the old neighborhood until we eventually revisit it, perhaps incognito, perhaps only in our imagination, in order to fill the breach in our heart. How many times have you not been able to wrench free of old loves, even the ones you no longer love? We try to separate by increments, and when that doesn't work we take a dramatic leap, and spend some of our lives filling in the gap of our leaving. Vocally as well as emotionally, a leap is hard work.

Back at the keyboard, still with one finger, compose a succession of tones that are *mostly* steps but take leaps at just the right moments, taking care to fill in, directly or sinuously, the area leapt over. As you follow the story of what you are playing, you can hear the drama of the leaps, and the resolution of filling them in. Then, in a reflective mood, you can wonder about the leaps of your life, and the living melodies, smooth or turbulent, sensible or inchoate, you have wrought thereby.

Counterpoint and Relationship

Counterpoint, also called *polyphony,* is a conversation among a group of musical voices wherein each voice individually makes sense, yet greater sense is made by the group as a whole. When you listen to a string quartet playing Beethoven, for instance, or a fugue by Bach, it's easy to imagine that you are witnessing individuals sitting around a table working out their collective destiny employing highly refined social skills.

In addressing the parallel between human relationships and musical voices, let's limit our discussion to melodies played by two instruments only. Although the musical codification of counterpoint, that is, its rules for relational etiquette, reach back historically for over seven centuries, we will attempt to summarize its rules of behavior in a few brief paragraphs. To begin, consider that every melody has motion: it may rise, it may fall, or, by using sustained or repeated tones, it may remain stationary. If there are two melodies playing at once, there arise four categories of relative motion.

Oblique Motion: When one voice sustains or reiterates a single tone and the other voice moves either up or down, the relation between them is called *oblique* motion. This is the most easily recognized relationship between voices. It is very much as if one person were talking and the other saying "uh-huh" for a while, and then trading roles back and forth. This kind of relationship falls so easily on the ear that it can be effectively improvised between two players: the only rule is that the player not sustaining is free to move. Grab a friend, get him or her to sing a single tone, and improvise a few tones of undulating melody, conventional or not, against it. Then, at a signal, it's your turn to hold a tone while your friend sings some tuney thing. Keep trading roles and you are improvising a piece of two-part polyphony in oblique motion.

Contrary Motion: Oblique motion has the politeness and accommodation of good conversation—one speaker is active and the other passive, with a frequent and willing exchange of roles. But what happens when both speak at the same time? In music, this can result in three additional types of motion. *Contrary* motion is when the parts move simultaneously, but in opposite directions, that is, when one part moves up, the other moves down, though not necessarily by the same distances. It's as if two dance partners spontaneously agree on the proper distance between them, either separating or coming together by combinations of various steps or leaps. In relationship, contrary motion is easy to comprehend but not so easy to implement. Should we each leap apart? OK, I'll take a little step away and you take a big one away. Now you take a little step away and I'll leap away. Now you leap back and I'll step back. Now let's rush into each other's arms...and on and on. Is this not unlike flirting? If the distances, anatomies, and certain other conditions are lined up just so, this is how we make babies. Wait, it gets even more interesting.

Similar Motion: In the remaining two types of motion (similar and parallel), both voices move in the same direction. In *similar* motion, both move in the same direction but by different increments. We both move up, but you leap and I'll step. Now I'll take a little leap down and you take a big leap down. This is like the latter phases of negotiation: we agree on the direction but not on the quantity. In human relationships, this is delicate; in music, it is marginally difficult to hear. The directional sameness can be confusing. Why? Read on.

Parallel Motion: Parallel motion means that both parts are always moving the same way at a fixed distance apart, like close ballroom dancing, or a unison dance routine like the Rockettes. In personal relationship this can mean a deeply resonant inti-

macy, or it can become a dangerous mimicry: too much sameness threatens autonomy, a basic condition for relational health.
Likewise, too much parallel motion between two musical voices
destroys the polyphony. The voices become not two but one,
and although this may be a supreme union, it is no longer a
relationship. Two people speaking in dead unison are not con-
versing. So in polyphonic music, the rule is: use only a little bit
of parallel motion, and only the kinds most easily untangled in
the mind's ear.

The anathema of polyphony is homophony: lots of voices
moving always in the same direction. Some of the music we love
the most is extremely homophonic. Certain country music harmonies, vocal groups who swoop up and down in complete synchrony and, most notably, the five-part saxophone sections of
mid-nineteenth-century jazz bands. Such homophony is sometimes called the "thickened line," and indeed the polyphony disappears and a single strand of gorgeous, fat, looping melody
takes over. These are some of my favorite sounds in the universe, but they are not conversations, there is no exchange of
melodic content. These synchronous sounds can be powerful
and moving, but they can also get old and treacly. Sooner or
later, we miss the cross-talk.

The Four Motions Combined: In a piece of two-part polyphony,
the four motions are richly interwoven. At certain times, the
two dancers are alternating between moving and not moving
(oblique motion), at others they move in opposite directions
(contrary motion), every so often they move uni-directionally
but for different distances (similar motion), and occasionally they
move exactly the same way (parallel motion). Clear polyphony
(and good relationships) both seek the most engaging mix of
these motions, the ideal balance between difference and sameness, hetero- and homogeneity. Thus has the polyphonic motion
of music instructed me about life; just as surely the relationships

in my life have given me to understand how polyphony, embedded in the psyche, produces powerful responses in listeners.

Although there are many kinds of polyphonic music in the world, the specific procedures of counterpoint as we have been discussing them are European in their historical genesis, and have left their cultural legacy, directly or indirectly, over a wide swath of the globe. Africa may own rhythm, Asia may own modality, but Western Civ has cornered the market on polyphony. Since composers usually prefer three- and four-part polyphony, exemplary compositions in two-part counterpoint are less common, though they abound in the motets and masses of Josquin Desprez and Orlande de Lassus. Closer to home, a good place to start is a recording of Bach's Two-Part Inventions. Better yet, sing some rounds with a friend or two or three, including, incidentally, *Frère Jacques,* which works in four parts. The most amazing thing is the way well-crafted polyphony can remain translucent even in four or five independent parts, how the full complement of complex relationships remains functional for the attentive listener. For my money, polyphony is our richest cultural icon, a magnificent metaphor from which we are learning still to govern not only our lives but also — *E Pluribus Unum* — our nations.

Don't Do Two Hard Things at Once

Most of the rules in music can be condensed into these seven words: Don't do two hard things at once. In real life this is good guidance: don't get shingles and divorced in the same month; don't declare bankruptcy and fall off your bike on the same day. Don't sing Schoenberg driving in a blizzard. Don't learn calculus in Turkish. Or, if you do any of these things, be prepared for the extra labor in regaining equilibrium. This is the credo by which music (given its diverse dimensions of rhythm, melody, harmony, and polyphonic motion) retains its clarity. The trick lies in knowing, in each dimension, what is "easy" and what is "hard."

Simply put, in rhythm, *boom* is easy and *chick* is hard. In melody, steps are easy, leaps are hard. In harmony, the low ratios of octaves and perfect fifths are simple, and the complex ratios of whole steps and half steps are hard. In contrapuntal motion, oblique is easy and parallel is hard. Here is a table of what is easy and what hard (reading down the page) in the four dimensions we have discussed (reading across):

	RHYTHM	MELODY	HARMONY	POLYPHONY
EASY ↑	*boom*	steps	unisons octaves fifths	oblique
IN BETWEEN	strong beats weak beats	thirds fourths	fourths thirds augmented, diminished intervals	contrary similar
HARD ↓	*chick*	leaps	seconds (steps) sevenths	parallel

Before proceeding further, let me say more about the notion of "rules" in music. Musical rules are not laws; there is no penalty for infraction. Rather, each rule is actually an "if → then" clause, formulated in the interest of maximum clarity, flow, and beauty. For instance, "the more stepwise motion, the smoother the melody" does not obviate the use of many leaps, perhaps many consecutive leaps. If you want a jagged, bounding melody, leaps are the answer. "For clear polyphonic motion, do not leap *into* or *away from* dissonance" is the so-called rule, and it is indeed the most efficient way to maximize the music's clarity and flow. But what if you want the music to be rough and tough, with some clouds and fog? Life isn't all about clarity and flow. Leaps *into* and *away from* dissonance are hugely affective; toughening things up for the listener can evoke deeply felt emotion. Of course, pedagogical strategy usually insists on learning the smooth and clear ways first. That is a good way to teach, and it is also a good way to listen. Music for kids, some of the sweetest and most carefree music we have, is the way it is because it steers clear of too many hard things at once. There is no right way to make music; the "rules" always return to the one that must never be broken: If it sounds good, it is good. Everything depends on how you want it to sound.

That having been said, it is amazing how the thickest books on compositional procedures can reduce to the dictum that, in the interest of maximum clarity, if you do something too far down in any one column of the table it is best to be high up in the other columns. As a teacher, I am always looking for good metaphors to clarify this formulation, and, unsurprisingly, most of the good ones come from students. One day I was explaining yet again "Don't do two hard things at once," and my student, a young mother, said, "Oh, I see! Surround your ouches with yum-yums." I think, if we are really moved by some outrageous leap or the excruciating beauty of a harsh dissonance, the chances are that we were otherwise abiding in a warm cave of yum-yums, that is, our leap into dissonance (ouch) occurred on a strong beat (yum) in a clear harmonic context (yum) and resolved by a step (double-yum).

A real-life version of this rule is called tact, which can be found in the form of "good news/bad news." Don't tell Aunt Ellen that her car was towed until her nose stops bleeding; then tell her about her tax refund; then say about the car. Music is a quintessentially human expression. When we listen to it we are Aunt Ellen, so thankful for the yums among the ouches.

It's Not Where You Go but How You Get Back

In my early teens, when I was first learning to compose, my jazz teacher (Walter "Buddy" Hiles) often reminded me, "It's not where you go but how you get back," and that has remained true guidance in both music making and in life. In largest life terms, one can never really leave home—the project of reconciling the growing child you left behind with the emerging adult you now are is never finished. Even if a piece of music ends far from home, the beginning of a piece is never really left behind. *Never look back* is another way of looking back. In the musical realm, place of origin is never forgotten. I have learned, for example, that the "leaps-tend-to-get-filled-in" rule (which we've just discussed) is a special instance of "how-you-get-back." Every dramatic leap in your life has a bungee cord attached to it pulling you back even as you propel yourself forward. And if you ever do get back to where you began, the "return" must reconcile the dramas of the past with the narrative of the present. All music, but especially the richly tonal music from Bach to Brahms, displays this concern with the continuity of musical narrative, as do novels, as do we ourselves when we reflect on our life story. In this way, the compact narratives of music provide a lens to focus the sprawling drama of our lives.

⇒ SURPRISINGLY LIFELIKE BEHAVIOR ⇐

A subtext for a composer's process is *how much* information is being played out over a given amount of time. This can be understood as a judicious application of "you can do only three things." Too much too soon will overwhelm the listener. Not enough and too late will bore, and ultimately lose, the listener. How much newness is enough? Typically a small piece of information (obviously incomplete) is followed by its repeat or near-repeat (even more obviously incomplete), followed by some hint of completion, which in turn opens out into hereto-fore unimagined territory. This can be experienced as parallel to the kinds of relationships in life where people test one another's space, in turn holding themselves back and then bringing them-selves forward—withholding, then revealing. With new cou-ples, this is flirtation; with domestic partners it is negotiation; in music it is composition.

It is interesting to listen to music, especially through-composed music, from the view of the composer-fisherman playing out the fishing line enough but not too much—just the right amount, in fact, to hook the listener-fish. This strat-egy of exposing just who you are and what you intend takes on a special meaning when you consider your own personal relationships, especially new and significant ones. Am I being too forward? Too shy? Why not just blurt out the whole truth? Or should I bide my time and appear mysterious? We don't want to scare people off but we do want them to see us—just enough. Artists who work in a temporal medium—novelists, playwrights, comedians, filmmakers, composers—have similar concerns, and your appreciation of this aspect of their art clari-fies the artful strategies you yourself employ in everyday life.

Two Social Models

Music highlights two complementary social models. The first model is the individual separate from any group: a lone musi-cian speaking from the heart. To hear an instrumentalist per-forming a solo is to witness the covenant that player has forged with his music and is sharing with you. The second is the musi-cal ensemble, an expression of the social unit: partners (duo), family (band), and tribe (orchestra). The intricate dynam-ics of music allow these models to be publicly and formally played out.

When you sing in a choir, the intimacy of the communal bond is palpable. For instance, if you are singing alto along with eight other altos, not only do your unisons with the other altos have to be true, but the alto section has to blend with the basses, tenors, and sopranos in order for the music to work. Furthermore, the altos are typically somewhat submerged in the overall texture, separately discernable to only the keenest outside listener. Why would anyone want to sing alto? Because the reward is extreme. To be a single cell inside such a human construction goes beyond sound waves into the essence of evolutionary cooperation. By temporarily giving up your individuality, you become more than yourself by far.

For a few terrifying, glorious months in 1959, I was a part of the trumpet section of the Stan Kenton band, a brass section known for its high precision and great power. It was terrifying because the other four trumpet players were much better than I was (I'd signed on as a composer/arranger and the trumpet job fell in my lap), so I had to play at the top of my ability and beyond. Glorious because there has never been anything in my long life since the Stan Kenton band to match that powerful mixture of musicality and sensuality. The exultant shouts of the very loud, high brass climaxes exploding in your ears amid the pandemonium and excitement that the band usually created, all conducted and drawn out of you by a highly charismatic (and very tall) man, made your body an organ in a beautiful musical monster. It was over-the-top manic, and it was gorgeous. At age twenty-two I had a pretty chubby ego, which it took a lot of intense vibration to absorb, but absorbed I became, a willing part of Stan's ambition and his hefty contribution to American music. Nowadays, when I carefully observe a second desk, second violinist in a symphony orchestra, her bowing arm in absolute synchrony with twenty-one other bowing arms, one part of myself asks, "How can she live with her loss of identity?" but another part of myself knows.

Subtle and Overt

Before I studied with the North Indian raga singer Pandit Pran Nath I thought I knew about subtlety in music, but his raga teaching showed me a deeper level. The vocal technique called *meend*, akin to *portamento* (for strings) and *glissando* (for keyboard), means "to slide." For the raga singer, the meend is usually an unbroken curve between one tone and another, getting softer as it travels, and then blossoming suddenly as it sounds the target tone. Guru-ji showed me how to sing a descending, diminishing meend that would all but disappear as it arrived at the target tone, which itself was sounded briefly at the vanishing point of audibility. I think the intention was to *point* to a tone with such a precisely fashioned arc that the designated arrival tone, though unsounded, was nevertheless heard—a sort of aural illusion. The target tone simply slipped beneath the surface of the background drone of the tamboura and the ambient sounds in your ears, a vanishing act. So when you sing it back to your teacher, do you sound the target tone or not? Guru-ji would never explain. "Like *dees*," he'd say, and sing it again, but differently enough to open up the possibilities and deepen the mystery.

I had thought I could glance at a face and know the feeling behind the face, be sensitive to the slightest twitch of an eyebrow or quickening at the corner of the mouth. I knew that people are mysterious at root, but the lesson of the vanishing meend took me further into the limit of my sensibilities than could any body language or tone of voice. Perhaps this is because the end points were musically prescribed: start here and disappear into there. Or perhaps because the entire phenomenon takes place in a realm already enchanted by the beauty of the *rag*. In any case, when I first studied the technique I was struck—and am still—by how deeply it dives into one's unknowable center.

There are many examples in music of extreme subtlety. In bebop there are "ghostnotes," placeholders in a melody's rhythmic flow that are played but scarcely pitched. This happens also in the deep folk music of the Middle East and Eastern Europe, and I delight in trying to bring it off as a pianist. In the middle of the sustain of a loudly struck chord, was there a little ghost music? If you question me I won't tell, but I'll play it again, just differently enough.

You don't have to look far to find a person who is very gruff and forward, perhaps even gross-seeming, who nonetheless, if you live through the barrage, displays a delicate lacework between the furrows. Some of the most powerful music we have does that. There are countless passages in Beethoven, Wagner, Mahler, even Mozart, that are bombastic, arbitrary, and (if you don't stop it right *now*) terminally boring, which give way to passages of savvy, subtle complexity. We treasure companions who can thunder and purr without compromise or apology, and the music that shows us a cogent panorama of these sensibilities we treasure also. Beethoven's fierceness can make us cringe, his gentleness bring us out from hiding. Miles Davis also. Bartók too, and The Grateful Dead, and all of us who have known to reveal the extremes of our humanity through musical means.

The Great Tuning Compromise

The lovely thing about compromise between opposites is how often a solution arises that is beyond the domain of either alternative. In the history of European music, this happened most dramatically in respect to our tuning system. Before the Renaissance, the low-prime ratios of just intonation were more or less universal in the world, although their application—how the harmonies were coarsened or refined—varied widely over the globe. But toward the end of the Middle Ages, the European ear became restless for more and more harmonic territory, which meant more and more tones in one's chosen harmonic field. A wide palette of differently tuned notes is OK for singers, but not for fixed-pitch instruments. Where should one drill the holes in flutes, tune the strings of violins and harps, place the frets on lutes and guitars and, most critically, tune the tones of fixed-pitch keyboard instruments like clavichords, organs, harpsichords, and pianos? The choices for these instruments are limited by their design. Eventually, twelve tones to the octave became the standard and in the eighteenth and nineteenth centuries the question of how to tune those tones became the subject of passionate debate. More and more, the road of compromise was taken: we'll have some notes exactly in tune, and for the others, we'll just split the difference between neighboring rivals. (Such tunings are called mean-tone temperaments.)

Gradually, the compromise took the form of dividing the octave into twelve precisely equal parts (the system is called twelve-tone equal temperament). This is the tuning system we use today for fixed-pitch instruments, and it is our culture's standard of reference. When the piano tuner comes to your house, he doesn't tune your piano, he de-tunes it, but in an extremely precise way. The octaves (2:1) remain OK, and the fifths (3:2) are a teeny bit too narrow, not enough to start a war; but the harmonies of the other crucial ratio (5:4), the major thirds, are egregiously too wide. That's enough to cause a chronic itch in the Western ear. But hold! If you accept this compromise, the old harmonic field that used to be a flat plane is now a sphere, and you can use your twelve slightly skewed tones to travel anywhere and everywhere in the sphere. Like Magellan, we have circumnavigated the territory. If you leave your house by the west portal and travel long and far enough (by twelve perfect fifths, for instance, or four minor thirds, or three major thirds), you will arrive home by the east portal, only slightly battered by your not-quite-in-tune journey.

The battle between just intonation—(everything sounds great, but you have only a limited number of tones and you can't go very far from home) and twelve-tone equal temperament (nothing sounds quite right, but you can go everywhere)—has seemed to many like an either/or proposition. The spokesperson for just intonation says: "This is the music of our ancestors. One doesn't really need to travel far from home. Home is where the heart is, and besides, how could you ask *anyone* to sacrifice the sacred resonances of just intonation *simply* to fly about from place to place? Your tuning system *sounds* wrong, and it *is* wrong." The spokesperson for equal temperament replies: "I'll send you a postcard from each lovely place I visit."

This debate was being waged over several centuries by millions of musicians during the same period when Western civilization was in fact learning to circumnavigate the earth, to dramatically increase its territory of influence, to mass-manufacture standard-sized goods and, indeed, to fly. But few could foresee the compromise that was finally reached: We use both systems at once. This solution depends partially on a serendipitous psycho-acoustic phenomenon: although the ear demands that the musical *foreground* be well in tune, it more easily forgives tuning approximations in the *background*. This means that the discrepancies between (for example) a perfectly in tune singer in the foreground and the equal-tempered piano accompaniment in the background will be more or less forgiven.

But what about a solo piano? Well, I'm sorry to say that pianos are enough out of tune that some things don't sound very good on them. Equal-tempered major thirds, somewhat too wide, sound a bit raw. If you play middle C together with the E directly above it over and over again for long enough, you will find yourself uncomfortably christened by modern times. (Were the two tones in just intonation, the result would be far more pleasant.) However, craftsmen have accumulated centuries of skill in piano manufacture; musicians have sorted and re-sorted the harmonic possibilities, tending toward those most musically rewarding; and pianists have established a high standard for piano technique that favors sonority and beauty of tone—all of which makes possible the transcendent sonatas of Beethoven, the romantic essays of Chopin, the rhapsodic flights of Keith Jarrett, and the countless lives lived in deep devotion to the instrument including, incidentally, my own. Speaking only for myself, though, I did have to learn to sing raga in order to keep my musical sanity intact.

The greatest blessing from our modern tuning has been our gradual awakening to its innate possibilities of ambiguity and resolution. In spoken language, a single word with more than one meaning can generate a pun, the meaning of which must be decided by context. For instance, the difference between "half a pear" and "have a pair" can be deciphered only by knowing the rest of the story. The mind will seek *the best fit* according to context. In the riddle "What is black and white and red all over?" the contexts suggests that "red" is a color, which renders the syntax nonsensical. When it learns (or figures out) the answer, "a newspaper," in that moment "red" the color becomes "read" the passive form of a verb, which is *the best fit* for a new context that does make sense, and the cognitive dissonance is resolved.

Because there are a large number of possible harmonic meanings in music (more than thirty) yet the number of tones in the modern tuning system is limited to twelve, similar types of ambiguity arise often in our music. The resolutions of linguistic puns are usually groaners. But the resolution of harmonic ambiguities could be called *swooners* in that they result so often in a deeply moving emotion. In music, the pun-moment is often felt as a turning point in the flow of feeling, a moment of sweet discovery. In music, *the best fit* is not so much a logical resolution as an affective one. Thanks to equal temperament, the harmonic field is now *round* and there is a new dimension of possibility: you thought you were west, which *feels* a certain way and then, not unlike Magellan, you discover yourself east, which feels a different way. (This amazing dynamic is the central topic of my thick, heavy book, *Harmonic Experience.*) For now, when you hear a ✺ chord progression that fills your heart with a sudden knowing, the uplifting benefits of our tuning system may well be coursing through you. It is the surprising beauty of our modern beast.

PASSION AND DISPASSION

Through experience, musicians inevitably discover that music without feeling becomes lifeless. At the same time, we recognize that if we are totally absorbed in feeling we will lose our musical coordinates. Soaked in passion, yes; absorbed, no. For the artist, there always must be some remove. A master performer gives the public impression of being utterly swept away, and perhaps the goal is to give that impression. But the little beady eye at the back wall of the hall is always open. How does one practice walking this wire between immersion and objectivity? At home, among friends. Falling off the wire in your living room is good work. Over time, you develop a kind of leathery (but permeable) outer skin. Yet even if you perform often, it could take years to find your balance onstage.

As listeners, we can tell when music becomes syrupy, gushy, over-the-top, and we can tell likewise when the blood drains out of it, and it sounds dry, emotionally empty. Everyone has his or her own idea of the balance. From my own listening seat, I like to drown in feeling, but I also like to listen coolly to the lacework of well-crafted music. I want to have it both ways.

In life too, we get to practice the line between passion and dispassion, also among friends. Losing your dispassion in private or in public results in the many varieties of "losing it," from a petulant toss of the head to road rage or, on the other hand, from a blurted compliment to an ill-advised elopement. Our methods for learning dispassion in life can be painfully interactive, but we also have safer practices to rely on: we listen to teachings of moderation, we pray for guidance, we meditate.

For me, music has been a reliable teacher of the balance between passion and dispassion. As both listener and musician I try to find the balance between emotion and the no-motion of being centered. Especially in this regard, practicing music is life practice. It is like walking the floor of a valley. On one side are mountains painted by Van Gogh, heaving with color and emotion; on the other, glaciers, shining and still. Sometimes you may find yourself exploring the turbulence on one side, sometimes the crisp clarity on the other. Or you can walk in the middle and hear the music from everywhere at once.

6

Music as Story

In Igor Stravinsky's music for the ballet *Pétrouchka,* there is a particularly memorable moment. The circus puppet Pétrouchka, who has fallen in love with the circus ballerina, is, after a long and exciting chase sequence, slain by the Moor, his rival. Although the music for the ballet has many flamboyant and boisterous passages, at the moment the Moor's sword pierces the puppet's straw body, the orchestra becomes suddenly still and, as Pétrouchka falls dead from parapet to ground, we hear a single sound. In Stravinsky's score, the instructions to the percussionist are as follows: *Tenir le Tamb. de B. tout bas au sol et le faire tomber,* which translates to "Hold the tambourine low to the ground and let it fall." When I saw the ballet, this was chilling. Passion had become sticks and straw. The association of the *chink* of the dropped tambourine with the sudden obliteration of a beloved romantic-comic character is an aesthetic choice the composer made, and it now has become an indelible connection in my ear. Whenever I accidentally drop a tambourine I can't help thinking, *There goes Pétrouchka — snuffed again.*

All too easily we associate music not only with puppets and their romantic escapades, but with every imaginable story. Music

whose purpose is to tell a story about something external to itself
is called *program music*. Music, however, knows also how to be
its *own* story with no external reference—the woof and warp of
musical sound is the sole narrative line the listener follows. The
somewhat stern term for such music is *absolute music*. For over
two hundred years, musicians, listeners, and critics have been
extolling the merits of one kind over the other, though clearly
there is room for both. Why should listeners to Debussy's *Images*
be deprived of their images? Conversely, do I have to make up a
story to enjoy Bach's *Art of the Fugue*?

I would like to suggest that program music and absolute
music are not mutually exclusive, that an extreme example
of either contains the seed of the other. Let us imagine there
is a continuum of experience from the stories and pictures of
program music to the intrinsic formal refinements of absolute music, and that each listener at each moment is moving
somewhere along this dialectical line. In this chapter we will
be examining, among other things, how the entire continuum
looks from various points within it.

WORDS AND MUSIC

We are discussing music, not poetry or lyrics, and the stories we
are talking about are told in sounds, not words. But as a kind of
preface, let's briefly consider words and music together. Song
and speech are indeed branches of a single tree. Language is
made of pitched vowels and rhythmic consonants. We refer to
the music of speech and the grammar of music. What we call
song has arisen over tens of millennia as an intensification of
speech—language vivified for special purposes. This intensification can work two ways, by contraction or by expansion. The
natural rise and fall of speech can be contracted into a mono-
tone, the natural rhythms corralled into an even pulse, thereby

channeling body rhythms into a trancelike state, a technique used today as a ritual practice to bring everyone into one vibrational frame. On the other hand, the natural cadences of speech can be expanded by exaggerating the pitch range (rendering the high tones higher and the low ones lower), and by lengthening the vowels while sustaining their pitches. This heightens the natural emphasis of language, underlining the meaning and increasing the expressive content. In prehistoric times, that is, before the invention of writing, the keepers of the stories of tribes and peoples, the early bards and poets, almost certainly used varied pitch as a memory aid to keep their creation stories and cultural narratives alive.

As writing evolved, music was gradually released from its mnemonic function; it was, so to speak out of a job. Purely instrumental music — wordless music — is probably a relatively recent phenomenon, although nonpitched or quasi-pitched percussion music — the prehistoric version of a drum jam — is likely ancient indeed, maybe going back to more than a hundred thousand years. But the playing of pitched instruments is probably only forty thousand years old, and instrumental ensembles are relatively recent — maybe a few thousand years, though these time frames lie between intuitive and more or less educated guesses. We *have* discovered a thirty-five-thousand-year-old bone flute with musically placed holes, and it's probably not the first one ever made. A public concert of purely instrumental music, where listeners gather and musicians play, is commonplace only after the early 1700s.

What primarily concerns us here is wordless music. It is precisely because music and speech were joined at birth and in modern times have become separated that wordless music has so robustly developed its own intricate grammar. Instrumental music can remind us of speech — amazingly so sometimes — but it is not speech. And yet it has found a way, over many centuries of longing, to say precisely what we mean. What follows is a consideration of the many ways that music tells our story.

Music as You
You Alone

You alone are in your room, let's say, watching a good mystery thriller. So absorbed are you by the film that you don't realize the role of the score in drawing you in. In fact, if you do happen to notice it, it's probably intrusive. The thought *What a great score* would take you out of the movie. Ideally, the music for a film, especially a mystery or an action flick, should merge with your physical responses. The effectiveness of a good film score is best realized only after the movie is over, at which point you might want to see it again, the better to appreciate the skill of the composer, not to mention the director, the cinematographer, the actors, etc. But the virgin view gives the viewer an opportunity for total immersion in the story — that's the magic of the movies.

Now let's get into the mind of the film composer as he or she sets about to score the movie. To be truly effective, your music should not be listened to (especially at first) in its own right. This extreme, though common, model of program music includes all forms of theater from drama to juggling acts. (Remember this is about wordless music, which excludes opera and musicals.) So the composer needs to get it just right: the music needs to heighten the mood and intensify the narrative without calling attention to itself.

One aspect of the movie composer's skill is creating the score with appropriately shared cultural references — styles or types of sound that associate with commonly held archetypes. Thus, the Elgar-like fanfares of John Williams in the *Star Wars* series stand for the grandeur of space travel. The cool jazz of the '60s set the scene for a Woody Allen cocktail party. These references, shared by the intended audience, are part of our culture's story. The scores for car chases, sad farewells, stalking villains, are not works of overt originality but more-or-less efficient references to recognizable archetypical situations, characters, and moods.

As the pianist for the original company of Chicago's Second City, I learned this lesson in the trenches. At twenty-two (in 1959) I was the baby of the company, in awe of the actors, their improvisatory skills, and their compelling personae. Early on (1960), Severn Darden and Barbara Harris were working on a sweet, funny, and tender scene between a college English professor and his daughter, who is about to confess her just-lost virginity. I watched silently from the piano bench for a few minutes, then director Paul Sills said, "OK, take it again from the top. Go, Mathieu." I played something or other to set the scene, just guessing really. The actors began, ran into trouble right away, Paul stopped the scene, gave notes to the actors, and said, "Top again. Mathieu, go." I began again with something I thought more sweet-funny-tender, but this time Paul stopped right away.

"The music's all wrong."

"What do you want, Paul?"

"Play the music from the glider movie."

"What glider movie?"

Exasperated with this kid pianist unable to grasp the *simple* basics of theater, Paul raised his voice: "There *is* no glider movie, man — *as if* there were a glider movie!"

So now I had to set the scene for two made-up characters in accordance with a movie the theater director was imagining as he projected his sense of it onto the scene. Strangely enough — and this was the genius of Paul Sills — his direction was right on, I found the music immediately, the scene developed into a favorite and played for hundreds of performances. The striking part of this story is that although I recall the scene I've forgotten the music, except that it sounded a lot like the glider movie.

Back to you. Your film is over and it's not yet time for bed, so you decide to watch the DVD of a ballet Aunt Jane gave you. It is called *Connections,* let's say, and you've never heard of the composer, and whatever narrative exists is played out solely by the patterns of human bodies in motion. In contrast to the film you just saw, this score seems to be much more prominent, more able to be enjoyed for itself. The dancer's bodies, their costumes, the lighting, all allow you to imagine that you are actually seeing the music. Although you are comfy on your couch, your body is, in an inward way, resonating with the bodies of the dancers. You can both see and feel the music's embodied intelligence.

In this example we have moved considerably along the continuum from program music toward absolute music. The story is in the patterns and weavings of bodies, light, color, and sound. Although most ballet music is written collaboratively by a choreographer and a composer, some music originally intended purely for listening enjoyment, for instance a movement from a Bach *Brandenburg Concerto,* has been subsequently choreographed so that the dancer's bodies become a visual kind of music. And the dancers, who are definitely not sitting quietly on couches but leaping about in lighted space, fully embody the music. So the story of such music is still the story of itself, but it can live viscerally in our bodies, thanks to the bodies of the dancers.

Most music intended for dancing is more fun to dance to than interesting to listen to, though there are many magical exceptions. *Pétrouchka,* for example, is commonly played as an orchestral suite and is hugely rewarding as such. Although someone who hears the score without knowing either its title or the story of the ballet could find it quite wonderful, it's likely that once you know the plot, or have seen the ballet, the music will be forever merged with it. For me, will the *chink* of that tambourine ever not be Pétrouchka's skull breaking? It is even less likely for a film score to work as absolute music. Most people who listen to film music are referring to the movie as they listen. Nonetheless, these are all examples of listening experiences that shift subtly along the continuum connecting the external story and the intrinsic musical narrative. Every place you can listen along this line is a good place, yet there are valuable qualitative differences one does learn to discern.

OK, you again. The next night (it's nice to know you have so much leisure time) you decide just to listen to good music —Vivaldi, Ravel, and Keith Jarrett are your choices. First, the Vivaldi. The sprightly, well-ordered sound of strings skitters across your consciousness. You stretch out on the sofa and within ten seconds begin to think about your day: the really disturbing call from Daniel that woke you up—must call Anne and warn her about Daniel and Lisa—owe Lisa lunch, it won't happen—car appointment at 3:30 tomorrow or perish—why was Jonathan being so damn nice in the lobby?—find *and return* his drawings—more tired than I thought—better check e-mail: must be more than fifty of 'em, I'll answer three—what is this? Oh yeah, Vivaldi, it's nice. Ends nice.

The music, which this time around you scarcely heard as music, served with great success as the score for your clear and present autobiography. In my experience, this is the way most people hear music most of the time. When I go to a symphony concert, I look at the rows of people in front of me and imagine opening little doors at the back of their skulls to see the screen playing their movie. So many lives, so many lists, so many imaginary scenarios, so many real appointments to keep, so many wounds to salve, promises to break, tears to hold. The music streams on and on, score to a thousand films playing on a thousand screens near you. A perfect film score is not so much heard as *used* to heighten the story; similarly, what most of us bring to the act of listening is a heightening of our own story.

The story that music heightens is not confined to the near present. Music can be a potent and specific jog to deep memory. For me, the sound of Louis Armstrong singing "Hello, Dolly!" renders me twelve years old, experiencing copious sweating and wild leaping in my mid-parts while dancing close with Susie Bloom. I can't hear '50s Miles without being haunted by my high-school longing to be an authentic musician, like him. Regardless of its context, every Beatles song smells like weed. Every last one of us has these musical historical markers, where memory and music are fused.

OK, next, the Ravel. You don't know which Ravel you've chosen, and decide not to look at the title. This time, as you close your eyes and the orchestral sounds begin to drift and shift shape, you see amusing and amazing things — waterfalls, translucent forms looming in mist, mysteriously floating creatures. The music is guiding your visions.

Enough of that: now a solo piano track by Keith Jarrett, a long, gospel-inspired riff with pianistic displays and compelling rhythmic grooves that you visualize as bright patterns against dark ground. The patterns feel wonderful inside your skin. By the end you are exhilarated. Although you weren't following a program external to the music, through its agency you made up picture-stories and passed through changes of mood — a psychological narrative of sorts. So the music was still about you; you were the program, not in terms of specific events like appointments and phone calls, but in the more ephemeral realm of images and feelings. It seems quite natural to appropriate the music of another as our own autobiography. Back in the day, a person's life and character could be read by his or her collection of 78s, then LPs, then cassettes, then CDs. Now your life is described by what's on your iPod or in your iTunes, not to mention your ring tone. We carry our sound tracks with us to enhance the programs of our lives.

You and Hero

A step removed from music's autobiographical function is its biographical one. The entire life of a composer (or songwriter, or improviser, or performer) can be studied through his or her music. As one can attest by the plethora of goopy films about composers, many folks identify more with the life story of a composer than with the music itself. It is fair to say that for most of us, music is vitalized by the composer's or performer's story. Many musicians are cast as triumphant heroes, most are perceived as tragic heroes, and a few, even, as antiheroes. Beethoven is the archetypical triumphant hero, succeeding in forging from the deepest adversity and isolation a music that has guided the world's spirit for generations after his death. Most great musicians are perceived as tragic heroes, especially the many who have died young or "too soon": Chopin, Charlie Parker, Coltrane, Jimi Hendrix, John Lennon—the list is long. Perhaps even more fascinating are the antiheroes, Gesualdo, Miles Davis, Kurt Cobain, whose dark energy filled their music with dangerous truths and a powerful kind of light. We identify more or less with heroes of all types because someone else's biography is a measure of one's own autobiography. Each hero's story is, in certain and particular ways, both your story and not your story. Your interpretation of the composer's (or performer's) story as it merges or diverges from your own, though an indirect way of listening to their music, is a revelation of yourself. Through their story, you yourself are revealed.

I say *indirect* because knowing about a piece of music is not the same as listening to it. It is an interesting pursuit to set up a "blindfold test" for yourself by asking a friend to pick some music from various styles or sources with which you may not be familiar and then to plunge into the unfamiliar waters with no external map to guide you. This is one way of ferreting out whatever "absolute" aspects of the music are available to you. After all, what would a nondeaf, socially gracious Beethoven mean to your listening of his music? Mozart as a sixty-year-old late bloomer? Bix Beiderbecke as a kindly old farmer? Dylan as a doting grandpa who reads *USA Today*? It's illuminating to know how much of what you hear is text and how much is context.

Public You

For better or worse, music is just as mixed in with our public space as it is with a typical action movie. Culture seems to compose its own score to public life. This is the case worldwide. As we've mentioned, in Bali the sounds of gamelans and drums are woven into public consciousness. In Istanbul, some flavor of Eurasian pop seems to be everywhere. In Congolese forest villages, singing and drumming arise without seeming effort from the activities of daily life. In the United States, music seems to occupy every available public niche. Even the relative privacy inside the space of your own closed car becomes public when drivers crank the volume and open the roof, turning their vehicles into careening hot bands. Commercial suppliers of music (like Muzak) provide a bleached, flattened-out music for every categorizable market including work spaces (to maximize efficiency), retail stores (to increase sales), and dairy barns (to stimulate milk production in cows). There are few places where music isn't, and the music we are dealt is typically homogenized, generic, canned, and piped into our ears through a tinny speaker *directly above* our private booth.

Much has been written about the soundscape of Western life, especially adroitly by R. Murray Shafer in *The Tuning of the World*. This subject will come up again (especially in chapter 9), but for now I am asking that you pay close attention (if only for brief, experimental periods) to what you may have stopped hearing—precisely because it is everywhere. Next time you're in a restaurant listen to the room, and notice how the music in the air is modulating the quality of the room's vibe. How does the music mix with the sounds of the silverware and crockery, the conversations, the ambient noises? How does it mix with the gestures and relationships of the folks in the room? In a store, especially a big store, feel the whole space as a dimension of the music someone else somewhere else chose to channel into your ears. What would your choice have been? There is nothing as effective for understanding the quality of the American experience than listening consciously to the subliminal, obligatory soundtrack of its public life.

Unconsciously heard music has the power to temper a chaotic conscious. Some dude with his car stereo at 95 dB and his woofer leaving dead cats along the road pulls up alongside me in the adjacent lane at a red light. He is keeping time with his upper-body spasms while metrically cracking gum. At this particular moment, this man is not wasting his girlfriend, nor is he totaling his car. His mind is entirely modulated by gangsta rap and, ear-splitting as it is, that's OK by me. Here's the question: What is the story of that rap track we're hearing? In one sense it's the story of the lyrics, of the rapper, about how some guy has more power than some other guy. But in a larger sense, given the market savvy of the bottom-line music industry and the fierce desires of American consumers, the story of that piece is the story of the guy at the red light. Intuitively he knows his psyche needs to be tamed by this dark, loud, ancient, and perverse embrace. He is relying on the deep pulses, the complex rhythms, the power language, the perfect synch of the musicians, the mastery of the engineers, and the ear-splitting volume to somehow ricochet him from depression and violence to functional if brash behavior in the real world. The music is his story, and to the extent to which we are all in the same American boat—and even if we maintain a high level of individual choice, we pretty much are—it is our story as well.

147

MUSIC AS US
Music as the Cultural Story

Given our diverse and fragmented culture, it is instructive to study the music of so-called indigenous people—populations who have stayed geographically close and socially tight-knit for millennia. There aren't many such populations left. One of them, in a small region of ancient Nubia, now southern Sudan, has recently been dispersed, thanks to the rising waters of the Aswan Dam. The Nile River village of Toshka is presently submerged under the waters of what is called Lake Nasser and its inhabitants have been relocated, but in the early 1930s, playing in its streets, running in its fields, and swimming in its sacred river was a kid named Hamza El Din, whose unusually sensitive ears were recording the sounds around him. He did not know at the time that his village would be drowned, or that he would become its aural emissary in the years ahead.

Sixty years later found Hamza a master world-musician, playing the music of his village over the radio waves of the planet. One of his most celebrated songs features a forty-eight-beat clapping rhythm that in his childhood would be heard continually for three days on the occasion of a wedding that is the first for both bride and groom. Everyone in the village knew this rhythm, and the various songs and dances it supported; if one group tired of clapping or drumming, another began, so the pattern was continually in the air. This music was made by the entire village as a joyous celebration of the continuity of life. It was not made by specialists, and it was not for sale.

Not that our culture is bereft of its rituals and affirmations— we do have them. But there are two primary differences. By and large, our music is made by specialists. And it is very much for sale. Then again, we live in a culture that is nothing if not specialized and commercialized, so it is to be expected that our music mirrors the aggressive gloss of commerce. Although plain folks making their own music is far less common than customers consuming packaged musical products, if you explore far enough below the surface of American life you will be heartened to find that music is still the language of, by, and for the people. There are community choirs and orchestras, surgeons' string quartets, neighborhood polka bands, Monday night jazz bands, not to mention a vast community of guitarists and pianists, acoustic and electric, many of them improvisers and songwriters. Much of the music that is being made seems fairly to reflect the modern American zeitgeist, replete with its ambition, greed, violence, inventive narcissism, and plain old good times. Real love songs, honest introspection, genuine compassion, and authentic inspiration are in the mix, but you have to sift for them. Indeed, there is something for everyone. The American story, though defined by competitive marketing, is nonetheless admirably diverse. Our range and our variety have always saved us. As film music goes, I think we've scored our cultural movie pretty well — our music heightens and enlivens the American saga. My own aesthetic life runs counter to culture, but I'm *in* the American movie no matter what I say or do, and listening consciously to the underscore teaches me about my world. So I do listen deeply (if briefly) to everything I hear from every corner, including commercials (especially the most annoying ones), sound logos, video games, and most especially the hip-hop from the car at the red light, which happens to have a wickedly hot bass line. It's all the score of this movie I'm in, and I figure since I'm the star I'd better pay attention.

Ritual Music

To an outsider, a Balinese religious procession seems exotic. The participants prepare by prayer, dress in their flowing finest, walk in solemn single file balancing beautifully tiered flowers and food offerings on their heads, give homage to the gods under the guidance of the priest and, finally, disperse in laughter. Some Balinese guides will offer instruction in these ritual protocols so a visitor may dress, walk, and pray according to indigenous ways. Thus an outsider remains an outsider, but is invited inside as a guest. From such a vantage point, it is possible to imagine a life where this particular ritual seems natural and necessary. One way that travel broadens is in being able to imagine the quality of unfamiliar lives. An even broader experience can be in appreciating the deep similarities in human feeling, even when outer behaviors manifest disparately.

It is instructive to attend a public concert—let's say in this case a classical music concert featuring Beethoven's Ninth—while observing, from the very beginning, the ritualistic behaviors so integrated with the particulars of our lives that to us they seem both natural and necessary. Take note of the elaborate offering before the concert (your purchase of the tickets by phone or computer or at the door with cash, credit card, or check) and after (your applause and kudos); the careful preparation (what should I wear? how to get there?), the precision of assembly (ushers, seating), followed by the ritual itself: hundreds of people quietly frozen in place, all going through inner experiences separately yet in resonance, a public sharing of the most private chambers of our minds and hearts. To honor the communality of the space, decorum is uppermost. We hold our position and we hold our silence. Whispering is bad. Coughing is bad. *Sniffling* is bad. Yet there will come moments when everyone's concentration is so single-pointed that the ritual bond becomes pristine: hundreds of bodies and souls entrained in a complex, transcendent vibratory state.

If a young woman who has never left her Balinese mountain village were suddenly to find herself present in the tenth row during a stunning moment in the Beethoven, what would she make of it? I wonder if, notwithstanding the bizarre rituals of these strange people she finds herself among, she would be able to recognize the devotion, the focus, and the human bond. In ritual, people seek affirmation, they come together in agreed-upon formality, share communion through the agency of a medium, and disperse after a particular outcome. In the case of a symphony concert, the music is the medium. Let's subtract the music. Imagine the whole scene again but with no orchestra—just people gathering at a place, sitting in silence (no squirming), and leaving. Now ask this question: What does the existence of concert music owe to its function as public ritual?

On one hand, you could play the recording at home alone. This is not the same as public ritual, but to the degree you become engaged there can be a private experience of communion. On the other hand, Beethoven, who likely did not foresee recording, wrote the piece to be played and sung by a large number of musicians to an even larger number of listeners. Is the ritual intrinsic to the creation of the piece? Of *any* concert piece? How much am I missing by listening alone at home? Do we have to honor and obey the original intention of a piece to understand and enjoy it? I think the answers to these questions tend to evolve over time with your own experience. The questions themselves are stimulating. Posing them holds up for scrutiny the qualities of your listening.

Less formal musical rituals are all around us. Wherever people gather to listen, dance, or make music, certain modes of expectation and behavior are in play. There are specific cultures around jazz concerts, rock concerts, Elvis concerts, raves, square dances—not to mention Beatles concerts and Franz Liszt concerts, both featuring screaming and fainting. To the extent that these gatherings are expressive, the music takes on the role of bonding agent. Its value lies in its capacity to bring cohesion and affirmation to a certain group. The music is more than the score to the film—it is central to the plot. Consider the symbiosis between The Grateful Dead learning to play their exquisitely intricate acid jams and its audience learning to hear them. Or a

DJ guiding the vibe at a rave, where it's nearly impossible to separate the music from anything else that's going on: it's all woven into the tapestry of the unique night.

Music as Anthropology

Stories and music just seem to stick together. There is an expression, "Music is the best biography," which I've also heard as "Music is the best autobiography." It is true that a musician's music generally follows the contours of his life, but it is tempting to be too literal in correlating a composer's music with the specific events of his life: "This is the very chord where Gesualdo (supposedly) decided to murder his wife." A few years ago, during a period of suffering and emotional retrenchment, I reconnected with an old acquaintance who'd recently moved to the area. We had dinner and caught up on our lives. She's a psychoanalyst and gifted documentary film director, and was understanding and sympathetic. About a month later, in an exchange of e-mails, she asked "Are you able to channel some of what you are experiencing into your composing?" Here is my reply:

> I don't think composing operates the way your question (though I know it was meant in the most supportive way) implies. For me, composing is nothing if not a global process, and reflects that day's or that month's or even that year's activity not nearly so much as it reflects the whole history of one's life and thought, an entire life that gets poured through each decision, each note. These days, even these last years, make a small wave in a long line that goes back to the first cognized middle C, and earlier into infancy, maybe earlier still. The whole line of life is what truly inspires, not so much the emotional content of the day. Not to say I'm dead to what's happening, just riding it, including it—one might say *folding it in*.

Improvisation at the keyboard is different. If I feel happy or sad right now you'll hear that—BUT not necessarily through happy or sad music. Not surprisingly, sometimes opposites merge. When I'm happy, maybe it's really safe to express profound loss; when I'm depressed, maybe I need some joyous sound. The most ebullient music I ever made was just when I was most depressed. It's proved so tempting for so many to assume that works of art can be interpreted by what's going on with an artist's life during the time the art was made, but for me, at least, the reality has proved much less linear, much less easy to ascribe cause to.

Having told this cautionary tale, I admit that when one zooms out to a longer view and studies the rise and fall of musical styles of groups of musicians over a substantial period of time in a certain place, a special kind of anthropology does emerge. Crucial to this science is the art of deep listening to a considerable amount of music. Although we can track times and places and the conditions of the period, we must never be seduced by them, never leave the embrace of the music itself. We can take the long view and get the big picture, but we can never be out of earshot of the music.

I find several such periods particularly remarkable. The so-called Ars Nova period in France—roughly 1300–1400 but centered on the work of Guillaume de Machaut (ca. 1300–1377)—produced works with a novel rhythmic and polyphonic complexity, yet what strikes me most about that period, and Machaut particularly, is a new appreciation of the affective range of harmony. The trenchant, plaintive, often melancholy and newly discovered harmonic palette is what draws the modern listener in. Machaut's pieces don't sound like modern music exactly, but they do resonate with our contemporary, restless longing. Most people, especially in the United States, think that European music somehow begins with Bach—a kind of weird creationist theory of classical music. Actually (as we've already mentioned), there had been a good six hundred years of extraordinary music within an identifiable European culture preceding Bach, including (besides Machaut) Hildegard von Bingen (1098–1179), Gilles Binchois (1400–1460), Guillaume Dufay (ca. 1400–1474), Johannes Ockeghem (1410–1497), Josquin Desprez (1440–1521), Giovanni Pierluigi da Palestrina (1525–94), Tomas Luis de Victoria (1548–1611), Orlande de Lassus (1532–94), and Henry Purcell (1659–95), among many others. Have a listen, Gentle Reader—"early music" may satisfy deep hungers you never knew you had.

As has doubtless become evident by now, I am hardly a scholar, not even a proper academic, and my method of knowing and expositing knowledge is about as tidy as Beethoven's study. But I am a deep listener and, like any working composer/performer, know from my own inside-out point of view how music behaves. When I hear Machaut, I am so quickened that I want to be alive in the very moment *he* heard what he heard. I want to be with him in his chapel, in his boudoir, at his writing desk, in his conversations, only because he found a way of combining linear mind (melody and polyphony) with proportional mind (harmony) that for the first time sings of the searing tensions and keening pleasures of the modern psyche. Listening to his music opens a door to the leading edge of conscious feeling in his time. I want to be privy now to that then, and through Machaut's music I can.

A little closer to home is the period between the death of Bach (1750) and the death of Beethoven (1827). Bach codified and improved upon the wedding of polyphony and Baroque cadence-driven harmony, which by the mid-1700s had had six or eight generations to develop. When Old Bach died, it was as if Dad had *finally* left the house and the kids couldn't wait to make their own kind of noise. The new music of Mozart and Haydn ("classical music" to us) told a new kind of story: long narratives comprising many themes and motifs spinning and weaving through tortuous harmonic journeys that could be truly understood only by paying attention through ten or fifteen minutes of instrumental music without dropping a stitch. The opening movements of symphonies, concerti, string quartets—most chamber and orchestral music—are like novellas, placing the listener-as-protagonist right at the center of the dramatic narrative form. These stories weren't about anything external, they were about the listener's listening. Through this powerful magic a new sense of the validity of individual consciousness was being defined, just as surely as, through the revolutionary politics and wars in the late 1700s, the validity of the individual within society was being identified.

Bach to Mozart to Beethoven chronicles the evolution of societal values from the exalted other to the exalted inner. By the time Beethoven inherited the musical mantle, music was clearly about the listener's inner path. This is a new paradigm: Each one of us has not only a legitimate, defendable self, but an inner, sacred self as well. Even more strikingly, I sense that Beethoven consciously and deliberately exteriorized his unconscious; in this he is the harbinger of the modern mind. Participating in the drama of a late Beethoven string quartet is as exhausting and exhilarating as being engaged in a modern play or film and, especially in late Beethoven, can feel just as contemporary. Next, in a historical blink of the eye, came Sigmund Freud, and next came your therapy appointment followed by your meditation group. It was an enormous cultural shift, and if you listen to enough of the music of those times, you can feel your own near-history in it. Music is a plumb line to your ancestors near and far; it offers an intimate anthropology that neither pottery nor poetry can.

The three decades between 1880 and 1910 witnessed an amazing turn in Western culture generally and in European art music specifically. A useful comparison can be drawn between tonality in music and representationalism in art. In tonality there is a home ground, a tonic, unity rules, there is a definite place to put your feet. To the degree that art is representational, a horse looks like a horse, a face looks like a face. By the 1880s, Liszt, Wagner, and Richard Strauss had pushed the ambiguities implicit in the century-old tuning system of twelve-tone equal temperament to a point where the listener was, with both trepidation and pleasure, lost much of the time. Where is home? Will I *ever* get back? A similar thing was happening in impressionism: the familiar world was being challenged and morphed toward an unknown and perhaps frightening limit. One fine day around 1880, Claude Debussy sat down to the piano, played a whole-tone scale (which has six equally spaced tones, no major or minor triads, and no perfect fifths, and no single tone able to stand out among the others as a generating tone—it hangs in the air like mist), and said to himself, "That's not half bad. In fact, it sounds fine just hanging there. I like mist."

I think I might have maybe just made that up, but *something* like it was gradually happening to composers working on the expressive edge of their tonal language. It was increasingly OK to be lost. Debussy almost always found inventive ways to tonally resolve his whole-tone mists, but by the turn of the century, Schoenberg was using all twelve tones as equals—no tonal hierarchy, zero proportional mind, no unity, no home nowhere. This new world, the atonal world, was a new place where lost and found were redefined. By 1910, Schoenberg had composed a small body of such pieces whose influence spread rapidly through the minds and ears of the artistic elite. Meanwhile, in painting, image was losing ground. Abstract expressionism was spreading wings. In a lecture about the history of art, the late comedian Severn Darden explained, in a thick German accent, how artists used to paint pigs that looked like pigs. Then, shrugging his shoulders and turning up his palms, he asked, "Who wants to look at pigs?" By 1910, viewers were standing dumb-founded in front of color-dashed canvases. Angry listeners were bolting from concert halls protesting a world gone mad. And don't forget the concurrent advent of electricity, telephones, and automobiles, all within these few decades.

Much closer to home and even more compressed is the rapid change in American jazz from the late 1920s to the mid-'40s, a span of less than twenty years. By the late '20s, the edges of jazz's sources, especially its blues forms and processional rhythms, were being absorbed (thanks to popularity of recordings, the mutual influences of Tin Pan Alley, and ever-growing white audiences) into American culture at large. What came to be called Dixieland, a style only faintly tinged with post-Emancipation memories of plantation, levee, and prison, had begun to assimilate the harmonies and glosses of American pop. By the early '30s, a new, safer, and socially more neutral music called swing was being forged in Harlem, and big bands, both white and "colored," were becoming the rage. By the late '30s, the sound of white swing bands like Benny Goodman and Tommy Dorsey filled the airwaves, and piano bars featuring jazz standards culled from Broadway shows and pop hits became the night-time destination of choice. The emergence of the United States after World War II as the world savior, coupled with the heroic yet unacknowledged role of Negroes in the armed services, provided a ripe context for the arrival of a black musical zeitgeist of hyperindividualism, a spiky, aggressive manifesto of freedom. Slave days were ending (but not over), the civil rights movement was aborning (slowly), and bebop emerged like a shot in the early '40s as the voice of a black musical elite keenly aware of a new way of being in America. Whites had ears to hear it also, and by the mid-1940s the new music was being heralded by the white press as the music of liberation. Forty years later, the sound of muted Miles was in every boutique on Main Street. A joyously explorative solo by

Bird in 1945 was challenging enough to internalize; had it happened to be heard fifteen years earlier—in 1930—even a very sophisticated listener would have found it all but incomprehensible. The recording debut of Ornette Coleman, whom many still cannot hear with any clarity today, was, in 1945, only fifteen years into the future.

—

As seen through the prism of American popular music and jazz, the evolutionary shape of American culture is brightly limned —the more so if the listener resists the impulse to describe it in words. If you could listen to a recording of one piece of popular music from each year, from 1905 to the present and hold on *wordlessly* to your impressions—no discussion, no definition, just sound and feeling—you would get a sense of the American mind and spirit more intimate and revealing than a hundred history books. Whatever part of this experiment you can manage to do for yourself is a special kind of research, social anthropology from a vibrational source. Our music tells our story in a way nothing else can.

Ibony and Evory

There are many stories within stories. In American music, one of the most compelling is the racial one, the mutual influence of black and white. America has been very slow to give up its slaves, even in post-Obama times. A large body of our popular music deals head-on with race, putatively commemorated by Stevie Wonder performing Paul McCartney's song "Ebony and Ivory"—perhaps more appropriately titled "Ibony and Evory," because the stylistic mix has become so thorough it is difficult to track the complexity of the black/white feedback loops. There is a stunning moment in the musical *Dreamgirls* (about a Supremes-type singing group) when a black man and a white man are finalizing a deal. As they shake hands, the black man says, "You always wanted our *rhythm* and we always wanted your *Cad-il-LAC.*" "Our rhythm" refers to the innate intelligence of the body, of the village, of the natural world long lost to the citified, industrialized peoples of Euro-America. "Your Cadillac" refers to the development of an ambitious, success-driven intellect that had been exploding outward from central Europe for a millennium and landing, with Yankee greed and ingenuity, in America.

Consider the Afro-American feedback loops in the following tableaux:

- Al Jolson singing in blackface
- George Gershvin [sic], a Jew from lower Manhattan, writing perhaps America's best opera ever—about a Southern black ghetto
- Louis Armstrong singing "Hello, Dolly!" and it's a huge hit
- Elvis Presley on Ed Sullivan doing pelvic shtick to music he stole from (very poor) Southern rhythm and blues musicians
- Working-class Brits galvanizing the white world with pentatonic blues riffs learned from black players who themselves were cashing in on the hunger of white college kids in folk/blues clubs
- Canadian Gil Evans writing concerto-style compositions and arrangements for Miles Davis, who makes them soar
- Herbie Hancock playing beautifully well behind a white singer covering Joni Mitchell tunes
- White lawyers at their firm's lavish Christmas party, roasting each other in what they imagine to be rap
- Rap and hip-hop itself, a special language of power invented by blacks and purchased mostly by white suburban teenage boys who can't wear their trousers low

enough: did they ever know that prisoners on death
watch (mostly black) have their belts confiscated?

All of these images have complex soundtracks, redolent with
juicy history, and when you listen to them—and this is the
point—they are joyous and witty and affirming and challenging, full of moxie and the unashamed desire for union. We need
each other. If we lose our rhythm, our connection with our natural state of joy, we are lost forever and a day. And who among
us, Honest Readers, does not want a good-looking, smooth-
running, truly reliable, and ever-so-comfortable car?

The forging together of European-based and African-based
musical styles on American soil has resulted in one of the most
vibrant bodies of music ever made. Again, if you listen to enough
of it for long enough you can experience with great emotional
resonance the pain and wonder of an antagonistic symbiosis
evolving into a functioning, harmonious, swinging, brand-new
celebration of a vibrant culture.

Human Music

The story of the mutual influence of Africa and Europe is only one
of the many stories embedded in the history of American music,
just as the history of American music is only a part of the story
of human music. Beginning slowly with the arrival in the early
'50s of LP recordings, gaining speed via cassettes in the late '60s,
accelerating rapidly with the advent of CDs in the early '80s, and
exploding with the rise of the Internet, "global music" has become
a graspable paradigm. Now let's be very careful: By global music
we do not mean a homogenized Esperanto that everyone learns
to speak passably. We foresee a living music with fierce individu-
ation, limitless variety, and the capacity to ravish and astound its
listeners. Recently, a series of bare keyboard tracks of pop classics
(including "Stand by Me") were presented to dozens of musicians

worldwide, who added vocal and instrumental tracks while the sessions were video-recorded. The master recording with umpteen tracks was then edited and mixed down onto a cohesive and extraordinarily moving global effort, a compendium of compassion and tenderness, which was then posted on YouTube and seen by tens of millions of folks. Worldwide simultaneity, like rolling New Year's Eve broadcasts, are becoming commonplace. We are more and more plugged into a diffuse and fractal nervous system whose soundtrack is ever present, sometimes even front and center. "Global music" is still an infant, but the story of music is more and more becoming a matter of world history.

Humankind has had its musical expression long before there was a concept "music." If there exists a human body, mind, and heart, a human aesthetic will arise. (I think the same to be true for zebras and chimpanzees.) Even if our music is traceable back only thirty or forty thousand years, I suspect what we would recognize as musical impulses—our attraction to periodic pulse, sustained pitch, and resonance—goes back more than a hundred thousand years, maybe to the rise of *Homo sapiens*. Clearly, what we now call music is a very old tool. By studying the hair cells in the cochlea of the inner ear, it has been shown that hearing-related genes have been evolving along with human speech. Civilization brings with it increasing population density and the commensurate need for cooperation. The human ear has evolved to better understand what we need to say to one another.

Incidentally, the capacity to hear proportional harmony (that is, tonality) is probably a fortuitous by-product of this aural upgrade. We are preadapted to hear tonal harmony. Thanks to the demands of living closely together, we have acquired the equipment and the smarts; subsequently, tonal harmony arose as we needed it. And we did need it. "Tones remove the barrier between persons and things," to quote the musicologist Victor Zuckerkandl. "Music is the most natural solvent of artificial boundaries between the self and others."

Music is one of the most telling stories we have, going back to the beginning of any story we can imagine to tell. In this chapter we have looked at music as movie score, as ballet program, as narrative of images or moods, as a score for the autobiography of you the listener, as the composer's biography and autobiography, as the underscore of our daily environment, as varieties of social and transcendental bonding, as a carrier wave of cultural evolution, and finally as the story of humankind itself—a special kind of socio-anthropology. Yet even though our discussion has been wide-ranging, we have not examined the most compelling story of all, the one that music tells as its own self-contained and self-sufficient universe, as a self-revealing narrative, as itself.

Music as Its Own Story

Music does not give itself up easily. It doesn't play hard-to-get, exactly, it's just not a cheap date. If you want to get serious with it you have to pay a lot, and what you have to pay is attention. That means making a space, an inner accommodation in order for this quintessential, unique story to be understood. This is difficult because all the external stories that music can be heard *as* are most splendidly true, and they can sparkle. Yet they can be attractive distractions from a deeper truth. For me, knowing the story of a piece, it's intention, it's performance history, and appreciating the ritualistic aspects of its performance all help to draw me in to the bare sound of the music itself. The more I'm drawn in the more I hear, and the more the light dawns. Perhaps it is a paradox, but the more I know about the program, the more I can let these aspects go and appreciate the pure narrative of the sounds themselves. Context is homework. *Having seen* the context allows me (in most cases) to let it go and drop into the vortex of the music.

162

Composers (me among them) obligatorily spend a certain percentage of their allotted time on earth explaining how, for instance, the "Moonlight" Sonata is not what Beethoven had in mind. The title, as is well known, was a marketing device appended by the publisher. What Beethoven did have in mind was (for the first movement) a very compelling harmonic progression in C-sharp minor replete with Phrygian aspects, a slow-moving, predominantly stepwise melody, a simply arpeggiated accompaniment, and a tightly woven formal scheme all spun out in a tempo that would contrast well with the sprightly minuet and the fiery rondo to follow. Although some compositions are clearly meant to have an image, or a story, to frame the listeners' experience, in many cases composers simply *give in* to the general desire for such a frame. In 1960, the Polish composer Krzysztof Penderecki wrote an abstract work for string orchestra that he titled *8'37"*. After hearing the piece he renamed it *Threnody for the Victims of Hiroshima*. It subsequently became one of the most played pieces in the repertory. According to Allan Kozinn (in the *New York Times*), when asked why he renamed the piece, Penderecki said, "I was surrounded by propaganda against the American bomb. Living at the time, you know, I did it. And because of the dedication to Hiroshima, certainly, people found this interesting. Because I have other pieces for strings that are not so well known." Now, of course, it is all but impossible to hear the piece without the intensity of that reference. But when he composed it, Penderecki was writing abstract music whose story was the piece itself. My question is: Even though he has brought many listeners to the piece by renaming it, has the composer done his piece a favor? Has he done me a favor? I can't listen to the damn thing anymore—it's about people burning up. It used to be about string sounds.

So if music isn't essentially about the composer or the performers, and it's not about appended ideas, what is it? What *is* abstract—or pure—music? What is it that's so pure? And come to think of it, what, if anything, is actually abstract? Are we merely mounting a clubby intellectual conceit?

What's So Pure?

Pure, deep listening occurs automatically in real-life moments of heightened awareness: life-threatening danger, pivotal moments of personal history, a suspicious creak in the middle of the night—any time the conscious mind needs to be riveted solely on sound. Listening to music unadulterated by thought, image, concept, or judgment is what musicians practice when they are practicing, and what they attempt when they perform. In the making of music, there is no room for anything except the sound of music. Although most people have had this experience from time to time, it is difficult to sustain even for those who train for it.

Earlier we spoke of the continuum of listening that stretches from program music—music about something external to itself —all the way to abstract music—music that is self-referential. To intentionally cultivate your listening, the first thing to do is to step back from the experience of listening to music, even while immersed in it, for the purpose of observing how you scoot, or slither, or zoom along this gamut from story (it's about really cute elves) to image (lovely, scary, *ooh, aahh*) to the underscore for your own thoughts (*must* call Todd and make amends) and fantasies (these women have one horn, like *uni*corns), to the story of the composer (that poor, *lucky* man), or performers (*so* virile), to the setting of the scene you are in (*perfect* music for this party), or ritual (*so* sacred), to cultural history (the Bach is not at *all* like the Handel), to socio-anthropology (to think that just a few years ago we were blowing air through bones, now *this*), to the vibrational source of life (what *is* this stuff we are?), and finally to the sound of itself, where all the answers from the outside coalesce into a focused, bright inner knowing. The journey along this continuum is experienced as a journey from outside the sound to inside the sound, and finally abides inside you, *as* you. The "purity" in pure music is the purity of your listening. The abstraction in abstract music refers to the fact that you need nothing but the act of listening to appreciate it.

The range of musical sensibility is wide. Each person has his or her own palette of narrative preferences, and no one can tell you which are more fine or coarse, better or worse, high- or lowbrow. The secret is to experience the entire continuum for yourself, to sample everything at the feast. You are the research and the discovery, both. You define the music by the quality of your listening.

What's the Trick?

It takes practice to gravitate toward the music-in-itself end of the continuum. But the great gift of music, the miraculous, sumptuous beneficence of it, is that musical sound is an agent of attractive energy. It pulls you as you pull it. Musicians want to play for you just as much as you want to hear musicians play. We all fall in.

The trick is to use the music to listen to the music. Imagine that the sound has edges you can grab (a shiny branch), textures you can touch (a gauzy sheet), and then *give up* these images to the sheer experience of sound. Another strategy is to follow just one of the strata: the treble with its tunes; or better yet, the bass holding everything up; or, even better, the mysterious muddle of the middle, and wait for the whole sound to come to you that way.

But the best strategy—as good social listeners, practiced therapists, healers of every stripe, and experienced meditators know—is to simply empty out. Stop. Don't try to do anything.

Don't be following your thoughts, don't feed them, they're already plump enough. Wherever you look for *meaning,* that is where the music will become eclipsed. Like a hawk on a treetop, just wait, and listen with empty ears. Let your hunger for sound be your guide.

"Just listen" is like saying "Just be," which is, of course, the most difficult road of all to travel, the non-object of objectless meditation. But unlike objectless meditation, music rescues you from the fear of nonbeing in a most splendidly specific form. In this respect it is indeed an object meditation, that is, a collector of consciousness around a single object. The "object" in this case is streaming sound, which we humans have mirrored from the cosmos and extruded, in our finest hours, as music.

How Long Is This Story?

Listening to the story music tells requires, as does listening to any narrative, a wakeful memory. If you were able to recall only a single syllable at a time, Shakespeare would be babble. One sentence at a time would be a series of mysterious utterances. One needs to remember the whole play to comprehend it, and one needs to remember it over many months and years to make the best use of it.

From the neurological point of view, musical memory has many temporal orders of magnitude. In a kind of processing called *echoic memory,* the brain registers periodic vibration from a range of 20,000 cycles per second to about 20 cycles per second and consolidates them into the sensation of <u>pitch</u>. *Short-term memory* handles pitches and rhythmic pulses that last from a twentieth of a second to fifteen seconds or so (including brief <u>phrases</u>), and cognizes them as <u>patterns</u> of melodic and rhythmic groupings. From about fifteen seconds to an hour or more, *long-term memory* recognizes longer phrases of music, entire sections, movements, symphonies, and ragas. As musical experience folds into your life experience, the long arcs of your months and years are modulated by it, and long-term memory fuses into your quality of life. Diving into the sound of a piece of music can activate any or all of these states of memory, so for you the listener, the story of that music is as long as it lasts in you. The deep meaning of music is a function of your immersion in it.

—

I hope the words in this book will help tip you into the river. I know how to do this for myself and can do it any time, but I had to learn how. I had to learn how thoughts can be deafening, how they mask the inner light of sound. If you want to truly hear a piece of music, then think, reminisce, analyze, or fantasize before or after you hear it. Deep listening takes every iota of your consciousness, and music needs *only* your full consciousness of its streaming for it to tell its story.

So it appears, Ever-So-Ready Listeners, as though you have to give up. Give up your purring body, your fine mind and all its ideas about what you may find, and listen to the sound of sound. It is hard work to be fully awake to something and at the same time be totally empty. When you do this work, all the rhythms, the harmonies, all the patterns and connections among patterns in the music will come to you of their own accord. They are self-arising, self-explaining, and self-illuminating. When you do the work of the listener, the music will work for you. Given half a chance, the medium does the work. But you can't just dip a toe into this river. You must strip off everything, immerse fully, nothing dry, let everything be soaked with sound. Get naked! Get wet!

7

Music as Mirror

We are the mirror, as well as the face in it. . . .
the sweet, cold water and the jar that pours.

—Rumi/Barks

HUMAN REFLECTION

Have you ever seen those silver spheres, usually set on pedestals in gardens or on lawns? They are called gazing globes. Surrounded by the world, you are at the center of every image as it meets your gaze. Imagine for the moment that the *inside* surface of the sphere is silvered also, and that the space inside the sphere is clear and bright as the sky outside. If you were gazing from inside the globe, you could see yourself anywhere and everywhere at the center of a sea of self-reflection. Now with a further leap, imagine that this double-mirrored gazing globe is your own consciousness, thin-skinned and hollow, reflecting outward and inward. Nicely positioned at the center of the cosmic scale, you gaze outward and see cosmos; gazing inward, you see microcosmos.

168

A visual mirror is for peering, usually at yourself and your visible surroundings. Looking back at yourself can be startling. Looking at photographs and movies of yourself takes some getting used to (some folks never do), and watching people watch themselves on a TV monitor is as fun as watching monkeys, especially if you're one of the monkeys. But what about a mirror for the ears? Echoes are a kind of aural mirror. It's wonderful to listen to kids who've been let loose in a large space that has a long reverberation time. They squeal and shout and sing to their own voices coming back to them. Resonance itself, a "sounding again" that occurs in the everyday world whenever a sounding body causes other bodies to sound, is another kind of aural mirror. A most ubiquitous aural mirror is sound recording. When you hear a recording of your own voice, you get an overall impression of the person as well as the persona behind the voice just as, when looking in a visual mirror, you can see not only the discrete details of your hair and clothes, but also a more qualitative reflection: your stance, your attitude, your expression. What you thought was secret is exposed. Your reflection isn't you, but it can inform you in useful ways and even, if you learn to move in sympathy with your image, in beautiful ways.

It was the resonant musician in Inayat Khan who wrote, "This is a mirror land, living because mirrors are living." Music, by which I mean all music ever, can be heard as a human reflection. One of the most rewarding sensations you can have as a listener is to snorkel down into an attractive piece of music and discover something of yourself moving inside it. You are there, in that squiggle of light you see and hear in the music, and the squiggle is the small animal of feeling in your chest. That explosion in the high brass is your mind lifting off into the galaxy. As surely as when looking in a mirror you can point to your eye and say "my eye," when listening to music you can hear its motion and say "my emotion." Your feelings are feeding back to you: emotional feedback, one might say. It's almost like being in two places at once, observer and observed, a dreamer watching the performance of the dream. But then dreamer and dream unite. Listening to music can be so intense that the music merges with you—you as child and as adult, you as you were and as you are becoming. The double-sided gazing globe is now a globe of hearing that reflects the music coming from outside as well as the responses arising from inside, all combined in the spherical membrane of your consciousness.

How can music have this power? Even considered offhandedly, it seems to sidle up to the miraculous. I hope it won't diminish the wonder to point out that the music we folks have come so deeply to appreciate is produced by us very folks who appreciate it, some long dead, some playing fiddle in the street, some, still in diapers, learning to press down the keys with one finger, but all just like us. Music is a human extrusion. My entirely unromantic image: fresh dough being extruded from a pasta machine. We stuff experiential phenomena into our human shapes, transform it in our special ways, and crank it out in nourishing streams. Intelligence in, intelligence out. Feeling in, feeling out—but, like the mixture of water, yeast, and flour, transformed by alchemy. That is the wonder part: the alchemy is not in the music but in us. The music is just waveforms that your fabulous double-silvered listening globe reads, uses as it can, and, according to its nature, passes on. That's what composers do, that's what performers do, and that's what listeners do.

Music is not made by individual musicians, however, any more than babies are made by individual parents. In the same way that everyone has ancestors all the way back to the beginning of time, each piece of music comes from a swarming population of musicians with ancestors tracing back to the first motion in space. Even astonishingly original musical minds, like Beethoven or Bird, are, in respect to the music that has come before them, vastly more the same than different. So when we are immersed in a piece of music, we are reflecting and being reflected by the all of us who ever were. Music is our creation story, and we never stop telling it because we always have more to tell.

COSMIC REFLECTION

In a certain sense, the music any one of us makes is made by every one of us. It may be a bit of a stretch to believe this, but it is less of a stretch now than it was before radio, sound recording, and the Internet, thanks to which the writer J. G. Ballard said, "the entire human experience seems to unveil itself like the surface of a new planet." Most of us can be in touch with most any one of us by clicking a mouse. ("Clicking a *mouse*?" the Blondie of 1940 would have asked Dagwood had she awakened upon a twenty-first-century morning, "Whatever could that mean, dear?") So since we are all complicit in the music we make, it follows that we can hear all of humanity in human music. This is true not only for how we feel but also for how we think. We can hear our cognition of the-world-as-it-is, our worldview, being reflected back.

Some pieces of music announce their worldview in their titles. Taking cues from an ancient lineage of cosmological thought, Gustav Holst's *The Planets* suggests that our inner states reflect an energized, intentional solar system. Paul Hindemith's *Die Harmonie der Welt* (both an opera and a symphony) dramatizes the attempt by Kepler to discover the true harmony of the spheres. *La Création du monde* by Darius Milhaud is a kind of creation narrative. Some titles, like Charles Ives's *The Unanswered Question* pose existential quandaries. John Cage's silent piece *4'33"* asks that the role of music in society be reexamined. As Duke Ellington matured, he invited listeners into his increasingly spiritual view; John Coltrane ("Ascension") also. Each new rock band seems to project a new zeitgeist for listeners to buy into.

171

In some sense, every maker of music presents life, or some slice of it, to the listener: "This is how it is for me," and we listeners either buy it or we don't.

For me, the most revealing music (remember, we're talking about instrumental music, not songs) is music that doesn't tip its hand in the title. Titles like "Symphony No. 29," or String Quartet in A Minor," or "Piano Concerto No. 2" give no exterior clue about the "meaning" of the music. Such non–program music says, "This is the way it is" in the broadest sense. The meaning of the music is intrinsic to the music. It means itself. The composer is not saying "The world is *like* this," he is saying "The world *is* this, at least for as long as you are listening to my piece." In such abstract music, a wordless world is reflected in our gazing globe. I see myself everywhere in such music, I am the center of each moment just as surely as I'm at the center of every silver globe. Everywhere I listen I find myself in relation to the human condition, and humanity itself in relation to the universe.

One of the oldest cosmological paradigms is "As above, so below": the earth is a mirror of heaven, the phenomenal world is a (usually degraded) reflection of the pure forms. "The music of the spheres" is an expression of this: earthly music is but a pale reflection of the true, perfect music of the cosmos. In modern times we understand in more detail how the mirror model actually does obtain at each level of cosmic scale. The mystic's view as well as the scientist's view and, increasingly, the just-about-everbody's view is that the as-above-so-below model is OK so long as you don't value-rate it. Every octave of existence is sacred, and every octave has its sacred music. We honor each level, a distinctly un-Platonic view. According to this way of mapping the world, each littlest thing is a giant clue to the whole. In a grain of sand can be found the universe, and in this leaf also, and in Newton's apple, and anywhere and everywhere. In each part, some version of the whole is embedded. But if we are to understand clues to the universe, we must put ourselves and our search for clues into the mix. There is no better clue than one's search itself. "When you look for God," Rumi says, "God is in the look of your eyes."

Of all the beneficial uses of music, this one is the best, at least for this listener, for whenever and wherever I hear music, even the smallest snatch of it — a jagged note, the touch of a drum — can lead directly to the silence at my center, and all the way out to the sphere of the cosmos. I truly do not know if or how anybody else parses this, but for me music is an abundance, a wealth of clues. One can be clueless, in the presence of music, about what the music means to others, but one will never be without clues to the nature of his or her own world.

My raga teacher taught me that you can distinguish one *rag* from among the hundreds of *rags* in the North Indian legacy by the first tone alone. How could one tone impart such distinctive information? The answer is that a single tone (especially a sung tone) is a complex phenomenon, and in the hands of a gifted musician contains fairly precise coordinates of the raga universe. One of the characteristic properties of holograms is that if only a part of its recorded information is used to reconstruct a three-dimensional image, the full image nonetheless reappears, albeit with less resolution than if all the parts were used. The more parts used, the more fully can the whole be seen, but in each part is embedded a more or less complete version of the whole. In the holographic model, the whole is not the additive sum of its parts, but the result of many smaller wholes. Since each fragment of well-made music is a reflection of and a response to every other fragment, such music can be heard as an aural hologram. Not only can one infer the *rag* from the first tone, but to some extent the whole movement from a brief passage of Mozart, the whole solo from a few notes of Bird or Coltrane or Miles or, especially, Thelonius Monk.

I think God thought, "I'm going to make humans such that

any one of them can get a good read on Me from any part of My text. I'll make everything look like clues in a mystery, and let them invent mystery stories so *those* will be clues, and so on until someone gets it. I'll just sit up here and watch while they stumble on things and shout *Eureka!* from time to time." And of course, every once in a while one of us does get it, and that is His little entertainment, sort of like us watching for supernova explosions. He did laugh out loud about Newton, though.

Here's how I look for clues in everyday life: I imagine my gazing globe at different orders of scale. From the vantage point of a cell in my heart muscle, I can look inward and feel the push and pull of chemical reactions in my organic molecules, and I can gaze outward to the cosmos of Heart and the booming rhythms of Its Colossal Pumpness. As the sun, I can feel inward toward the dense plasma hearth at my core, or feeling outward to the tugs of the moons of the farthest planets. I could stand anywhere at any scale of magnitude—the head of a virus, the tail of a comet, a falling hailstone—gazing inward and outward, each perch a different parsing of the whole.

To look for clues in music, you can likewise place yourself at different orders of magnitude. If you latch onto a note, you can see outward from there into the phrase, the section, the movement. Or you can gaze inward to the energy of the sound waves and the mandala they make out of your eardrum. Or you could hone in on the intention of the music makers, why this particular sound has been put into the world, and follow your gaze outward to the human need for music of every kind. Or you could look inward to find your own need right now. When you focus on the feeling in the music, the emotional intelligence of it, you can appreciate how such qualities belong to everyone while at the same time they are profoundly yours. You can feel simultaneously the flood of human feeling and your own emotional uniqueness. Music feels out and feels in—that's why it feels good. You sense that the information coming into your spherical mirror from out there is actually you, and that your personal spark is everyone's.

⏤

There exists a cadre of scientists, neuroscientists and transpersonal psychologists among them, who think that consciousness transcends physicality, that we are not our brains. When we are in the grip of a piece of music that has about a billion other people in its grip, possibly at that very moment, it is easy to subscribe to this view. Hildegard von Bingen, who conceived God as an all-pervasive creative force, intimates as much in the text of her antiphon "O quam mirabilis est."

> Beloved, your way of knowing is amazing:
> the way you recognize every creature even before
>   it appears,
> the way you gaze into the face of a human being
>   and see
> all of your works gazing back at you.
> What a miracle to be awake
> inside your breathing!

When you listen to music you can feel, from your central seat, the universe gazing back at you. In my teens in Chicago, when I was first enjoying a concert hall of enlightened listeners transfixed by a Mozart piano concerto, I thought I understood the scope of the "gazing back" experience. But a dozen years later in the San Francisco of 1967, hearing "Here Comes the Sun" from an open window was like having the whole sky waving back at you. I thought I could hear all of humanity in those times, and that may have been true. I came to the notion then, and am still of the notion, that consciousness is spread out over being and we are hitchhikers being given a ride. Sometimes music is the ride.

175

OUT THERE . . .

About forty years ago the idea of a "holographic paradigm"
began to surface in the scientific community. It posits that reality is a living hologram and we, as fragments of the hologram,
represent a unique version of the whole. The reality of a person, or indeed of any seemingly separate thing, can be seen only
as a unique version of the entire universe. Objects, from subatomic particles to galaxies, *appear* separate from one another
because we perceive only the separateness. Actually, each particle is a representation of a deep underlying unity. This rings true
when listening to music. In the same way that matter *seems* to
be in particles, music seems to be in "pieces," and consciousness
seems to reside in individuals. To the extent we invest the fruits
of our human evolution into a piece of well-crafted, deeply felt
music, that music is a high-resolution version of the whole we
are part of. I know this as a composer and improviser, and I
think, on some level, every musician knows it as well. This piece
I am making now is just this moment's scan of all the music I
have ever made or heard. All of this information is cross-related
in my piece as it streams through the unique present. The piece-
ness is a convenient illusion, as is any separateness. When you
think about this it may boggle your mind, but when you are listening to the streaming wisdom of music, it can arise as a self-
evident, even simple, notion. You shrug. "Sure, right on." But, as
when watching a movie, you *think* about it only afterward.

Perhaps the most amazing scientific thought of recent
times has come from the inward/outward gazing on the part
of many adherents to string theory, which posits that the vibrational states at the smallest possible scale determine the large-
scale behavior of matter. Here is an elegant quote from Brian
Greene's book *The Elegant Universe:* "With the discovery of
superstring theory, musical metaphors take on a startling reality, for the theory suggests that the landscape is suffused with
tiny strings whose vibrational patterns orchestrate the evolution of the cosmos. The winds of change, according to super-

string theory, gust through an aeolian universe." The author is
referring to an aeolian harp, whose strings are activated by Aeo-
lus, god of the winds. The winds of change, I think, refer to how
the vibrational patterns are modulated by their environment.
Like consciousness itself, the reality of these most tiny strings
comes not only from what they are but what they do. A stone *is*.
A wave *does*. A particle-wave *is-does*. The problem with string
theory so far is that it can't seem to find a mathematics high
enough to fully describe it or make predictions based on it, and
there are only hints of empirical data to support it. Correct or
not, however, string theory is hot. Whenever I read about it, I
hear a real live symphonic string section swelling away, and it
sounds terrific.

However we may eventually imagine and experience the unity
of the cosmos, scientists are presently panting in pursuit. Just
before the Planck satellite went up to measure more carefully
the cosmic microwave background radiation (a record of the
earliest, subatomic moments of the big bang), Michael Turner,
a University of Chicago theoretical cosmologist, said, "Just the
idea that you have the subatomic world projected on the sky
today is mind-boggling." This is true for me too, except when
I'm listening to music, at which times I shrug, "Sure, right on."

COSMIC/HUMAN REFLECTION

There is a Sufi custom of saying to another person, "Ya Az'm"
(ya á-zum), which translates approximately as "I see the light of
the Beloved shining through your eyes," often accompanied by
a mutual nod or small bow, with the right hand over the heart
and the left hand over the right. When you are feeling the truth
of it, it's a strong, elevating practice. To recognize the best in one
another feels good.

For the mystic, the light of God is the recognition of being-
as-it-is. That recognition can appear through every imaginable

form: mineral, plant, or animal realms; and through sexual, social, or spiritual bonds. A highly intentional form of the practice is called *darshan*, literally "glance." In darshan, teacher and pupil (or any two people) first bow slightly, then look directly into each others' eyes for a few brief moments, then look down again, as if to concentrate *Ya Az'm* into an eternal flash. During my first darshan with the Sufi teacher Samuel Lewis, all sense of self fell away, and there remained only the connection of souls. My teacher's darshan has been a part of me ever since.

The music mirror is darshan through sound—the light of being-as-it-is is made recognizable in a form we can embody, sing and dance to, and feel lifted by. In darshan with another person, your eyes need to be open, of course—it's about recognition by visual means. Likewise in music, your ears need to be open—darshan needs your intention to recognize what you hear. And just as visual darshan can occur in many forms if you are open to it, so sound darshan can occur when you allow it to. The metal upon metal of rung bells and brushed cymbals can be darshan from the mineral world. The organic stream of resonance that comes from the wood of guitars, double basses, cello, violas, and violins; the enduring appeal of a piano's mix of metal and wood; the jitterbugging, break-dancing mammal in us who responds to music with physical joy; the society of trust that arises in the mosh pit and the concert hall; and the tears of gratitude for seeing the face of the Beloved in the "Lacrimosa" of Mozart's *Requiem*—all these are musical darshan from their respective realms. The ears as well as the eyes can be windows to the soul.

I'm like you—I know love, I know aversion, and I know what I want and don't want in my life. So if my life is some kind of darshan with a holographic universe, I can't help but wonder what photons want. What do stars want, or the nuclear soup at their cores? And I can't help but see that there is desire and aversion in every form, that desire-and-aversion is the *con-*

dition of form, the nexus around which all octaves of samsara spiral, the energy fields of the relative world. But in darshan we get a glimpse, a taste of the illusory nature of separateness, and go past desire and aversion into union. And so it is likewise in music when the ears are open, and the intention is pure, and the song and the night and the company all agree.

AN EVOLUTIONARY MIRROR

In the early 1940s, when I was quite young, our family still had in its possession some of the first phonograph discs manufactured, circa 1915, by the Edison Company. Like all phonograph records before the advent of LPs, these were played at 78 rpm. The early Edison discs were recorded on one side only and were about a quarter-inch thick. We had three. One was an aria sung by a soprano, which I liked; one was a march, which I didn't much like; and one was a chant by a Native American shaman, which, when I first played it, gave me a nasty moment of sangfroid. It was a simple song sung on only five tones, accompanied by a rattle and a deep drum. The man's voice was a sound I had never heard before; it certainly wasn't from my cozy, suburban culture of southwestern Ohio. The voice, in an unknown language, had a mysterious power that seemed to be coming from my inside my body. Was this the boogeyman? Some guttural intruder?

The shaman's song quite likely had roots connecting back to Asia untold millennia ago: Five? Ten? More? Five-tone chants survive today in various cultures, yet it was the *quality* of the voice itself that reached back, an invocation to ancient gods that penetrated my very pristine five-year-old eardrums. I was confronted with my own evolution and it scared me. The medicine was too strong.

As an adult, I, along with most of the rest of us, have come to cherish what has survived of our ancestral voices. We receive wisdom from our ancestor's music in the same way, as children, we are guided by our living parents. If things go well—and they often do—we soon enough become parents and grandparents who deepen and widen the wisdom of those who raised us. That's how, as a species, we learn to get on. That's why we read Aristotle, Chaucer, and Shakespeare, and listen to Hildegard, Bach, and Stravinsky. As a composer, I have listened to the wisdom of every ancestor I can trace, from the shaman on the Edison disc to Ghana's master drummers to the Sudanese Hamza El-Din to the cantors of my childhood to Schumann and Lester Young, and when I compose my own little piece of wisdom I am simply retelling theirs with whatever jot of my own has come through the experience of my life. This is true for every composer and improviser who has taken his progenitors seriously: we know that we are little cogs in a great wheel. And as listeners, when we listen to music historically, that is, with awareness of what has come before (and sometimes after) whatever we are hearing, we are witnessing the soundtrack of human development. We can listen back only a few thousand years at best; to go back farther, we need to listen to chimps and whales and birds. But the music we do have access to is at least a shard of an evolutionary mirror, and it gives us perhaps the most direct view of who we are and what we might become.

We are a woman at her dressing table putting on her best face, finding and exteriorizing her inner beauty and her secret intention for all to see. We keep changing our image, fussing with the details until we get it right. We objectify ourselves so we can reconcile inner and outer standards. In a visual mirror you pat and pamper until the image is as good as it can get. In the vibrational mirror of music we practice and alter, and notate and edit, and practice some more until it *sounds right*. Our best sound is our best wisdom. Imperceptibly, the wheel turns.

In these modern times of ubiquitous musical information, we are able to gaze into the music mirror from whatever angle we want and witness any point in the evolution of civilization. Never has our communal history been so important to us. Never has there been a time when it has become so necessary to listen to the voices of our ancestors, to resonate with them, and to go them one better. Music, our standard of wisdom, folly, and despair, is an inspiring and loving teacher. As an agent of the evolution of our deepest states of consciousness, music unites the wisdom of the past with the promise of the future. Will there ever be another composer who deepens our self-knowledge like Beethoven? I hope so. An improviser who carries us farther than Bird? Can the voice of a long-dead shaman from the central plains of Turtle Island transform a frightened suburban boy into a serious person? Stay tuned.

PART THREE

...And Everywhere

8

Music on the Zen Elevator

I am obsessed by paradox. "All day I think about it," says Rumi, "then at night I say it. . . . I'm like a bird from another continent, sitting in this aviary." For me, there is a persistent feeling of impossibility, as if there were no way my life could be happening, yet all I have is its happening. My obsessions are alleviated by music, by meditation, by loving in the moment, but the questions always come back. Not to complain too much — paradox is mentally engaging. "Truth without a veil," says Inayat Khan, "is always uninteresting to the human mind."

For me, paradoxes lie primarily in two areas. The first is in science, particularly physics. Although I almost chose physics as a career, as it is I am merely a semi-educated layman, fascinated as the next reader of *Science News* by the newest data and the most outrageously paradoxical terminologies to show up in print. I was first drawn in by the energy/mass and wave/particle debates we undergraduates were introduced to in 1955 (by which time they were antique), but these have been updated and refueled by such ongoing concerns as locality/nonlocality and existence/nonexistence. "One must become familiar," cautions a recent

Scientific American article, "if never quite comfortable, with phenomena that seem paradoxical." It goes on to describe the appearance of a particle/antiparticle pair. "Oddly, the pair emerges directly from nothing—from the vacuum." Yes, oddly.

Music is direct. Its quantities and qualities can be sensed without rational thought. My body vibrates without having to think about vibration. I have feelings I don't have to describe. Yet as soon as I rain descriptive sentences down upon it, paradoxes spring up like weeds. How do a bunch of discrete tones form a compelling phrase, or a phrase open into a symphonic poem? What is the *whole* that a whole piece is *of*? These questions dissolve in the act of pure listening, in the surrender to the vibrational experience. As the sensibility of music arises from its pure sensations, the paradoxes seem as distant concerns, toys left behind. But when I'm *not* listening to music, when I'm thinking *about* it, the underlying paradoxes, real as they seem, have been modulated and softened by the transcendent nature of musical experience. This chapter discusses how music can guide us experientially beyond the paradoxes of the intellect.

The other area of paradox that continually engages me is language, especially the language that meditators and mystic poets use to transcend paradox. Language is made up largely of terms, as in the *term*inal points of a line. When we "define our terms," we stake out our positions along a continuum between end points: not really scalding hot, just lukewarm. Since I study and practice meditation, an activity in which there are, ultimately, no terms to define and no positions to take, I've discovered that the very language the teachers and translators use to guide these practices, and how this language has been refined over the brief history of such teaching in America, is a teaching in itself.

Ultimately there are no words for experience, especially the experience of wordlessness; that is where music comes in. The difference between word and tone is that a word generally signifies something, means something beyond the sound of itself, whereas a tone is precisely and blessedly itself. Words can ring *like* a bell, but a real bell's tone rings your whole world. Instrumental music does have certain characteristics of language (as we've already mentioned), a grammar of sorts based on the mind's capacity to find patterns in its periodicities and contrasts. Indeed, music sometimes strikes me as a special kind of talking—a confession, a casual conversation, an important essay—but it is a language innately empty of words.

Music doesn't *solve* paradoxes or release us from their intoxicating confusions. Rather, it is a tool for making sense of the world, a guide toward the inherent harmony of opposites. How does that work? And how can we take advantage of it? Chapter 4, "Feeling Mind, Thinking Heart," was concerned with attainment —partly with the aid of music—of an abiding truce between often fractious roommates in the human boarding house. Now we will be searching farther afield for similar treaties in a broader world.

FIVE LOVELY PARADOXES
Discrete ↔ *Continuous*

The photographer Richard Avedon once said, "In art, every time you make a choice you tell a lie." I was electrified when I first heard this, but I didn't know why. Being a deep fan of Avedon's (he died in 2004), I knew that within the frame of his portraits he was an expert choice-maker, as was Henri Cartier-Bresson (he of *The Decisive Moment*). So how could these heart-capturing moments be lies? Because, I eventually realized, choosing when to click the shutter takes you out of the temporal continuum. The photographer creates meaning by capturing and freezing his subject, thus lifting subject, photographer, and viewer up out of time's flow. Native Americans knew that a photograph sucks out the soul from the body, and I suspect everyone with a camera has sensed a twinge of that feeling from both sides of the lens.

What is this feeling? I think we are experiencing the paradox between the continuous and the discrete. This paradox is an elephant on the table that never goes away. I (and my generation) had to think about this seriously if we wanted to become engaged even a little bit in twentieth-century science. Are we particles or waves? Matter or energy? Is experience sliceable? Is time quantized? Is gravity? Where is the elusive graviton, the gravity-particle *thing*, hiding out? Is there structure beneath quarks? It would be quite musically lovely to discover that the universe is made from vibrating strings, but what are *they* made of? (Brian Greene, in *The Elegant Universe*, points out that these fundamental bits of existence are not made of anything else, since if they were they wouldn't be fundamental.) As the wished-for strings vibrate, each kind of particle corresponds not to a thing but to a characteristic vibration, much like different pitches with various timbres. But alas, as we've mentioned before, so far there is precious little empirical data to support this, and no mathematics as yet conceived to fully describe such elegance.

Indeed, the very purpose of math, at least in its "lower" forms, is to discretize nature. The number "7" means "not 6" and "not 8" and indeed excludes everything in the universe except itself. As math becomes "higher," it recognizes more and more the "lie" of making discrete choices, and approaches more and more the continuous: negative numbers, irrational numbers, limits, pi, calculus, imaginary numbers, transcendental numbers, and so on into ever higher mathematics. Numbers are truly useful tools, but if the universe is truly continuous, if everything is connected to everything and there is no way of considering a discrete part without considering all of it, then numbers will lose their utility as you approach some extreme edge—the unimaginably teeny strings singing at the heart of things, the mysterious singularities of black holes, the very constancy of cosmic constants. Then the metaphor of number doesn't work anymore—there is always a crumb of humble pie left over.

The paradox of the discrete and the continuous shows up as soon as you begin to cognize music. At first it is a blare, a busy hum, a stream of Brahmsian moonlight. Gradually we learn to beat time to the timeless river. The stream of sound is made of phrases made from bits of melodies fashioned from separate tones. Learning music begins with tones and moves to the emotional power of elegy or sonata. Zoom in to the bits and pieces, zoom out to the whole piece. Music doesn't resolve the energy/mass paradox, it straddles it by turning the thing of your body into continuous waves. In physics, we don't fully know how energy is equivalent to mass, preoccupied as we may be with knowing it. In music, all we have is our experience: our massive bodies with music coursing through them—energized bodies.

The discrete/continuous paradox was addressed famously by Zeno of Elea, who demonstrated more than twenty-four hundred years ago (in what was to become known as one of "Zeno's paradoxes") the logical impossibility of motion and multiplicity: an infinite number of parts cannot be added up to a finite whole. Aesthetically and intuitively we know this as "The whole must be greater than the sum of its parts," and nowhere is this more clear than in music, which must be heard and played from the perspective of multiplicity and motion at once. So the discrete/continuous paradox, which is stimulated by thinking, can be transcended by music.

Another version of this can be seen in Noh drama, wherein the more passionate is the dancer, the more still the dance. Our word *passion* derives from the Latin *passio*, which means exposed to suffering or strong emotion, that is, being acted upon by them, and relates to *passive*, meaning emptied out and acted upon. As the dance stills and empties, it is filled with feeling. My mantra for music making is "Listen actively, play passively." Listening actively takes great effort, but you will then be filled. That's why audiences listening to a Beethoven string quartet are so still: that's how hard they are working to hear and feel how the music moves.

Dimension: Point ↔ Line ↔ Area ↔ Volume

The paradox of motion leads to the paradox of dimension. A dimension is something by which we measure or quantize; the four dimensions of common experience are line, area, volume, and time. A point on a line has zero dimension. It exists only as an abstraction, "an act of taking away...stealing...a withdrawal from worldly things," according to the *Oxford English Dictionary*, which defines abstract as "separated from, not concrete." When I think about it, I wonder how I could have lived this long without recognizing that dimensions, and the numbers that measure them, are concepts only, incomplete stealings from the world as it is. (The reason: I believed my fourth-grade teacher.) Maybe it is the existential oddness, the downright mystical, woo-permeated *weirdness* of contemporary physics that has given me the courage to investigate this for myself. Here is what I've come to: Just as there is no such thing as a point, there is no such thing as a straight line—try to find one. A physical line's boundaries will utterly disappear into atomic and subatomic irregularities in just a few zoom-ins. A few more clicks and we're into unbounded fields of force. And what is an area? Just as points on a line won't add up to a line, any number of lines won't multiply into an area, unless you expect to wind up with a surface that is *infinitely* thin, which means what, exactly? And is volume a bound-up space? What if space is a function of time, which it seems to be, and time is continuous, which also seems to be the case. There is no such thing as line, area, volume, or time without all of them interconnecting continuously. When you have all of them forming a continuum, and they still don't seem to quite add up properly, more and more dimensions can be imagined. It seems to me that the difficulty lies in that first abstraction, the concept of "1." From there on we have systematically "alphabetized the goddess," that is, made discrete in our minds what is not discrete in nature, thus stealing us away from the ground of being.

In the twelfth century, Hildegard von Bingen helped us along the way toward inventing Western music notation in the way she used *neumes,* curvy symbols that represent tones not as points but as moving shapes in space. She and her transcribers did their best to preserve in notational form the fluid grace of her music. But that notational system could not survive in a civilization increasingly shaped by the discrete conceptualizations of the Western mind. Modern Western music notation is based on the note-head, which originated as the puncture of an inked quill into velum, a *punctus,* our old friend the *point,* as in *punctus contra punctum,* point against point or, as we know it, *counterpoint.* Savvy contemporary teachers of Hildegard's music teach first by ear ("through the ear to the heart"), then by neumes, and never even show their students modern transcriptions. As a listener, it is easy to distinguish those singers who have learned Hildegard through modern notation: they sing from note to note, and the music sounds (unsurprisingly) angular and stiff. Singers who have learned the music by ear have found the original suppleness; their music is literally moving. That is not to say that note-head notation will necessarily defeat musical flow. Bach was the apotheosis of counterpoint; in his music the seeming paradox between discrete and continuous, multiplicity and motion is, of all musics, most transcended.

Paradoxes show up in music just as much as they do in science or in natural life itself, but in music the resolutions to paradox are achieved not through rationality but through feeling, the feeling of harmonious balance. For me, the harmony of music is not an end in itself, but a touchstone for facing the world. I trust musical harmony. I trust the way musical dimensions blend and wrap and morph into feelings of vitality and beauty, so much so that when I turn around and walk into the world I have something to look for, and a little more faith that I might find it.

Time

Music especially elucidates and integrates the dimension of time. A point on a line is equivalent to an instant in time, a photograph. Is time quantized in little time-houses a fraction of an attosecond in duration? What do we mean by *now*? Points on a line are like seconds on a clock. Some people sleep better in the presence of a ticking clock—it's reassuring: I'm OK-tick, it's OK-tock, I'm OK-tick, it's OK-tock. Others, like me, go mad. We like to experience the unmarked flow, the danger of the course, the quality not the quantity. According to the Tibetan Buddhist teacher Chögyam Trungpa, "One might say that *now* exists always beyond the concept of relativity. Since all concepts are based on the idea of relativity, it is impossible to find any words that go beyond that. So nowness is the only way to see directly."

Such things are easier to say and hear in America now than they were fifty years ago. A movie released in 2009 called *Watchmen* features a character named Dr. Manhattan (naked, bald, blank-eyed, ghostly blue) who possesses the superpower of perceiving every moment in time—past, present, and future—as a *continuous present*. This celluloid pastiche of mysticism and culture is from a big-budget Hollywood studio shaping the minds of our American boys and girls right here in Springfield!

Indeed, recent neurological research suggests that the reason our perceptions seem to flow past us is this very mingling of past and present experiences in the brain. Such involvement of the entire brain has been called a "global brain state."

The more global the state, the more conscious the experience. Hyperconnectivity in the brain results in what might be called an *expanded present,* a sense of time that opens outward in both directions from immediate perception into memory and pre-science. Music listeners rely on the expanded present for music to accomplish its work. And performers of every stripe, especially improvisers, learn to be aware of the *now* at every order of magnitude from note to piece to entire concert and beyond. As an improviser, I can feel all the way back to source, and all the way out to an indefinite future while processing the complex quality of a single chord. My favorite *now* is in the silence just after a long, coherent piece of concert music has come to a close, time stops, and the entire experience seems magically to hang in the air.

Sometimes my North Indian teacher Pandit Pran Nath would sing tones quieted down to an uncannily steady state. He once sang a *re* (a D against a C drone) so perfectly that it stood me absolutely still. Nothing moved, nothing ever had moved, nothing ever would move, and nothing needed to. If there were such a thing as a perfect musical moment, that would be it for me, except there isn't one, of course. My college professor Grosvenor Cooper used to say (in 1955), "That's one of my ten thousand most favorite places in music."

Real ↔ Abstract

The abstraction of all the dimensions taken together has engaged painters and sculptors for over a century. Perhaps the development of our capacity for abstraction is inherent in the evolution of perception. From the earliest known cave art, to the pure forms of Plato, to Arabic algebra and ever higher forms of math, and all the way up through Picasso, Pollack, and Rothko, abstraction seems to be an innate baggage of the human mind. "The longer you look at an object," said the British painter Lucien Freud, "the more abstract it becomes and, ironically, the more real." You can look at a giraffe and lift out (steal away) its essential forms and motions—where's the giraffe? You can look at an abstract canvas and be mystified, then—oh, it's a giraffe—then go back to no giraffe because it's better that way.

Or you can look at a giraffe and sense the *music* of its form and movements, the grace in the reach of its neck, the rhythms of its lope. But then—no, it's a giraffe. Or you can listen to music and be reminded of a giraffe galloping over the savannah, but then—oh, it's just a flurry of notes lifted utterly away from anything nameable into its own precious, unique reality. Lucien Freud implies that abstraction is an aspect of our perception of objects, and I think that happens in music as well. Imagine listening to Tchaikovsky's *Swan Lake* without thinking about swans or lakes or even ballerinas, hearing nothing but swirling sound waves, the rushes and gusts of sonic wind between your ears. Now imagine the reverse: you are listening to "pure" music, say Bach's *Art of the Fugue,* and you are following the intimate weave of musical conversation; but then you turn your mind one crick to the left and nothing makes sense, it's a passion dance of a mind on fire, just blazing color. I love it when that happens, because when I "follow" the music I think I'm smart, but when, within this utmost concentration, I lose the giraffe, the swans, the fugue, I'm beyond smart.

I realize that earlier I've used "abstraction" in the sense of a "point" on a "line" and identified it with the "discrete," that which is separated out, as opposed to continuous. But just now I have used abstraction in the sense of a lifting up out of the specifics of the musical narrative to a higher level of wind and fire. *Abstract* can mean a stealing away, but it can also be used in the highest sense of continuity, as in "abstract sound," as we shall soon discuss. These associations of seeming opposites feel very much to me like improvising at the keyboard, a musical play of ideas. I don't know what I'm going to say next. I hope you don't mind. I do know that there are twelve notes in each octave, eighty-eight on the piano keyboard, and that I've played them all before, learned and relearned myriad configurations so they fit my hand and my hand fits them. But then, as I play through this worn-down and well-mapped territory, each tone opens out into unknown others, and those in turn open into starry possibility. I know everything and nothing. I'm stuck in the sound of the instant and expanded toward inner and outer horizons. And that is true for these words on this page as well: I know and I don't know, which brings us to the next paradox.

Known ↔ Unknown

There is a dark, built-in irony to science, the physical sciences in particular. *Science* is from the Latin *scire,* "to know"; scientists are empiricists who look for patterns in nature from which "laws of nature" can be derived. But is the innate nature of the world an order that is predictable, or is it unpredictable change? Scientific irony consists in the probability, in nature, of an irreducible randomness. Thus "probability," a certain kind of unknowing, is at the core of modern knowing. Where will this end? Maybe, as suggests the theoretical physicist Lee Smolin, the laws of nature change with time. The Hindu poet Tukaram thought so; he reported in the seventeenth century that God said to him, "Even I am ever-changing—what I have once put my seal upon may no longer be the greatest truth." Maybe, as Dennis Overbye, a wonderfully clear science writer, speculates, "the dichotomy between forever and emergent might turn out to be as false eventually as the dichotomy between waves and particles. Who knows?" He goes on to consider the position of the scientists themselves: "They have no choice but to play their cards as if they can win." (Which is what I'd say about us and free will—we need to behave as though we have it.)

Musicians confront the issue of certainty and uncertainty

continually. By rote we learn rules of harmony and counter-point, only to learn by experience how and when to bend or abandon them. We must be predictable or run the risk of may-hem; we must delve into the unknown or be boring. Thus we learn the musical boundaries between knowing and not know-ing. As a listener, you can ask yourself as you listen: Can I pre-dict what is going to happen? Do I expect something? Am I being gratified for being able to sense the pattern, or am I being surprised? "Both at once," is the usual outcome of this experi-ment. We are attracted to the music we love largely by how satis-fied we become with the mix of known and unknown.

Unknowing has a new *cachet* these days: we educated West-erners are more willing to give it a try. Pema Chödron's wonderful *Comfortable with Uncertainty* has framed the scene. Through such teaching we can learn to recognize just how quick we typically are to revert to knowing. "Meditation," says Donna McLaugh-lin, a teacher in the Mahamudra tradition, "asks us to stay with unknowing so the full display of possibilities has the potential to manifest." In the fourteenth century Rumi was asking,

> Why talk about all
> the known and the unknown?
> See how the unknown merges with the known.

The merge is what Rumi asks us to appreciate:

> Look at water and fire
> earth and wind,
> enemies and friends all at once.

Contemporary art and music often test viewers and listen-ers as to how much unknowing they can tolerate. This takes some courage, some evolution, perhaps. Say we are some fishes in the ocean having a discussion about something called "water."

One fish who always swims close by her neighbors says, "I don't know what you mean. How can I understand this 'water' you've been talking about?" Another fish leaps out above the surface and splashes back noisily:

"Like *that*!"

"I still don't get it," says the complacent one.

It's the flying fish and the dolphins who go out so that they may return—the sages of the ocean. That's what musicians and listeners have to do: break out of knowing in order to come back. Nothing is more stimulating than a patch of sound that doesn't make any sense, then suddenly makes a lot of sense. That's what keeps our love of music fresh.

The Zen Elevator

We have been shuttling between the terms of our favorite paradoxes, sampling them like chocolates, mixing them and letting them melt in our mouths. We ordinarily think of a continuum as a horizontal line, but if we upend the line, the shuttle we've been riding becomes an elevator. The most discrete, bounded experiences are now at the bottom floor; at the top a connectivity so seamless that there are no longer any "things" to connect. We can call this the Zen elevator, though the Zen of it doesn't fully manifest until the elevator disappears, as we shall discover. For now, it is important not to consider higher and lower as worse and better. It is only that, as one rises, one's view changes.

There does seem to be an awful lot of lurching up and down on this elevator. We are born into form and make what use we can out of it whether or not our questions ever get answered. "Seems like we're just set down here," says a woman from West Virginia, "don't nobody know why." Yet there are those among us who report unexplainable experiences. Their view widens, and they talk about it, guiding us with crazy language toward new experiences of our own. Twenty-five hundred years ago, the view of the man soon to become known as the Buddha became so wide that he started to preach about *four noble truths,* the *eightfold path,* and the *wheel of dharma.* Plotinus had experiences of *unification* which, he taught, were not possible through thought, but only by losing the restraint of bodily form and entering into an *ecstatic state of immediacy,* a knowledge of the *One.* (He claimed a total of four such experiences over the course of his life.) Because I am a musician, and have my own kind of ecstatic realization through a nonlinguistic medium, I've become very curious about such language. It gives me a conceptual handle on the Zen of my own music, a way to think and talk about the music on my elevator. Here's what I've learned from my forty mostly truant years of meditation practice and about twenty minutes of reading, more or less.

First and foremost, realization is experiential, not conceptual. The best and only thing that words can do is guide you toward wordlessness. Words take you so close to the truth, it is said, because they are what led you away from it in the first place. An effective meditation teacher knows this in the same way that an effective music teacher knows it. It is the best reason for having instrumental music on your Zen elevator—to remind you where the words stop and the view starts to get really good. Teachers inundate you with words, usually specialized in bizarre ways (like Buddhist philosophy or music theory), and then devise cunning strategies to wean you from them.

If you teach, a good strategy for weaning students from words (and the concepts they contain) is to model what you teach. "Enlightenment can't be taught," said Buddhist sage Joe Miller, "it's got to be caught." A spiritual teacher can teach spirit only to the point of his or her own realization. The same is true for music. I play and sing for my students, and lead them to other teachers whose sheer immersion in musical vibration is their truest teaching. The other thing I've learned about transcending language is just how important linguistic clarity is. Clear talk is self-dissolving just as surely as pure mind is self-arising.

The ground floor of the elevator is thingness, the stuff of the world, the thwack of the Zen stick on the shoulders of the student with a wandering mind: "Start here, with *this*." "This" is *samsara*, the world of life-and-death duality. In music, the most sensible thwack is the downbeat of the drum, which strokes your body into relationship with our best and biggest thing, Earth. This leads directly to the two-step of the boom-chick, the universal mantra of bipedal samsara, the walking tempo of the world. Walking opens out into dances that rock and roll in every dimension, and on into soundscapes as heavy as metal. Music that shakes and shocks the body is earth therapy for minds and souls who seriously need to stay here now. And, speaking of salvation, without the blues of every color and origin, we surely never could have come this far.

As the Zen elevator rises there is no measuring the altitude or the progress, but the view does get wider. Riding up from brute thingness, one becomes preoccupied with scale, orders of magnitude, zooming in and out: we were *there*, but now we're *here*. How far have we come? How high does this thing go? Simple things seem to take on a larger meaning. Trinkets become somehow imbued with sacredness. My individual self begins to feel connected to the landscape and to other selves. My "I" seems to be moving around, to be more than itself. The perceived center is searching for itself.

Meanwhile, the simple repetitions of dance music and minimal music become hypnotic, focusing the world through a small space that seems expanded—a way of being stoned. The sound of a solo cello becomes a world in itself. You can hear the years of skill and refinement in the cellist's bow, and the centuries of instrument building that produced this river of sound so dark and so sweet that you can tolerate the sorrows of your life. Things are more than they are, and sounds are more than one hears. As the view widens, your "I" becomes more and more inclusive, unlimited: you are everyone more than you are someone. You get flashes of oneness with everything, a taste of nirvana. You begin to look forward to your next oceanic experience.

In music, this is the place where individual tones seem magically to coalesce into gorgeous melodies, and melodic phrases conjoin into living communities of phrases. Individual chords combine into streaming harmony. Beauty comes in. You recognize how, in the long history of vibration, you and the cello are siblings. And the elevator isn't yours anymore—everyone else is on it too, sharing the music and the view. The emotions you're experiencing aren't yours either, but belong to all the listeners and viewers, somehow crowded together like this, sobbing and sighing, one revelation after another.

Paying attention, you notice the view expanding slowly now, but certainly. The sense of union seems to be shifting around: whose unity with what or whom? Everybody is reading Rumi and Hafiz, and the poetry is making perfect sense. People have insights: "God is Experience!" Heads nod, eyes glisten. Someone says, "When everything is God, there is no need for God," and someone else says, "Wow!" There is a deeper seriousness and a higher joy.

The music seems to have quieted down. Even in its roughest, loudest parts you can hear a deep, fixed intention. The music seems to be a reflection of the view, and you can do what King Lear admonishes us to do: look with your ears. Classical sonatas and symphonies begin to look like cross sections of the human mind. The aesthetic economy of Bach fugues, the unity in the plurality of their polyphony, look like prophecy. The ragas of North India place *samadhi* in your body in the form of timeless harmonic states. In the heart of the music you feel Rumi's *Beloved*, Buber's *Thou*. Late Mozart is how everybody ought to behave, and the voices of Bulgarian choirs are no longer sounding but pulsing with light. The pain you hear everywhere in the music is the seal of its authenticity. "This is what *is*," you say, and everyone nods.

Stuck ↔ Unstuck

Certainty has arisen, and for that very reason we've come to a most tricky part of the ride. As viewers, we can look beyond the horizon and plainly see for ourselves how everything connects to everything, there is no particle of the universe out of touch with any other. As listeners, we have selected our music: good music reflects the panoramic unity of our vision, and healing music, obviously, heals us. This is one of the places where the Zen elevator most likely can get stuck. It is in places like this that I, who am a musician and not a scholar of comparative philosophy, am thankful for the sincere efforts on the part of spiritual teachers in clarifying and refining their descriptive language, while at the same time cautioning us repeatedly that realization occurs by paying attention to experience, not by understanding descriptions of it.

I am especially partial to the phrase "the all-concealing truth" as a characterization of this phase of the ride. The "truth" refers to the perception of universal connection among all things. The concealment occurs because what is putatively connected is *things,* that is, separate parts. The stuck-ness consists in persistence in the belief that Zeno's paradox is solvable by chopping discrete things up small *enough:* even though we find ourselves in a relative, discrete world, it can be minced into an infinitely fine gruel. The all-concealing truth might be called an infinite relativity. When everything is connected to everything, we are still in a thing world.

As the view expands, there comes at last a glimpse of the falling away of thingness. The time has come to ask sincerely what precious baggage we need to jettison in order to lighten up and continue onward. Of course, I can give no substantive answer to this question. Instead, let me repeat back to you some of the words that have been said to me—carefully winnowed words that have guided me into ephemeral but life-changing experiences.

What could "a falling away of thingness" mean? Language, made of terms, must be fashioned into describing a termless existence. Invoking self-canceling terms is one strategy for this. For the experience of ultimate continuity, for instance, we have *no-self*. For the joy beyond joy we have *non-joy*. Likewise, reality is *unborn;* there is *no form* and *no void*. No longer dwelling in our expanded minds (*mindfulness*), we are in a state of *non-minding,* that is, dissolved in the expanse beyond mindfulness.

But there are also descriptive words that are neutral, or have a positive side. Non-minding is the bliss of *nirvana,* also called *one taste*. In the sense that nirvana is empty of the discrete, or relative, or substantive, it is called *emptiness,* which is far from being a negative term. Asha Greer, a wise leader of spiritual practice, says she likes "to fill the full with empty in order to make more room." Used in this way, emptiness is a highly refined version of our Latin-derived *passion,* an emptiness that can fill, finally, with *being-as-it-is*. Repeatedly we are reminded that the experience of these states can be fleeting indeed, a *glimpse* of the *Absolute*.

I experienced "the glimpse" through music long before I realized the experience in plain life. In this I can name two great mentors. The first of these is Hazrat Inayat Khan, widely held to be the first Asian-born teacher to bring Sufism to the West. He was a consummate musician called upon at a young age to continue his education in the Western world and teach Sufism on its soil. Inayat Khan had a deeply musical view of the world, and a mystical view of music. *The Mysticism of Sound and Music,* only part of a large oeuvre, has influenced many musicians and nonmusicians alike, guiding us to deep listening experiences and giving us a useful conceptual framework with which to continue our inner work.

The second mentor was a variety of psychoactive substances, especially the occasional LSD trip, but also (in my youth, of course) copious weed. On acid (and long before I knew what a Sufi was) I had a core experience: the realization of sound as a three-dimensional, palpable mandala of airwaves within which I could hear, see, and follow extremely complex, almost unbearably beautiful patterns. My entire understanding of harmony (touched upon in earlier chapters and expounded upon extensively in *Harmonic Experience*) came from an epic moment in my mid-twenties when, high as a kite on a tab of Owsley, I saw, in acrylic colors, the air mandalas formed by Beethoven's C-sharp Minor String Quartet. Since the feeling was part of the mandala, I realized that there was more to music theory than I was being taught. As far as marijuana is concerned, it simply focused my hearing down to a resolution fine enough to be able to hear what expert early training would probably have taught me on the natch. None of these drug-induced experiences were anything even close to a glimpse of the Absolute, nor, of course, was the reading of any book. Not close but, perhaps at some distance, parallel. Like any useful teaching, these episodes provided the guidance I needed at the time. Subsequently I found real live teachers to model the inner life, to show me how awareness is innate. But such vivid experiences can be, one might say, a glimpse of the Glimpse.

Deeper glimpses came later on. The "music is waves" experience became more connective and meaningful over time. Streaming waves are not *things,* exactly, though they may be the result of the interaction of seemingly concrete things, like hammers on strings. Waves reside as vibration in the body and the mind, and expand and refine into spirit by their nature. Great composers and performers have shaped these waves into structures so vast in our minds that they transcend cognition. When musical cognition stops, when the urge to *name* and *understand* is overcome by the vastness, you stand under the music, and deep listening begins. You hear how experience enfolds opposites, transcends seeming paradoxes. If you look inside motion you can find stillness; inside sound can be found silence, at least in glimpses. Mary Oliver mentions "a silence as comes to all of us in little earfuls." An artist friend reminds me that beauty is silent. We don't know why we are struck dumb by beauty's extravagance, but at a crucial threshold *now* becomes *forever* and music becomes a silence inside sound.

Behind the noise music makes in the world of trumpets and ears is a little earful, a glimpse of the source of all vibration. The Sanskrit word is *Shabd,* and it can mean pure consciousness, the vibration that permeates everything. *Shabd* is the "Word" of "In the beginning there was the Word." Our very own scientific creation myth, the Big Bang, could also be seen as the first manifestation in the "created" world of the source behind it. Inayat Khan says that creation is the music of God, and that what we normally call music is a picture of God. He goes on to say that "earthly sound is so concrete that it dims the effect of the Sound of the Abstract [what we have been calling the "Absolute"] to the sense of hearing...When the Abstract Sound is audible, all other sounds become indistinct to the mystic." As far as my own experience is concerned, I can tell you that there are times, not many, but there *are* times when, listening to music, my ears become tuned to the Shabd, the expanse beyond mindfulness, a glimpse of the Absolute. One cannot expect to dial this in, of course, but a good strategy is to stay awake long enough not to miss your turn.

Teamwork

Whatever happened to the Zen elevator? Gone! But the ride continues. We live the life we have, which means living in the world where others are living, a world where choices need to be made, where we must discriminate between this and that. For this we need teamwork between the discrete and the continuous. The relative and the Absolute need to function in plain life. We need a valley road.

A Buddhist term for discernment in the relative world is *cognitive lucidity,* or simply, *lucidity.* A corresponding term for the open and boundless experience of pure mind in the Absolute is *being-as-it-is,* or *emptiness.* For me, the key phrase that shows their mutual function is *lucidity and emptiness co-arising.* The relative and the Absolute are functions of one another. They arise together, and are called *co-emergent.* The transcendent experience of their co-emergence is called *co-emergent joy.* Another word for such realization is *liberation.* Liberation is the experience of lucidity and emptiness co-arising. In other words, when *we* learn to be empty, the true nature of being appears by *it*self.

MUSIC AS COMPASSION

For us humans, the "true nature of being" has the quality of human feeling—it is a human nature. And just as the nature of being is self-arising, compassion is self-arising in human nature. *Com-* means "with." *Compassion* means "with the feelings of others." If there were a God in Buddhism, its name would be compassion. The seal of enlightenment is compassionate, co-emergent joy. Also called *loving-kindness,* compassion is not a theology, but rather the experience of people who have *fallen awake,* to use Joe Miller's words. Enlightenment, characterized by loving-kindness, demonstrates that compassion is innate to human beings. When we feel compassion arising, we understand how we are innately, primordially connected.

Musical experience models this point of view. For me, the authenticity of music consists in the quality of its connectivity. Music that connects people and helps them live useful lives—that is the sound compassion makes. This sound has arisen always and everywhere, which is why music is called "the universal language." Where does this language come from? Music arises from the Shabd in the same way that compassion arises from emptiness. One might say in this sense that music is self-arising. I find this idea utterly amazing. I know that my own music is a message sent through me directly from my silence through sound waves to your ears and back into your silence. What is so remarkable is that—aside from sixty-five years of practice and the commitment to show up as often and awake as possible—I'm not *doing* anything except listening. I'm being done to. I'm listening actively and playing passively. Music, this amazingly self-arising form, is an audible message of being-in-itself. Loving-kindness and music are both innate to the cosmic whorl.

I love these crazy words and this way of talking. They make me want to dig deeper into the present tense of my life, the ever-present possibility of being more fully awake. But I don't think I would have been led to this teaching were it not for an intimation of such experiences through music. When you know how to be immersed in it, music can be a heaven world, capable of cosmic transport. You can lose all boundaries of self and time inside it. Sound can turn to a stillness that surpasseth understanding. This world, in brief, stops, and the next comes to get you. There is only one problem, however: such experiences last for about two bars, max. Then you cannot help but notice that you are lost, that your fellow musicians are waiting for their cue, that your hands are doing something very confusing and you are blushing in public. When you are doing music, you can't go cosmic, at least not for more than a taste. Making music is about thwacking and strumming on things, pushing air through columns, working your fingers in complex, ever-changing patterns. Musicians know that music is crucially about their very own muscles and organs vibrating in refined, exotic ways, and the more you keep all this together, the greater are your chances for meaningful experience. As far as co-emergence is concerned, music plays both sides of the fence, also straddles the fence, and finally, victoriously, rises up and over it into the empty sky above the fields. You never have to leave heaven, but you can never leave earth either, not for long.

Merely listening to music is a lot safer. In the privacy of the ear, there is no limit to the heavens. Yet most of us, most of the time, listen to music in connection with any number of adjunct activities that are braided into it, from dancing to dreaming. As a listener, the only advice I can give you is to notice the many dozens of ways you have of listening to music, recognizing especially those times when you are doing nothing *but* listening, thus experiencing yourself and your world focused in a very particular way. There are only a few times in my long life of deep listening when I actually entered the expansiveness of the Shabd, and these were mostly in conjunction with music suited for, or intended for, the purpose: North Indian raga, some music by the American composer Terry Riley, the polyphony of Guillaume de Machaut and J. S. Bach, and notably long passages of a concert I attended in 2005 by Ornette Coleman, blessings be upon him. Music can't listen to itself; it needs you, its true meaning comes from you. You have to meet it, to help it be alive in the *now,* and that is hard work.

Fellow Rider, the elevator may be gone, but we can't undo the view. When we reenter the world, there is no erasing where we've been. The more expanded the view we've had, the more we hear the validity of all music that connects heart to heart. From the co-emergence of lucidity and emptiness, alloyed with its innate quality of compassion, arises the discerning, awakened life. If unbounded being is what *is* is, then discernment in a cluttered world is what life is about. "A Bell Ringing in the

Empty Sky" is the title of the most frequently performed piece in the repertoire of Shakuhachi flute music, and indeed, music at its most affective is like a thing, a bell, vibrating in the continuous sky of human being. Bell and sky, co-arising. We listen. Inside, someone nods.

9

The Enlightened Listener

This chapter focuses on real-time methods for the appreciation of music as a vital energy at the core of your days. What follows are a few practical suggestions for listening to music (primarily instrumental), for claiming sovereignty of your ears and, if so inclined, for making your own music.

LISTENING PRACTICES
Balancing the Ears with the Eyes

We are a visual people. Most of our understanding comes through the eyes. The ears, for us, play second fiddle. Here is a practice that will help to balance the ears with the eyes. When you get to the end of this paragraph, take a moment to close your eyes and welcome into your ears every audible vibration. As the sounds flood toward you, notice the light on your newly blank screen, a kind of sculpture shaped by sound but lit from within. The bird to catch is that first whoosh of aural clarity, the slow-motion moment of opening to sound. End of paragraph.

Practice listening with your eyes open, then closed, noticing how your world changes accordingly. The primary responsibility of your mind is keeping you safe. We spend most of our conscious life visually locked in, checking out the world, and that vision is expensive—it burns the greater half of our mental energy. Assuming for the moment that you actually are safe, closing your eyes releases you into your soundscape, vibration by vibration.

A variation on this practice: With closed eyes, put your fingers in your ears and concentrate on the inner sound; then listen with ears open and eyes closed; then open your eyes and listen normally; then close your eyes and cup your ears with your hands to gather distant sounds. When you repeat this four-step practice a few times, you can experience how each way of listening changes your sense of the world. Here are the four steps:

> Ears closed, eyes closed
> Ears open, eyes closed
> Ears open, eyes open
> Ears cupped, eyes closed

This practice clues us to how, generally speaking, we are not aurally locked in. We see most of the time, but we hear and then we don't hear—we're too busy looking and thinking. When you listen to music with closed eyes, a magnificent world is revealed. What if you could learn to remember to hear in the thick of the plain-old, eyes-open world with that same magnificence?

Remembrance

An amazing variety of spiritual practices have come from the notion of remembrance. For religions, what is remembered is God, or Allah, or Brahman, or our relationship to whatever is held to be sacred. Remembrance practices are usually relegated to times periodically set aside for prayer, but the ideal is to never not remember, to walk always on sacred ground.

In meditation, you release yourself from following your

thoughts; the stilled mind opens to the true nature of Mind. You keep remembering your true nature, or one might say, re-Minding yourself. The ideal meditation is being able to walk through the world with a mind both lucid and calm — meditation in action.

A practice central to Islam involves a repeated, highly intentional, mantric prayer called *zikr;* the name translates literally to "remembrance." During my Sufi training, zikr became a powerful form of connection to my inner life. Since music was central to my lineages of Sufism (Chisti and Mevlani), my fellow students and I had the freedom to invent musically elaborate forms of the practice. Over the many decades of participating in the mantric power of zikr, the ideal of its practice gradually revealed itself: the outer form of the zikr may change, but the inner form, the remembrance, is constant.

A musician trains his or her entire life to never not listen. Ideally, our ears are always open, even when it would be much more convenient to hear selectively, or not at all. For instance, if music is playing in the background of a conversation, my response to "How's your family?" might well be "There goes a wrong note in the French horn." But on the positive side, musical training allows one more fully to hear the full palette of the soundscape, from distant farm machinery to mid-city birdsong. When sound stays alive in waking life, the connection to all vibration stays alive as well. Each sound is connected to every sound, and all sound reaches back to its source. You might call this "sound *zikr,*" the path of the enlightened listener.

For me, sound is sacred, which doesn't elucidate much because as far as I'm concerned, everything is sacred. But sound is so close to the marrow for me, such an opening in and of itself, that my impulse is to show you how to *fold* it closer into your own experience. It's easy, so I say. Start by closing your eyes, and hearing what you hear. Then open your eyes and keep going.

Bird to Bowl

Sound allows you to inhabit the interior structure and quality of the thing sounding. To knock on a wooden door is to release the song of the wood from its fibrous prison, to make the inner and outer dimensions of the door sensible. A door is rigid, but sound is vapor; it changes shape and travels the room in a blink. Imagine this: I am sitting in meditation at the home of Shabda, a Sufi friend. He has found a lama from Dharamsala who, after having spoken for a while in Tibetan-tinted English, has been sitting silently with the roomful of us for a quarter-hour. I notice that there is light around his body—how do they do that?

For the last few minutes, I've been listening to a bird outside the house in the throes of morning song; now I have become that bird. Now I am its syrinx, vibrating tremulously with territorial braggadocio. Then suddenly time is up—the lama strikes a small bowl gong. I go from inside the metabolism of bird to inside the crystal structure of metal. This particular bowl gong is super-refined, with a gently piercing golden sound, an unwavering chord of four or five tones that are mysteriously harmonic. I am ancient. Now I am eternal. Now Shabda speaks, his soft voice warm as flannel, and I'm back in a room among friends. Ten years later, during a meditation at the home of Donna, my Mahamudra guide, there is another morning bird, but this time I go back and forth between the bird and the true nature of mind, that is, bird as no-bird. The nature of sound thus realized is: it catapults one beyond sound.

We embody sound so deeply that we ourselves can feel like the sounding thing. When we hear consecutive sounds from disparate things, we have morphed with the ease of mist from rigid thing to rigid thing: *sound morphing*. I went from the territorial cries of a living bird to the crystal lattice structure of a metal bowl simply by changing waveforms. That kind of serious embodiment requires focus but, Patient Reader, it's worth it. The effort loosens us up, opens our boundaries, gets us closer to the all-wave model, to our connective possibilities and thus our compassion. And of course, all it takes to turn this stuff into music is a little pattern-making and a few low primes, and sometimes not even that.

Thinking and Listening

In this book we have already grappled with the complex and mutable relationship between thinking music and feeling music. A simple example: Most everyone can count time to music, but to really feel it, you have to stop counting and enter your moving body. In complex pieces of music, the metric and rhythmic structures often have to be analyzed and practiced cognitively until their intuitive body-life takes over. This is true for melodic, harmonic, and formal structures as well. I like to do my thinking about music before and after I play it, and as little as possible while I am performing it. The same holds for listening to music. Generally speaking, cognitive knowledge increases the scope and alters the flavor of listening, but it does not necessarily increase the intensity or the depth of the real-time experience. In fact it could easily pull you away from the music.

Consider the difference between speaking passionately using your native language and speaking passionately in a language that is new for you. If you need to look up every other word, you can't attain much eloquence. Although music is a kind of language and resembles spoken and written languages in most intriguing ways, it is quite distinct from spoken language, and absolutely unique in at least one way: Spoken language denotes meaning from outside itself, whereas music fills our need for a language whose meaning can be self-contained. Music, though it may have any number of referential meanings, can also mean itself. Many people prefer their music, as well as their visual art, this way. Too much stuff attached to art can kill it. Susan Sontag, who could always spot a worthy battle, nailed this when she said, "Interpretation is the revenge of the intellect upon art."

The special niche that musical language plays in our lives can be appreciated obliquely by a little experiment. In a quiet space, clear your mind and see how long can you go without thinking of a word. Now try the same while listening to engaging instrumental music. One can learn to listen to music—or even just the air and what's in it—from a neutral place, like a microphone: no judgment, no response, and no story, only waves that your body registers.

However you prefer your mixture of thought and music, the goal of the musician and the listener alike is for the hearing to be louder than the thinking. Each person between each pair of ears must dope this out for herself or himself. The recipe changes for each piece, maybe many times within a given piece, and most certainly over one's lifetime, but the focus needs to remain on the health and vitality of the listening faculty. If your listening body stops breathing, the parasite has killed the host.

Concepts, thoughts that combine concepts, and the linguistic syntax that frames them all come packaged in labeled boxes inside labeled boxes. Non-conceptual wisdom, the streaming wisdom of music, reminds me of Rumi's characterization of "God's joy" as it moves from "unmarked box to unmarked box, as rainwater down into flowerbed, as roses up from ground." Joy hides within these morphing forms until "one day it cracks them open."

Notice Any Aspect of Your Response in Any Dimension of the Music

A two-edged way to focus on listening to music is to choose a single dimension of music (the bass line, for instance), and

214

a single aspect of your response (your degree of tension/relaxation, for instance) and consciously track just that particular combination of it and you. The music will simultaneously reveal itself and yourself. For instance, concentrate on the bass only, the lowest-sounding aspect of the music. Rivet your mind there; forget the higher stuff, seductive as it may be. At the same time, track the tensions in your body—all over your body—and witness how they arise and dissolve. This is clearly an analytical method, by which I mean we are breaking down experience into component parts so as to reassemble them later into a more complete whole. The value is that you are likely to hear and feel things you may not have previously experienced or witnessed. We could call this the selective witness technique.

Another example of the same practice: While listening to a piece of orchestral music, notice only the density of the texture—how thick or thin the sound is. This is a dimension that composers have to be particularly aware of but that casual listeners do not ordinarily track. You may notice that the density changes at different rates of speed, sometimes gradually, sometimes quite suddenly. At the *same* time, track your level of concentration on the music versus when your mind wanders. Is there a correlation? Maybe, maybe not, but you will be riding a particular ray into the experience of listening that may be new to you. And when you return to normal listening, some of the heretofore blank spaces may now be filled in.

Yucky Music and the Culture of Darkness

The reliably clear Buddhist teacher Pema Chödrön says that trying to live as though everything is all smooth and nice "is death, because it involves rejecting a lot of basic experience. There's something aggressive about that approach to life." This zeros in on and ferrets out the quality some find most annoying in proselytizing, smiley-face music. There seems to be a deep sadness in such willful covering up of suffering. Truly jubilant music—where the smiles are real and not pasted on—knows what to do with sadness: it has opened its arms to it and worked through it. Can you distinguish these qualities by simply listening to the music? Yes, I think you can. Maybe you'll change your mind one way or another over time, but the point is to listen deeply for what is true in the moment of listening.

The other side of this coin, the music of grief and suffering, also has two aspects. A grimace can be pasted on as easily as a smile, and since anguish sells, a kind of commercial angst is sold to Americans, especially teens, as a stand-in for the actual horrors of the real world. This is not to say that the authentic pain is absent from commercial music, only that the more you can sell your bad trip, the badder you can paint it (which often, ironically, becomes a self-fulfilling prophecy). This is in contradistinction to, for instance, Delta blues and other musics of enslaved and decimated populations, where the music is made not for commercial release but for actual liberation from imprisoned lives. So why put your ears in the middle of such a stream of anguish? Because just as there is an acceptance of pain in jubilant music, there is in the music of grief and cataclysm a joy so profound and so hidden that only through the darkest sounds can it be expressed. As long as we are in the throes of music we're still alive, and the cries of those closest to the dark are the most piercing. Music that resonates with our deepest demons can guide us toward gratitude for the lives we have.

Let this be a plea: Listen to harsh beauty. When I had just turned seventeen, I attended the University of Chicago as an ambitious, immature, precocious virgin of a freshman. Inside of a week I'd fallen for the long, blond goddess Joanna, six months my senior, twice as smart, ripe for her age, poetically articulate, and intrigued by my musical mind. In the deserted dance studio of Ida Noyes Hall, she danced her life up to and including that afternoon while I improvised at the keyboard, one half of me salivating, the other half playing music I'd never heard anyone play ever. We took long walks; I almost fainted with desire; she laughed and wept. Joanna was the first person my age to actually recognize me, and she saw enough to want to bring me further along. One fall day after a crisp walk to Lake Michigan and back, instead of heading for the dance studio she steered me toward the library: "I want you to hear to something." She walked me into the listening room and sat me down. From the stacks, she pulled out an LP recording of Schoenberg's Fourth String Quartet, a fiercely atonal work written in 1937, the year of my birth, so at the time it was just as new as I was. Alone in the room, we sat across from each other at the far end of a long table. We put on our headphones. She dropped the stylus on the shiny black disc, then grabbed both my hands and held them tight. Not only was this my first goddess but also my first Schoenberg, and when the silver slivers began to shimmer and slice my brain, the overwhelm and shock of a swirling new universe was surrounded by the flickering patina of love. I tried not to grit my teeth, to stay open, to love the music as much as I myself was in love. We kneaded and clenched our hands moist with the intimacy of sharing such excruciating intensity. Halfway through the first movement, Joanna's eyes met mine, and for the duration of the recording we sat in a hormonal darshan of exquisite, ecstatic love and pain.

In the following decades I digested a large amount of difficult, atonal music including Schoenberg, analyzed much of it, learned to play my share of it at the pianoforte, spent ten arduous years composing it, and finally learned to fold its brilliant, spiny aesthetic into my natural ear. I'm glad I did. It opened the possibilities of beauty arising not from the low-prime resonances of tonal harmony, but from the intelligence of intervallic patterning, the sweep of gestural noise, and the pure aural land of timbre per se. When, in 1960, I heard my first free black jazz from New York, I immediately embraced it and even had the sense to rave about it in *DownBeat,* for which I was writing criticism at the time. The saxophonist Archie Shepp, the pianist Cecil Taylor, and other free jazz players became major influences in my life. Their liberation through a savage medium felt welcome and necessary in my musical landscape. I was fortunate, probably, that my ears and my heart had been opened years before, but even without an enchantress, and with only a well-spoken piece of music to guide you, you can train your mind not to drift away, to keep the lens steady and clear. Is this what twentieth-century composers were asking us to do—to face the century's pain? Is this what Bartók and Berg need us to hear in their most difficult works? I've never been in a war and I wasn't born black in America, but music that transcends these conditions embeds compassion and understanding in any listener who hears, and that is something of this world, not nothing.

Intelligent, difficult music is marginalized because it requires us to face unknown, feared aspects of ourselves; its perpetrators can thus seem like a threatening, self-appointed priesthood. Yet there can appear an unexpected shining in even the darkest, most fearsome sound. Yes, there may be posers among us, but deliberate listening can discern what is authentically transcendent in dark music. Today's anguish has a way of becoming tomorrow's beauty, so give yuck a break.

Pushing the Threshold

There is at least one more good reason to listen to challenging music: it can push the envelope of your cognition. This is true not only for the unfamiliar sounds of contemporary music, but for every sort of difficult music. The tunings of Japanese court music might seem too alien, the counterpoint of Bach organ fugues too impenetrably dense, the intrinsic rage of a metal band too threatening, the outpourings of free jazz too chaotic, the pieties of gospel music too pat. Yet if you pinpoint your resistances to these sounds, you can often enough find a point of entry into a useful experience. Weird new experiences have a way of turning into enjoyable habits. Preferences come and go, which is a good thing because when your tastes crystallize, the stimuli that formed them in the first place begin to cloy. Then you need to change the menu, and that takes courage. Be a brave listener. Try new stuff, even if it seems to offend. Let yourself be influenced by a changing world. Keep safe, friend, but not too safe.

A strange thing about the evolution of our musical tastes is that it so often proceeds historically backward. Kids usually want to learn the music of their immediate culture, not some dude named Schumann who wasn't even *alive* when Granny was born.

The same kid is going to discover Copland's *Appalachian Spring* when she is in college, with a Beethoven epiphany close behind, followed by revelations via Bach, Josquin, Machaut, Hildegard, and many others. I didn't fall for medieval music until I was in my fifties, but then I went head over heels. And this is just the Western canon. Each culture and style has its history waiting for us to travel back through it. Given the arrow of time and the place we are positioned upon it, backward seems like a perfectly sensible direction to proceed.

There is one more special reason to extend yourself by listening to difficult music, especially music that is intellectually tough, like richly layered polyphonic music. When you push the limits of your concentration over the span of a work, and do that repeatedly, and then come back to relatively simpler music — Mozart, for instance — an amazing transparency ensues. What had seemed murky or at best translucent becomes fresh and clear, a meadow after rain. For the dedicated listener, hard work pays off.

What Are They Telling Us?

If music is communication, who is communicating what? What are the musicians themselves trying to tell us? Although there are an indeterminately large number of answers to such questions, the questions themselves are fundamental, and keep popping up in the minds and conversations of listeners and musicians. At one level, the answer is obvious: what you hear is what you get, and if music means anything, whatever it means to you *is* the meaning. But let's go further.

In listening to music, regardless of its style or origin, try making the assumption that the music makers are speaking to you directly, even calling you by name. Try to listen for what the players, composers, recording engineers, and producers are actually telling you. There are two sides to this: What are we being given? and What are we being asked for?

What we are being given is the music, of course, but also the time, money, and care (or lack of those) that went into its making. What we are being asked for is a more complex issue: our attention perhaps, but how deeply are we being asked to engage? We are usually being asked for our money, but not always. Is our approval wanted? Our love? Are we being persuaded to have a good time along with everyone else within earshot? Are we being propagandized, brought to some allegiance, or point of view? Or imbued with courage so we can destroy the wicked enemy? Maybe we're supposed to buy a particular brand of beer, or simply spend more money while we're in the store. Maybe the intention is to guide us to some higher realm or other. Or is it to scare the bejesus out of us? Maybe this is a test to see if we belong to a certain club whose code is this very music — if we can break the code, we're in the club; if not, get lost. Music is a powerful tool, and powerful people have learned to use it with great skill.

This could be a fine subject for an entire book, but my only interest right now is in presenting questions that you might find useful to ask when listening to various kinds of music. The intention isn't to distance yourself from the music, although asking such questions might seem to do so at first. The idea is to point out a personal dimension of listening that could be easy to miss. When somebody asks me for something, I want to be clear about what is wanted. Following are some questions that have come up for me, across a variety of musical styles, about what I'm being asked for and what I'm being told.

Pop—What is our fascination with the glossy cover, the saturated surface, the magnified and amplified persona? Who's on that huge screen, him or me? We need to adulate some version of ourselves—self as Guitar Hero—but how does that affect the way I actually hear the music? Even though I've felt my own self succumb from time to time, I've never understood the psychology of Superman or Superwoman. I do know that music marketers understand it well enough to make millions for themselves and others. I do know that the image of a world in love with me, me, me is a very compelling one, and I know how that makes me a fair mark for exploitation. I know also that I want to be part of a group that loves the same music as much as I do (whether it's small: the Machaut Motet Club, or huge: the Mainstream Miles Club), because then I'm part of a mob of like-minded souls, we are all in love the same way, and I feel safe. But what about the musicians themselves? Don't they all want love, just like me? It couldn't be power only, or could it? I'm not so sure. What is Madonna saying? What does she need? What did Michael Jackson need, for God's sake? Or Elvis? Or Judy Garland? Are they victims or heroes, or both? It's complicated. That's why it makes sense, at least sometimes, to ask them directly while deeply in the act of hearing their music. They just might let slip their little secret, or yours. Would you then hear them differently?

Rap and hip-hop—We seem to be listening for some vestige of tribal power and connectivity, and yet rap is just as equally about how those very values so easily turn chaotic in Western civilization. We need an affirmation of a certain kind of primal power and are confronted with its attenuation and dissolution as it is multilaterally exploited in the marketplace. Maybe it's better to just get out there and dance: go along with it, don't make trouble. American popular music is a very complex business. The questions do persist, however.

Electronic music—Using the most general definition, all recorded music, from wax cylinders to flash drives, is electronic music. Whenever the music is neither live nor acoustic, there is a human/not-human cusp. My sense of the contemporary music scene is that more often than not we are being asked to weigh in on the angst-filled issue of how OK it is for humans to be controlled by what is not-human; and judging from the bionic nature of much contemporary music, the plurality seems to swing well into the "It's OK" side. But my question is, isn't this some Faustian bargain? Aren't we sleeping with the enemy because it seems so practical and safe? Doesn't that sort of... turn you into them? If the medium is the message, and electronic music, especially computer-generated music, flattens the message and increases distance from inner knowledge, aren't we, more and more, stimulating a visceral response to otherness? Isn't the whole range of electronic music a modern confrontation with virtual soul? Isn't that some sort of modern diabolic possession saga? If there is *any* bell of recognition in these questions, Dear Reader-of-Shambhala-Books, how does it affect your listening to electronic music? How can you personally ask a synthesizer what it is telling you, or asking from you? Well, you ask the very person of the synthesizer *player,* of course. Yet how can the player know what the computer is saying? Well, he listens more or less carefully to the patch—that's his way of asking the programmer. And how does the programmer know? He asks the marketing folks up on the sixth floor. And how do *they* know? Well, they ask you, of course. And how do *you* know? Hence these questions you might ask.

Dance music — To understand the meaning of dance music, ask your body while you are dancing; it will know. If you don't dance, ask the dancers; they will ask their bodies and show you the answer. For dance music, I think, what the music is telling you, and what it is asking of you, are one and the same.

Concert music — What we consider "art music" — music that is intended to be listened to, originally in salons or concert halls, for its own sake — is the music that allows you to question it most directly, because that music was generally composed to fully engage, amuse, fulfill, and uplift the listener. Reciprocally, listeners typically have been willing to give such music their full attention. So a certain transparency is written into the contract. The upshot is that when you ask a piece of "serious" art music what it wants to tell you and what it needs from you, and ask the same questions from the players who are in the act of performing it for you, the answer is usually pretty simple: *Your best ears.* But music is made by humans, and the limitations of the human condition are rarely fully suspended. Mixed into the pure intentions of concert music are the ambitions and career moves of the music makers: the need for recognition, further commissions, tenure, approval, and love. Love my composition, love me. And if you don't like my piece, you clearly don't understand it, so you're not in the club, too bad for you. In the last generation, much has been done to give the widest possible range of listeners a sense of comfort in the concert hall (it's called *outreach*), with predictably mixed results. If you want to find out the future of concert music for yourself, go to a concert and ask the music — really ask it — what it is telling you and what it wants from you.

Mozart—Mozart is a special case. He is the one composer I know of who sounds absolutely wonderful when you listen to him (especially the later works) and absolutely wonderful when you don't (in a restaurant, or daydreaming). I've been studying how this could be true ever since I was ten, and although I can talk about it for a week, I think the reason I can't explain it is the same reason that it's true. Mozart simply knew what I wanted to hear when I wanted to hear it. End of subject.

Music tangential to Western culture—This category includes Turkish pop, Thai pop, Bollywood, Japanese punk bands, European jazz, and so on—that is, all music that has been more or less influenced by Western music but retains its own distinct flavor. The temptation for the Western (especially American) listener is to feel proprietary about "our" music, which can lead to unfavorable comparisons. It is sometimes difficult to come enough to terms with a foreigner's accent, or his downright butchering of our language, to hear the truth of what is being said. So in the case of music that is only half familiar, your questions, "What are you telling me?" and "What do you need from me?" need to be especially sincere.

Music outside the influence of Western culture—Yes, there is still quite a bit of it, though you might have to search beyond your usual paths of discovery. Indonesian court music, Indian raga (northern and southern), tribal and indigenous music, ancient or contemporary are all available by searching the Web. Nonesuch Records, the Smithsonian, YouTube, Amazon, plus many, many Web sites will guide you if you look. Since some music of the wide-flung world is quite distinct from anything you've likely heard, an honest inquiry into the intentions of the music makers is especially illuminating. The stranger the music, the greater the need to know, and the greater the need for deep listening. A given piece of music might objectively *sound* the same from one culture to another, but perceived quite differently from culture to culture. So, can you listen with another culture's ears? Or anyone's ears but your own? Maybe not. But I know that the Edison Disc shaman (who appeared at the end of chapter 7) was too much for me to understand when I was a child because I was too busy being scared to ask him what he wanted. As it turns out, I didn't have to be scared.

Listening at Every Order of Magnitude

Wave by wave, human consciousness is jostled awake by sound. Your whole self is a symphony of response to distant thunder, a single footstep, the sound of skin on skin — these are the sounds of the human theater. The sounds of the cosmic theater are mostly out of human range, but we can intuit them. With respect to our vision, however, we don't need to pretend, since we have microscopes and telescopes and can see the molecular and galactic landscape for ourselves. Now imagine how life would change if our ears could quite naturally hear at the scale of an electron microscope. And what would we hear at the surface of the sun? What would you hear if the sun were your own body?

This is an amusing fantasy, but it can be useful in learning to hear music more completely. What would a violin sound like from the point of view of the bow? Or from the vantage point of the wood cells inside the taut bridge? What would you hear if you were an air molecule inside a flute? Or a sodium ion carrying an electric charge inside your brain? Would your tree-body hear thunderstorms as jam sessions? What siren songs does the black hole at the center of our Milky Way sing?

Sometimes I zoom out and zoom in like this while I'm listening to music. The purpose isn't to arrive at some other place, but to come back home. Even if I've been gone for only a second or two, the sound of home is then so much sweeter. Our greatest music is only a tiny piece of this universe, and it never sounds so fulfilling as when we've just returned from the road.

The Real Work

The core work of the enlightened listener is not so much about listening as about consciousness—consciousness focused through the ears. This is inner work, more rewarding as it becomes more familiar.

When I was in second grade, my teacher would knock her knuckles on her noggin to embarrass some vacant-stared boy who could not answer a question. "*Nobody home,*" she would crow to the class with a baleful wink. That was mean. Now, sixty-five years later, I think somebody *was* home, just not where *she* called home. But she did get the metaphor right. I like the idea of *home* for where your conscious mind lives. Consider this right now for a second with your eyes closed. What could be more homey than your sense of how it feels to be alive in your skin at this moment?

I don't sense my consciousness as a home full of rooms, though. It's more like a vast territory—partly known, partly unexplored—full of beloved landmarks and shifting boundaries. Most of the time we let what we are seeing and whatever we are thinking lead us through this territory of ours, as though we were walking through a gallery of images while holding on tightly to a string of thoughts. Yet you can learn, even in a noisy world, to let sound—not the images you see, or the thoughts you think, but what your ears hear—be your trusted shepherd though your home territory. And with some practice, and some well-considered choices, the music you love becomes a trustworthy guide through your native land.

RECLAIMING THE GODDESS
Pernicious Ubiquity

Imagine a country where hugging and kissing strangers is absolutely mandatory—on elevators, in corridors, in restaurants, whenever you're shopping or walking in the park. You can scarcely be in public for a moment without a squeeze or a big smooch from anyone who wants to have one, whether you want them to or not, whether they've been eating a hot dog with mustard on it or not. With nothing to say about it, you have to give away your choices for intimacy and affection, your autonomy. Sometimes this works out quite well—a beautiful kiss, a loving hug—but your personal space is no longer personal. That is how I feel about my culture's obsession with and addiction to its musical soundtrack: I have had to give away my ears.

Life's ubiquitous flood of recorded music offers me two options: deaden my ears or change my attitude. If I deaden my ears, then music tends to flatten out, the spacious landscapes of the master painters become wallpaper, and what has been dear is now cheap. One does not want to be put in the position of being forced to not listen. That would be like not feeling someone's touch. But because background music is so often a mandatory condition in public, it is a very difficult position to escape. After all, there is *music* in the American air, better by far than bursting bombs. On the other hand, if I accept what comes, I'll probably be a more docile camper, and maybe I'll even learn to exercise compassion for those obsessed rather than react against the object of obsession. So the option I seem to have chosen (and I think I'm not alone) is a little bit of both.

Ever-present recorded music has indeed given my ears a kind of chronic exhaustion, like aural jet lag, but I retreat to silence whenever I can, choose acoustic music when there is a choice, and pick the recorded music I actually do listen to with great care. I protect my ears, but at the same time try to accept the constant jingle of commercial music as a characteristic of human life here on this planet at this time. It seems to be just as much a part of being a contemporary human as the sound of our breathing, so what's wrong with being who we are?

Goddess as Sex Slave

Taking the historical view, however, music has definitely lost some of its guidance cred. Up until a few decades ago, music was the harbinger of momentous transformations of the cultural zeitgeist, the deepest expression of the survival of populations, and, generally, a repository of what we have collectively held to be our best knowledge. Music has been Our Goddess of the Guiding Vibe. However, as recorded products have become more compact, convenient, cheap, and available, and as broadcast music has become more and more prevalent, our dear goddess has been sold in a million markets to the highest bidder. We've captured her and used her for our innocuous or nefarious purposes with scarcely a thought toward her lost honor. We've trapped her in strategically placed overhead three-inch speakers so we can sell more frozen pizzas. We've compressed her onto our iPods, where she can be either a welcome companion or an engine of escape, whatever works, as long as her pimps get paid. We use her as a shield against having to actually experience our inner lives, and as a barrier to what is present in the outer world. One night we treat her like the sacred being she is, bathe ourselves in her wisdom and generosity, and praise her bounty. The next night we abuse her without looking back. We are both alarmed and amused at the caricature of isolated preteens wrapped hermetically in their earbuds and game boxes, oblivious to the living world just inches away, but the caricature is far more applicable to adult culture than most adults suspect. Music as a way of avoiding our deeper selves is not terribly destructive, really, just a waste of human potential, an evolutionary drag.

Live Music Gives Live Energy; Electronic Music Gives Electronic Energy

Part of the reason you can get energy from listening to acoustic music is because music emanates from matter, from stuff, and imparts that stuff's energy. So we can feel the wood and wire in the piano when we listen to live piano music. In recorded music or amplified music, the stuff is electronic, and it comes over plasticized cardboard speakers, so we get electronic energy through stiff chemo-paper, not caloric energy generated by living tissue. Even in recorded acoustic music, the acoustic energy is translated into electronic energy, and some essence is lost in the translation. The more the medium is electronic, the more it becomes the focus, and when the medium is the object, the subject has changed. In this case the subject has become the bionic relationship between human listener and electronic source. Typically today, a kid's first reference is not Mozart, not the Beatles, not even 50 Cent, but the soundtracks of video games.

Just as responsible eaters should know where their food comes from, responsible listeners should be conscious of where the sounds they hear are coming from. A forest animal is completely invested in tracing sounds to their sources. What could be the consequences of losing that investment entirely? How many degrees of separation has civilization placed between a living source and the music we hear? Listening on earbuds, in the car, in airplanes (even with fancy earphones) are all simply more degrees of separation from acoustic, live music played by living beings. Just as processed food is removed from the field, my recorded voice is removed from your ear.

You can't listen to everything you hear, and you can't not listen to everything you hear. Your task is to strike the right balance, but that task needs to be preceded by an awakened curiosity about what indeed is in the air. The first question to ask is, Do you care? The second is, How much? The next thing to ask is, What is electronic music really telling me, and do I choose to hear that? And finally, What do I have by way of reply? The aim isn't to change the world, but to pay attention to what is present, and then, if necessary, to develop a strategy to protect what is rightfully yours. That is one way that world change happens.

Mary Oliver and Nature

In her books, the American poet Mary Oliver demonstrates a kind of ideal relationship between life and nature. She walks into the woods most every day and then comes home and finishes her poems. Nature has become such an intrinsic part of her life that when she writes about nature, she is writing her life. I want to extrapolate back and forth between life and music the way Ms. Oliver does between nature and poetry. To some extent I've done this: I live in the country where it is mostly quiet, spend most of my time at home doing mostly contemplative things: practicing, composing, writing, teaching, and being domestic. I mix only marginally with the big world. Pretty much I own my ears, and that is pretty much the most precious thing I can say about my life. But what if I lived on the Lower East Side, or near a noisy factory, or across the street from a 24/7 air conditioner screaming atop a Safeway roof (that did happen), or in the slums of Delhi? What kind of music would I compose? What kind of poetry would Mary Oliver write if she walked in the South Bronx every day? Maybe Ms. Oliver would be a better poet (although that is difficult to imagine). Maybe I'd be a better composer, or write a different sort of music altogether, or none at all.

Folks have to navigate their own conditions as best they can. I speak of Ms. Oliver and her nature walks because we know how especially rewarding it is to carefully observe nature. But recorded music has become about as special as paint, and about as carefully observed. Gentle Listener, I don't want you to be discontent, but I do want you to care about what is precious, not just for your own sake, but for everyone else's also. How you listen to what is within earshot has significance beyond your own ears.

Plato's Mistake (and Ours)

Plato had a good idea about the reciprocity between heaven and earth, but he didn't see his own way of seeing as a part of it. As quantum physics has been trying to tell us for years, we are inexorably a part of the world we endeavor to describe. The light of your own mind illumines and frames whatever it apprehends, and that is true for sound generally and most particularly for music. Your listening to music is part of the meaning of the music itself, just as surely as your presence in the audience is part of the meaning of the play. The meaning of music and how you hear the music are two ends of a string. The sources *of* music and the listeners *to* music are swimmers in the same wavy mix. When you find and appreciate a piece of music that is right for you, you have found a part of yourself in the world, and to that extent, and in that quality, you have changed the world. The search starts with you and invariably comes back to you. "You think you are the seeker, and find you are the sought," wrote the Sufi teacher Sam Lewis, referring to one's search for the divine experience, into which category we now firmly place the music of this world, Plato notwithstanding.

THE RESPONSIBLE LISTENER

Fascinating and broad, the history of the world's music is the history of our far-flung evolution told in a wordless vibrational language. Music is an evolutionary feedback loop: it brings us forward and we bring it forward, the more so as we hear it deeply. You can locate your position in the loop by taking stock of the music you're attracted to. We humans are all pulling the same barge loaded with the same evolutionary cargo, and most of us end up choosing to throw our full weight onto the ropes. That means keeping our spaces clean, raising our kids well, honoring our parents, and giving back what we've been given, *plus* that extra little evolutionary sliver, that something gathered up and paid forward that is the purpose of each life.

Some music hangs around for a long time because it continues to define its listeners well after its prescient makers are gone. Those makers have served as the musician-guardians of our evolutionary intelligence, and we cherish them. At the same time, as we go forward we become more complex, and so does our Logos, and so do our codes of communication, including music. We look for guidance where we can find it, and the restless search for the newest music, the next thing, the freshest spark, the brightest beacon is what drives the pop mill. Beneath the frenzy of the Next Thing is the question: Who am I right now? And *now*, two hours later, let me look into a new mirror to see what I've become. Even music that has been around for centuries, like Bach, is still popular music. Believe me, when we don't need Bach anymore, he will go the way of Al Jolson (the 1920s, kids) or Frankie Lane (so soon you forget?). The hidden makers of indie music, the struggling composers of art music, the concert impresarios, the bestowers of grants and awards, all weigh in on the question: Who are we now? The time scale for "great" music might be flexible, but the driving principle is everywhere the same: we want mirrors that tell us who we are and intimate who we might become. Art music and pop music all do their part, because all music is part pop-mind, part wisdom-mind.

The culture's music can keep the evolutionary mind awake, but can any one of us afford to accept cultural choices as a done deal? Or are we obliged to fashion our culture's tastes to fit our own individual needs? The answer is that you *are* the culture, even and especially if you think of yourself as counterculture. The evolutionary impulse that brought us this far needs, in order to persevere, one thing only: your awareness. When you fashion your listening to your own best lights, when you become discerning and, in a word, *picky*, you are being responsible not only to yourself; you are also being responsive to the needs of all humans. All that is necessary is for you to make real choices that are truly meaningful for yourself. From that point on, your discernment spreads out in concentric circles beyond your family, friends, and social life to the quality of life on the planet. Does this mean that when you choose your music mindfully and engage in it willfully you participate actively in the evolution of the whole of humanity?

Yes, it does.

What to Do: A Fast and a Feast

How can you learn to appreciate the value of your own listening? I don't mean the intentional listening most of us already do, like your playlist, or the concert you shell out bucks for. I mean everything that life presents to your ears, willing or not. There are surely ways to take control of your ears that are gradual and kind. But let me suggest an industrial-strength method to reclaim your listening health and bolster your ears' integrity: Go on a hard fast. For a full week, stop listening to all recorded music whatsoever, all surrogates for the real thing. This means music in commercials, on TV, on the car radio, on CDs, mp3s, iPods, all music produced by any media machine of any kind, everything in fact except nonamplified acoustic music produced by living people in real time. Dial your time machine back to 1877, before Edison's first phonograph, when the clip-clop of horses' hooves were as common as rap beats are now. As a preliminary, close your eyes and try to imagine such a soundscape. No internal combustion engines! Live acoustic music only! Then, as much as due diligence will allow, try to reproduce those conditions in your environment. Do it 24/7, which works out to about ten thousand media-free, Amish-like seconds.

Of course, unless you actually are Amish, or a hermit, this is nearly impossible. In the process of trying to avoid it, you are bound to notice how ubiquitous recorded music is. Noisy neighbors, the roommate or spouse not thinking twice about TV ads (after all, who listens?), plus, of course, every public area under the stars. No wonder our ears are three-quarters shut. In the process of tuning in you'll discover how tuned-out you've become. Even if you can control little or none of your sound environment, however, you will begin to notice more and more what actually is there—everything there is to be heard, in fact—and that is a very good start indeed.

Abstaining from recorded music may give you an opportunity to notice music you may have missed. You could sing, or ask someone to sing to you while you actually listen, warts and all, no joke. With any success, you may find yourself thrown back to the days when the sound of a violin, or lute, or flute, or a gently sung, half-remembered tune was sweet as sun after rain and just as welcome. You may hear a strain so beautiful that you'll be amazed how you could ever have forgotten what you now so keenly remember. The resonances of real live bodies, real wood, real breath streaming through real pipes is so compelling and fulfilling as to make strong women weep and young men cry for no apparent reason.

When you do go back to listening to recorded music by choice, try to hear what you're actually hearing, which is, to some degree, the medium itself—the flattening and compression of the music, the artifice of the mix, and its spatial allocation to speakers. This is not to make you discomfited, just a bit more choosey. It *is* more possible to live well in the outer world if the inner world is awake.

There is one more part to this exercise. To fully reclaim music as your own, you need to be able to listen so deeply that you can hear your own stillness inside it, even inside the most turbulent, restless music. The exercise is to listen within yourself for what does not move. When you find that, then it is truly you who is listening.

234

The Proactive Listener

In a society that has almost entirely withdrawn its support from publicly financed music education, it is not difficult to find opportunities to be a proactive listener. First and foremost, support music education in public schools, especially the younger grades. Kids should sing daily under the guidance of teachers who are clear and joyous in their singing. Support legislators who favor arts education if there are any, and if there aren't, spearhead a constituency. Since this is not only a local issue, but a regional, state, and national concern, support arts councils at every level, especially in their efforts, which are legion, to encourage music to become once again part of the core curriculum from preschool onward. Politics is personal — make your views known. Volunteer to teach kids music if you are willing and able. Research in cognitive neuroscience has demonstrated definitively that we learn in proportion to our mind's ability to make connections and grow in response to its environment. Study after study has shown that musical training increases the mind's *plasticity*, its ability to learn across disciplines. The corpus callosum, which connects the two hemispheres of the brain, is larger in musicians; musicians also develop a relatively thicker outer cortex. This doesn't mean that musicians are necessarily smarter than other people; only that a given person will typically learn more readily if he or she is liberally exposed to music.

Think about this. Arm yourself with your own research into the value of music education in childhood development, then beat the drum for it. Beyond that, attend music events you like or suspect you might like. Take kids to grown-up stuff, especially symphony and chamber concerts. Encourage their interest (and your own) in *any* music in *any* style. There is no best music.

As far as invasions of your own listening space are concerned, complain about (or praise) on-hold music. Take your opinion to the supervisor and beyond. Make your preferences known about music in public places. Be adamant. It is absolutely OK to get restaurant managers to turn the music down, or change it, or even turn it off. Likewise in stores, or anywhere you might have a voice, which is, remarkably, just about everywhere. Keep your eye out for local sound-ordinance legislation issues. Lobby for your point of view, and get your friends involved. Don't be held sound-hostage by anyone—locally, regionally, or globally. Sometimes if you make enough noise you get some quiet in return.

The pages from here to the end of the chapter are meant primarily for readers actively engaged (or interested) in music practice. However, even if you are not presently practicing music you may discover that the concerns of active musicians are surprisingly relevant to your own life, so please feel welcome to these pages.

PRACTICING MUSIC AND MAKING MUSIC

While it is true that all musicians learn some version of craft, what is less obvious is that all craft, whether it be vocal, instrumental, improvisational, or compositional, depends on the Ur-craft of listening. Each musician could write his or her "Autobiography of a Listener," a personal history of listening epiphanies. In lieu of my own, here are a few comments focused on the listening aspects of practicing, composing, and performing music.

The Green Light of Listening

Almost everyone who practices music knows that the experience of deep listening comes and goes. A certain amount of practice time is spent half listening, or hardly listening, and precisely in proportion to how one is not fully listening, that is time wasted. How can you control your listening concentration so that you are learning (and enjoying) the music as fully as possible?

The trick is to wait. For one precious moment before you play, don't play. When your ears are not present, let there be a cautionary yellow light. Take a breath. When you are lost in thought or fantasy, let there be a red light. Get up, turn around, and sit down again. When your ears are clear, let shine the green, and you will be free to love what you are doing.

This is especially true when a lot of repetition is involved in the course of practice. Before each and every reiteration you must make a clear space for your ears to open and fill with silence. Don't proceed until the green light of listening is on. Wait for the moment of pure listening to arise, just as a pitcher waits for the moment of pure concentration to guide the pitch. You can train yourself to do this *on a single in-breath;* on the out-breath make music. In a kind of body-awareness training known as the Alexander Technique, thinking about the result instead of the action is called "end-gaming," which takes you away from the game's present moment. If you deliberately make an empty space for your listening to become focused, the path of the music itself will become clear.

The Open Secret of Listening

The open secret of listening lies in listening to really basic stuff. It takes a master musician to listen completely to musical elements. The reason such completeness is ultimately important is that the components of music, like the components of matter, are configured with exquisite interdependence. The complexities that arise in music can be fully realized only when the elemental components are clearly perceived and deeply held.

One of the best examples I know of this comes up very early in the study of music: hearing two tones at once. At first, the hearing of "intervals" is perceived merely as melodic distance: two tones are distant from one another by, for instance, "a major second," and that's all you need to know. But as music making becomes more refined, the ability to hear two simultaneously sounding tones independently becomes more crucial, and the student must pause and ask, "Am I really hearing this?" Next time you are near a keyboard, play (and hold down) middle C and the D directly above it. Be sure to strike both at the same time. Your first impression may be a thick braid of sound, but try listening first for the upper pitch, then the lower. Anyone can hear that two tones are sounding together, but only a clear ear can hear their mutual streaming *and* the independence of their voices at the same time. My secret suspicion is that I don't think *anybody* hears two tones at once: I think the ear scans dozens of times per second, like old TV picture tubes, and the *effect* is of two independent voices sounding simultaneously. As one of my advanced students says, "It really scrambles your radar." It is nonetheless possible to train yourself to hear two tones both simultaneously and individually, as if they were two separate beings utterly absorbed in one another, the union of lovers.

Gently play the two tones again and again, each time letting them sound for as long as they are audible, each time separating them in your ear, then putting them back together as a single harmony, then separating, then putting back together. Most of the music you hear is made up of hundreds of such events every minute. Polyphonic music especially is requesting you to do this work continuously — optional if you are a listener, mandatory if you are a player.

There is an overwhelming beauty in the syntheses of polyphony when you first begin to hear them. Yet it needs to be led by your intentional, energetic, cognitive act of analysis, of separation. Yes, it is difficult, but it's not the music that's difficult, it's getting yourself clear enough to hear the music. At the level of clarity I'm speaking of, understanding music and experiencing it are the same thing. Music, fully heard, is self-revealing.

Two Composers on Practice

Easley Blackwood: "Practice is the art of turning the impossible into the familiar."

Pyotr Ilyich Tchaikovsky: "What was difficult becomes easy and what was easy becomes beautiful."

Practice as Waves

In an essay titled "I, Poet," Maureen Hurley likens a poem to a stone thrown in the pond of our collective consciousness: a small splash, then concentric ripples spreading out into the conscious dimension of the larger pool of humanity. I think the same is true for any music you make, not just a symphony or a song, but a simple tune sung in the shower. This is also true for everyday practice, no matter how private you think it is. The truth is, waves make waves, and you don't know where they all go, or how they all connect, and you couldn't stop them even if you did.

Music as Teacher

As you learn music, it reveals who you are in relationship to self, culture, and the sacred. At first it is all about you, and you own yourself ferociously. Gradually, you begin to notice how music has been developed through others and given as a gift to the world you are part of, and you slip into that stream and discover your humanity there. Music then becomes for you the lens of creation through which you can give yourself up entirely into the nature of being. Who is the teacher here? All of us and none of us. The teacher is music, the teacher's teacher is sound, and when that has been learned you can begin at last.

Tough Love

True practice—when your listening is focused and your musical memory is awake—addresses the challenge of rewiring, or newly wiring, the brain. New habits are constantly being formed, which means that new circuits are being connected. We experience these new circuits as memory—we remember what we've learned, and we can retrieve it whole or piecemeal at any time. Musicians learn to remember everything from bodily coordinated routines, to scales and chordal patterns, to long rivers of sound transmitted aurally or from the page. Memorizing music makes you smarter, better connected and, all else being equal, healthier. It is an ameliorative for any brain, but most particularly the aging brain. Geezer brains (like mine) need new pathways to stay alive: it's grow or die. Learning music—not necessarily from the page, but simply the sounds you are working with, *really* learning them until they live comfortably in you—is for the most of us very hard work. Even the most loving teachers often have to be tough cops and insist that students do the inner of work of hearing. That takes courage for student and teacher alike. Sometimes the student's inner sanctum is so well guarded that extremely tactful strategies are called for. Whatever the case, for both teacher and student there needs to be an uncompromising concentration on consciousness through sound. Then the real teacher is free to teach.

Computer Mind

Gun lobbyists say that guns don't harm people, people harm people; the same thing might be said about computers. Having been born prior to 1985, I know nothing about computers,

I have no way of addressing the subject that isn't based on my own paralysis, not unlike my relationship to guns. I compose music as far from a computer as possible, and have my scores engraved in Finale or Sibelius (computer music-writing software) by my students in exchange for composition lessons. Not to change the subject, I write the first draft of all my prose manuscripts in longhand and edit them subsequently with a word processor. With continuous grumbling, I do use e-mail, though I lure my correspondents into real-time phone conversations whenever there is the option. I can scarcely remember the last time I sent or received a proper letter in proper longhand, much less the six-page confessional masterpiece that lays bare one's heart, and this makes me weep and cry out. That having been said, I confess to surfing the Web just as glibly as everyone else alive and to having become dependent on Microsoft Word to organize and edit everything I write. Indeed, I find it impossible to conceive how books ever managed to get turned out in the old, dark days before Word. As a writer, my only question is: Has word processing affected, generally speaking, the quality of writing? My answer is: Yes, for both better and worse, but I don't want to talk about writing. I want, double please, to talk about music.

A few pages ago, we were speaking — well, actually I was ranting — about the give and take involved in listening to electronic music of all kinds. Now we have come to the question of the effect of using computers in the practice of musical composition. Computers are used for composition in two ways. The first (and oldest) is to generate computer-shaped sounds of any sort that can be manipulated variously either for recording or for live, spontaneous performance. The second is to aid the composition of music by providing synthesized instrumental and vocal approximations in order to guide the ear of the composer. There is every sort of mixture among these two usages. Each used separately has influenced the aesthetics of modern music;

it is in their mixture that the most telling shift in the contemporary ear has occurred.

In regard to the first case—computer-generated music with no acoustic instrument interface—this listener experiences such use as sometimes ingenious, sometimes thoroughly engaging, and *always* cold, search as I may for warmth, much less compassion. For me, it's a chilly medium. Yet I think the chill is the point, by which I mean that it appeals very seductively to the computer part of *us*, which is, of course, an undeniable part. But our computer part is a weeny part, so I am always left wanting the bigger part, the heart part. Nonetheless I actively encourage my composition students, if they are computer-savvy, to experiment freely, because the investigation of the capabilities of computer algorithms, and the creation of new ones, plays directly into that messing-around mentality of creating your own infrastructure, and messing around is how one creates music. The only problem: many composers stop there, and *there* is not far enough.

In regard to the second case, computer-directed synthesis of sounds of traditional acoustic instruments, some considerable deterioration of compositional standards have occurred as a result of this widespread practice, or so I think. The culprit is glibness. Increasingly since the 1980s, composers have taken to improvising their ideas into the computer and then asking the machine to manipulate them until they sound OK. The result, more often than not, is that they sound OK. This is not inspiration. This is not listening in the dark-dark and trusting the muse. This is messing around with machines, and attractive as that may be, it is not an end result. When it is accepted as the same, the outcome is disappointing. When listening to a piece of music composed later than 1975, I can always tell the ratio between what is heard and what is computer-derived. I am now speaking directly to composers who use computers at any stage of the process of composition: DON'T FORGET YOUR EARS! Unless you want to turn into R2-D2, in which case I take it all back.

Perhaps the most interesting mixture of machine and natural resonance occurs when synthesized and computerized tracks are mixed with live musicians playing in real time. This is an intriguing version of sleeping with the enemy. So is jet travel, which compromises both walking and sailing, but gets you there in time for tea. When I hear computer sounds mixed tastefully with live acoustic sounds, I figure we might as well learn to live with the Blue Meanies, that is, master our symbiosis with the robotic mind. My life-and-death question to you, Mortal Listener, is: To what extent, if any, do we need to resist this? This is a real question, and in posing the question I've said enough. It's your turn.

Speaking for myself, however, I do honor my first drafts of prose in their everlastingly sloppy cursive. Whenever I write a first draft on a computer, the result is gloss, or terminally misshapen. And my musical scores always appear first in gleaming graphite. The act of typing sounds into a computer program, or improvising them at the keyboard into a notation program cannot ever (for me) substitute for the stream of internal hearing required for glyph notation. I need to have the words flowing into my hand and into the pen's liquid ink, and the tones running down my arm into a pencil making beautiful signs in a mystery script. It *must* make a difference, and it does.

Job Description

Musicians train to be continuously open to the sound stream, both audible and cosmic. We learn to never not listen. The more you recognize this, the more you recognize that your inner being was created to tune in and be present, not unlike animals, not unlike saints.

ONE LAST QUESTION FOR EVERYONE
Why is music like Pure Mind?

Because it's too close to be recognized,
too easy to believe, too deep to grasp,
too amazing to be understood by the intellect,
and is realized in practice.

10

Living the Waves

My primary purpose in this book has been to point out a more direct path to clear listening. This has been motivated partly by my pleasure in sharing aural delight—the wildness in a pan's clang, the plumb beauty of two simultaneous tones. Another purpose has been to point out how sound in general and music in particular connect humans to humans and humanity to the cosmos. Music is the throne of our kind, empowering us to appreciate how tiny we are, and how vast. I want you to have clear access to music's powers and, most of all, to recognize them as your own. In this chapter we will revisit, reexamine, replenish, and reflect upon some of the metaphors we've used for the connective and expansive powers of music.

THE BRIDGE METAPHOR

A bridge goes *to* somewhere and it also *is* somewhere. It is and it connects. When you are listening to music you are standing on a bridge, absorbing its vibrations and becoming its waves of energy. Its waves move outward, touching and connecting in every dimension. When you become waves of music, you can feel the connection between your bony body and your energetic mind. You can experience yourself as a splendid human among splendid humans. You can sense your relationship to all energy from the littlest to the biggest bang, from cosmically vast and long ago to vanishingly small and now. You are at once discrete and continuous, somewhere and everywhere.

The Alchemy of self and Self

Learning to listen, to practice, and to compose music can seem to be primarily concerned with something external, but it is really an internal journey. As your perceptions refine, your sense of self refines also, turning your dross to gold just as the early alchemists used the refining of lead into gold as a metaphor for finding truth. The elements of musical refinement are *your* body, *your* heart, *your* psyche, history, and life quest. During a recent discussion about her work, a poet friend of mine said, "What a lovely trick, to turn your raving hubris into poetry." I think this is true not only for poetry but across all the arts. Refinement of my own sensibilities from little self to sacred Self has surely been the focus of my own experience as a musician and a teacher of musicians, my own best shot at the alchemy of refinement—for myself and for the world.

Play, Practice, and Survival

Killer whales have been observed to teach their offspring techniques of beaching and escaping (entering and leaving shallows to capture seals) through play. Those who have learned these skills make better hunters. Pixel and Sunny, our two male kittens, spent several months ferreting out our socks from the laundry, tossing them in the air, catching them, chewing holes in them, and then dutifully presenting us with the carcasses. Six months later, in place of the socks were dead voles, rats, and baby gophers. Animals seem to play for a variety of reasons: to learn locomotor skills, to learn social behavior, and to learn specific tasks like hunting and courting. Through play, the wisdom of a species is passed on to the young. Many animals and virtually all mammals play. The larger the animal's brain, and the higher its metabolic rate, the more likely it is to learn, through play, the lessons of cultural transmission. Humans have a tenacious passion for many varieties of play: sports, dancing, and social games (Scrabble and cards) come to mind. Some of us even develop into playful people.

The arts, especially music, seem most essentially to have codified the many regimens of learning cultural transmission through practice and play. From a very young age we learn through practicing and playing music how we are connected to the minutiae of survival. Through music we encode our relationships with each other, with culture, and with the world. The courtship and territorial wisdom of the Swainson's thrush, for instance, is taught to its fledglings by the male birds' example. Each spring along our creek we hear the attempts of the babies to replicate the complex arias of their parent—to me they sound for all the world like kids practicing "Für Elise." By midsummer the songs have been learned, and by the following year the students have become the teachers. I learned Beethoven as a kid, and jazz, and popular music also, and through these I learned how to think and use my body at the same time, how human beings get along with each other, how we externalize our inner lives, and how to add my own two cents to this wisdom and to transmit my particular version of cultural essence to everyone within earshot. I bring the fruits of my hunt to the feet of my peers, just like our kitties matter-of-factly present theirs.

The simple act of listening to music puts you in the stream of human wisdom—sacred and profane—and the deeper you listen, the wider the stream. Music practice, reiterative and private as it may seem at the time, is no different than the baby thrushes learning to come back next year and carry their species forward.

EMPTINESS AND TIME

With only the slightest prompt, music will show you its emptiness. The prompt is the question: *Where* is music? You can be touched by music, but you can't touch it—it's made out of motion. It is not concrete, not substantial. It is full of energy but empty of substance. It's nowhere specific; the energetic waves of music keep on keeping on to everywhere.

A similar question is: *When* is music? Even if a piece of music is given only a single performance, it can live on in the listener and its energies continue to change form and function forever—and forever is not a *when*. What if a piece is played repeatedly and becomes an icon in the culture? What if it's always in someone's ear? When is Beethoven's Fifth? When is the Beatles' "Here Comes the Sun"?

THE SURGE

Teachers of meditation are like music teachers in the sense that there is relatively little *information* germane to their subjects. What they are teaching is experience, and experience (as we are fond of saying) can't be taught, it has to be caught. At their best, teachers teach by their own example, each bringing into the present his or her own vibe, whether that be a quality of music or of consciousness itself. Yet along the way there usually needs to be some cognitive guidance, some verbal and conceptual signposts, useful descriptions of experience that may ring a bell. One day in my meditation class, we were trying to literally *come to terms* with the "fruition" aspect of practice, that is, describe what happens when lucidity and emptiness co-arise, when the substantial world and pure Mind are in resonance. "What's that like for you?" can be a pretty tough question for a meditator to speak to, although that is, of course, what dharma does attempt to speak to. At one point the teacher said that during those moments she always felt a surge of energy accompanied by an inner brightening. She called it "the surge," and that term rang my bell.

Later I thought about the surge and how it relates to my experience as a musician. When I am making music, there are times when everything goes right, when earth and heaven are smiling actual smiles, the atmosphere brightens, and I'm a kid soaring in a glider dream. Kid and dream, co-arising. That's the way it feels.

SUBTLE AND GROSS

What I also know about music firsthand is how gross it is, how dependent on limbs, lips, skin and bones, reeds, metal and wood, and the wee yet violent air storms we call sound waves. Subtle as music can seem, it is generated by the harsh manipulation of matter: cymbals, gongs, gut, and wire set forcefully in motion, vocal chords beating against themselves, taut lips screeching into metal tubes, reeds pleading their cases under pressure — all transmitted by turbulent molecules slamming into the thin skin of our eardrums. From the standpoint of mechanically setting matter into motion, music is about as subtle as a locomotive. Yet somehow music chugs along, using its primitive, material means to forge our light, to evaporate our mass into energy. In this sense, music is a subtle science, a vibrational philosophy. Through experience it teaches that our bodies are made of waves, sheer poofery. It lets us live in not only our solid, familiar world and the motions innate to its nature, but also the weightless world of the essence of things.

MIND AND MIND

The cognizing mind will lead you back to paradox every time. Music uses mind to take you beyond mind to Mind. It bridges mind and Mind, and weans you from the notion that Mind *contains* mind, that the world is a box in which we rattle about. This is the same mistake as assuming that the Zen elevator has a highest floor. It is also the fallacy of Plato's Heaven of Perfect Forms of which we are the mere shadows. If you give it your permission, music can successfully guide you away from the incompleteness of any totem, wizard, or sacred idea that associates vertical (or concentric) forms with positive and negative values.

What existence actually *is* is how we have come to be here at all. Wisdom consists in our timeline, our history, the entire messy, evolutionary lot of it. The hidden wizard behind the velvet curtain is actually our ancestors in every dimension. Every consideration of this wisdom from whatever angle is some piece of the hologram our minds latch onto — filtered cigarettes, fast cars, doughnuts, Doonesbury, Madonna, Adonoi, Ram, Allah, anywhere we happen to look for clues. Remember, it wasn't even Dorothy who pulled back the curtain revealing the wizard's true identity — it was Toto who got it right, blessings be upon his doggy intuition. It's the everyday magic of our lives in the history of lives that we finally learn to live by, not some conceptual wizardry. Wholeness comes from something we sense but cannot be: the whole hologram. That is the very something that music brings us closer to if we enter into it. A piece of music with its illusion of wholeness is a resonator of the whole, something that allows us to *feel* the wholeness before we drive home through traffic. Some music seduces us even further by taking us beyond our intentional search and onward into a transcendental state, using intelligence, as is the case with *koans,* to transcend intelligence.

CERTAINTY AND MYSTERY

If you are casting about for definitive answers, the only ones you'll be able to find are the ones that deepen the mystery. But when you stop looking and start feeling inside, then you yourself, you with the inquisitive gaze, become the answer. What was once mystery is now the clear bead of the present tense. When you hear music, its long streaming moment somatizes the mystery. That helps bring you 'round. You surely don't *have* to have chords, grooves, and beautiful tunes to be enlightened, but when music that sounds beautiful to you happens to be in the air, it's a little easier to remember that "the answer" is what is happening to you right now.

CONNECTING THE DOTS: THE MORPHING MODEL

I can think of at least one good reason why continuously morphing forms—animation and computer graphics for instance—are so aesthetically amusing. We seem to carry around with us an abiding sense of one single universal energy that changes continuously from form to form. Once we recognized the elegance of the formula $E=mc^2$, something in humankind got jostled awake. We seem to be more and more eager to accept the notion of our insubstantial nature with each passing generation. Thanks to graphic techniques, we can experience what our grandparents could only hallucinate. Most of us nowadays just love to see stuff turn into other stuff, like shape-shifters and werewolves and every magical transformation Ms. J. Rowling could think up for the Harry Potter books, each and every one an affirmation of the persistence of energy and the impermanence of form. Especially when listening to music, we can easily feel ourselves as squiggly energy fields, the motion of *is-ness* with its unlimited possibilities for formal expression. This speaks directly to musical processes of motific development, which allows a single musical idea to elongate, shrink, hide or leap forward, turn upside down or backward, appear at any height or angle, speed or distance, and renders the eight centuries of composers in our Western canon as true pioneers of morph-consciousness.

TONES AS LIVING IDEALS

Sometimes, especially when I am singing raga, I can the feel the affect of the different tones of a scale with such intensity that they come alive inside of me. It is true that I am the one singing, but the tones seem like autonomous energies, breathing through my mouth. Earlier I said that they seemed like gods and goddesses, whom one worships by realizing them through the voice. You could call this a kind of neo-Platonism in that the heavenly ideals of proportion are mirrored in the imperfect, flickering forms of our musical realizations, but I think it is more than that. I think the ideals are alive in us, and take us by the hand as would any good friend. Beethoven thought of music as a kind of living world, as though the organizations and patterns of music were a formal dimension of life. He is said to have said, "Music is the vibration in which the spirit lives, thinks, and invents." What I say is that if you pay close enough attention for long enough, music becomes alive in you.

FROM SOUND TO SOURCE:
THE MUSIC OF WANTING

The process of listening is permeated with a kind of sound-perfume: the stretching out of the ear's listening, the mind's fanning out, searching the sphere—all this has the scent of wanting in it. Music itself is a kind of wanting, the same kind as in wanting to be alive. It may be a leap, I know, to connect the primal, wanting-to-be-here ground of life with whatever music is, but for me, and for many musicians, that leap is realized in ongoing musical experience.

The feeling of listening outward toward a farther and farther sound horizon is not uncommon—think of trying to hear distant birdsong, or listening fearfully into danger: the intrusive footstep, the dreaded snap of a dry twig. What you hear takes time to get to you; the farther out, the longer it takes. So when you hear outward you also hear backward in time, like seeing light that originated in a star a billion light years ago. What dawns eventually is your perception of a sound as moving backward to the time *before* the dead twig, back before the sapling and the nourishing of the seed, back through the formation of the soil, the cooking of the earth's crust, its condensation from stellar stuff, and before that, atom-less plasma, then, Bang, then racing back to now. Every sound you hear goes back to its origin.

The curious thing about the Big Bang, though, is that even though it led directly to the imprinting of the overtonal pattern of its waves (in the ratio of 3:2:1) on the heavens for us to observe 14 billion years later, there was at the time no sound as we understand it now, no media (like air) for it to pass through, and no us to hear it. The *first* sound was silent, get it? So: If we all are so connected up with the first sound, could that be what we mean when we talk about the silence inside the sounds we hear? Well, I don't get it myself, at least not when I think about it. I'll settle for listening to Mozart in the dark.

$$1 = \infty$$

Millions of us in dozens of tongues have said *God is One,* or have said it in the past, or have heard it said. We also say *one penny* knowing exactly what we mean. We also say *God is infinite.* So if God is infinite and God is One, why isn't one infinite? The answer is that we use *One* and *one* in different ways, yet the fact that we use the same word leads us to ask why and how they are different. Maybe there is a place where one and One are not distinct.

Saying that one equals infinity smacks of a cute bumper sticker. I know it can annoy rational people. It is a kind of mind-play that seems antithetical to analytical thought. What distinguishes the $1 = \infty$ model, however, is this: as a given component becomes more and more elemental, its connectivity to other dimensions increases. When you reduce to the most elemental level, what you were pursuing has vanished *as itself,* yet the connectivity appears multilaterally. This could be called a kind of transcendent reductionism. I suppose the most simplistic possible interpretation of string theory (that would be mine) to be that each string is potentially entangled with every other. The closer you get to the level of single string, the more potential for connectivity there is, so at the level of a single string can be found the greatest degree of connectivity. The Dalai Lama says, in *The Universe in a Single Atom: The Convergence of Science and Spirituality,* "Given the profound interconnectedness of everything in the universe, it is not possible to have total knowledge of even a single atom unless one is omniscient."

When I listen to music, the smallest bit of it seems to have the power to universalize my sensibilities. Even a single tone — *especially* a single tone — can make me feel energetically whole. A tone begins as an acoustic wave which, through its various transformations of energies, becomes a few ions flashing through in my brain, which in turn trigger my musical responses, which fan out to everything in my mind and heart and story including my evolution, and everyone and everything else's, and which inevitably lead back to Source and silence. I am reporting as accurately as I can what happens to me, even though these words themselves seem some sort of musty, leftover residue of something. Maybe infinities make us too light-headed for words, and we've gone as far as we can with them. Next subject, please.

LET IT RING

If you hold the rim of a bell it can't ring. If you touch the rim of a ringing bell, it will stop ringing. If you are listening to music so deeply that it is ringing your bell, thinking *about* it could be one way of touching the bell; judging, or being reactive, might do the same. When composers want a percussionist to allow a cymbal, or a gong, or a chime to continue ringing without being damped, they write *laisser vibrer* on the score. Aside from the beauty of the sound of the words themselves, the phrase has always been a cautionary mantra for me. When I am listening to music, the mantra reminds me: just let it happen, don't be too hasty to have some idea about it, or reaction to it. Let it vibrate — *laisser vibrer*. In this way, listening to music can serve as a splendid rehearsal for entering into the stream of life without needing to *change* it all the time. Sometimes you have to and sometimes you don't, but let the scene in front of you play out some, let it unfold. Give life a chance. Don't touch the bell.

WAVE THEORY AND PRACTICE

For thirty years, and with a persistence I scarcely understand, I've been waving to the few drivers who pass me on my daily walk along the country road where I live. Many wave back, each in his or her individual way: a flip of the pinkie on the steering wheel, a little smile with eyes fixed front, a high five, a condescending nod, a knowing guy acknowledgment, the toss of a blond pony tail, a proper salute, a simple open palm sweeping left or right. Each of these is a gesture of acknowledgment, a momentary realization of companions on the journey, a silent music of recognition. We are all one through this wave, which came all the way from forever ago to now, then straight back to the Wizard of Oz, then on back to Ahura Mazda, and Jehovah, and then out again to the Sacred Et Cetera. The wave you exchange with a stranger and your connection to Source are not separate. You are the bridge and you are the wave both, you are a bridge of waves, and have been all along.

I have been thinking about you, you who have been reading these words, and about how the words we are sharing are just little wavelets in my mind—and how they are moving now in your mind. We have waved to each other on the road. We have recognized one another. Now I can stop writing and you can stop reading and we can open our ears to what comes.

End Papers

One Hundred Ways to Listen to Music

There are as many ways to listen to music as there are of being alive. Here, organized somewhat arbitrarily, are an even hundred of them. We've discussed or mentioned some of them earlier. The others are snatched from the blue.

For Particular Feeling States

To wake up, to feel awake
To feel good, have fun, be mellow
To feel as if the music were playing you (just as a violin is playing music)
To get frenzied
To get a pheromone surge (as in drugs, sex, and rock 'n' roll)
To feel primitive (pre-language)
To soothe the savage beast
To witness specific emotional responses
As a counterirritant (a focus for all your irritations)
To calm down, let go, ease anxiety (at the dentist, in company, home alone)

To feel civilized (not hunting/gathering but at the concert
    in a state of leisure)
To listen without intention, just to see what will happen
To lift out of depression, to make it through the night
To gain courage
To ease pain, to heal
To pray
To become very still (*listen* and *silent* contain the same
    letters)
To escape thought, undo words
To cry
To be half asleep
To go to sleep

For Physical Activities

To dance
To work out
To walk or jog
To increase physical coordination, as physical therapy
To do yoga
To get or give massage
As pure energy, with no surfaces to grab onto

For Ritual

To get married
To prepare for battle, wage war
To grieve — for a funeral
To exorcise demons
To appease the gods
To help celebrate a red-letter day or holiday
To demonstrate patriotism
To act out class demarcation (all dressed up at the opera)

As a Soundtrack

As a soundtrack for TV, or a video game, or a movie
As theater cues that set the mood, cue lights and entrances
To accompany quotidian activity—homework, housework,
    reading, etc.
To think about stuff, solve problems, zone out
As a trip enhancer (pot, LSD, coke, Ecstasy, etc.)
To flirt and/or seduce
For sex
For eating
For talking
To fantasize, make up stories to, to express your own story
To shop
To sell stuff
To convince, increase patriotism, proselytize (Wagner by
    Nazis), as propaganda
To help protect the Good Old U.S.A. (In a low-profile
    U.S. government security building, while geeks hack
    cyber codes of potential enemies, rock 'n' roll blares out
    through large speakers, thus helping the hackers meet
    "one of the most serious economic and national security
    challenges we face as a nation," according to President
    Obama. An office gong heralds each breakthrough.
—*New York Times* 5/3/09)

For Getting into the Music

To become as engaged as possible, as if music were living
    spirit, and living in it
To identify with the composer or the players
To marvel at the talents and qualities of the performers
To be one end of a string: stimulus/response, expectation/
    gratification, give/take, and so on

To follow the written score
To follow layers or parts
To follow instruments
To track how things morph
From the bass up (a clue to how most composers hear)
To witness the mind as it cognizes musical patterns
To follow formal aspects
Repeatedly, focusing on one element each time, then every-
thing at once
To compare words/no words
To compare eyes open/eyes closed
To learn to play it

For Getting into Music History or Cultural History

To appreciate historical continuity (composer to composer,
period to period)
To imagine living at a certain time in history, or to expe-
rience the music as history (as in the wild premiere of
Stravinsky's *Le Sacre du Printemps*)
To appreciate historical context and change: to learn history
from old to new
The same, chronologically backward

For a Sense of Place and Context

To understand where you are and whom you're with
To ask what the music is telling you
To ask what the music wants from you
To help you get from place to place: Maestro, a little traveling
music, please

FOR PERSONAL REASONS

As a fetus through the womb
As your friend when you are by yourself
As if you were a microphone, to maintain a neutral,
    nonjudgmental state
As an object of meditation
To solve a problem
To reminisce or relive certain moments the music
    recalls
To say good-bye to someone, or to part of your life
To drown out other sounds
Loudly, to get back at the neighbors
To avoid something, including yourself, your monster
To impress someone
As a commodity: to market it
As an affirmation: proof of the existence of good
As if these were the last sounds you ever will hear
As if the music were listening to you
As little deaths
As a palliative for death and dying while revivifying life
As if for the first time, with virgin ears
To transcend the world, including music

TO ENHANCE OR DEFINE RELATIONSHIPS

To listen with someone else—to be in each other's
    listening
Eyes closed, holding hands
Dancing with a partner or partners
All alone in a crowd (for instance, standing still, eyes closed,
    inside a dance jam)
Alone together in a group: campfire songs

In a crowd, with the crowd's ears/in a crowd with your
   own ears
To feel yourself as one human in the whole of humanity

NUMBER ONE HUNDRED

Just because

Sources, Notes, and Comments

Although I do read academic music journals, for the most part my sources are those available to the general reader: the *New York Times*, *Science News*, *Scientific American*, the *New Yorker*, *Harper's Magazine*. To this add one perk: my wife, Devi, as well as being the soprano in my life, is a science writer and editor; among her tasks is the writing of the magazine *Physics at Berkeley*, produced yearly by the UC Berkeley Physics Department. For over a decade, her job has entailed interviewing some of the zaniest and most brilliant scientists in the universe, then representing the gist of their thinking to the engaged but nonspecialized reader. Through the years, as I've looked over Devi's shoulder, her arduous process of sifting through and winnowing the most mysterious complexities has allowed me to savor the intensity and vitality of the scientific work now being done, as well as the skill and passion of those who try to make scientific research accessible to the earnest, if nonspecialized, reader. In addition, several of my former students have become neuroscientists specializing in music. Such research is close to my heart, so it's nice to have spies in the field.

So I'm afraid you won't find an abundance of academic rigor here, just the normal hungers of a generalist living in the Near Boonies with his antennae out for news, especially news that further animates and illumines one's love of music.

—

Epigraph: *"Where there is listening there is love."* The maven of listening, Pauline Oliveros, has often said, "Where there is listening there is music." By changing one word, her protégée and collaborator, Jennifer Wilsey, has turned the phrase into a lovely collaboration, and a touchstone for this book.

Chapter 1: Music as Body

Page 7: *"...makes music a primary area for research into how our minds and our bodies are hooked up."* Much of what I understand about embodied cognition I owe to George Lakoff, whose *Metaphors We Live By* (Chicago: University of Chicago Press, 2003) is but one of several of his books to have shaped my thinking. Another is *Where Mathematics Comes From: How the Embodied Mind Brings Mathematics into Being* (with Rafael E. Nunez; New York: Basic Books, 2000), and another is *Don't Think of an Elephant!* (White River Junction, Vt.: Chelsea Green Publishing, 2004). Central to his thought is the tenet that abstract concepts have a literal core, that conceptual metaphors are grounded in everyday experience. Although Dr. Lakoff is a cognitive linguist by trade, the depth and breadth of his interests, and his clarity in articulating his ideas, have given him a wide following across many fields.

One of the most accessible books about the perception of music is *Music and Memory: An Introduction* (Cambridge, Mass.: MIT Press, 2000), which was written because its author, Bob Snyder, "needed a text to use in my undergraduate musical composition classes at the Art Institute of Chicago...to present an overview of a field that is quickly evolving." Although the book does not use music notation, it is written by a musically savvy scientist, is very readable throughout, and has provided me with some of the language I use in teaching and writing about music.

The map/territory relationship between mind, body, and world is eloquently addressed in *The Body Has a Mind of Its Own,* by Sandra Blakeslee and Matthew Blakeslee (New York: Random House, 2007). See also the note to chapter 4.

CHAPTER 2: MUSIC AS MIND

Page 17: *"the working of your mind..."* Although it is both fashionable and functional to speak of music in relationship to "the brain," I have most frequently chosen the somewhat more comprehensive term "mind." Mind has a large range: it can refer to the anatomical brain, or the brain plus the psyche, as in "making up one's mind," or—capitalized as "Mind" or used with an adjective as in "pure mind" or "high mind"—refer to states of heightened or transformative awareness.

In researching this book, I came across many music/brain sources but will mention only three here. *Music, the Brain, and Ecstasy* by Robert Jordain came out in 1997 (New York: W. Morrow). I will say more about this book in the section "More Books" at the end of these notes. The November 2004 issue of *Scientific American* contains an article by Norman M. Weinberger called "Music and the Brain," which fairly summarizes the field of inquiry up to then, and points with prescience to further research. *This Is Your Brain on Music* by Daniel J. Levitin (New York: Dutton, 2006), came out in 2006, giving the entire field a far wider exposure. See pages 289–90 in "More Books" for more about this book.

Page 39: *"...le principe de tout est un."* I have no idea where precisely to find this famous quote from Rameau in his far-flung *oeuvre,* but it is quoted on page 569 of Volume 15 of the 1995 paperback edition of *The New Grove Dictionary of Music & Musicians,* edited by Stanley Sadie.

Page 44: *"Ninety-nine percent of the music of the earth is tonal..."* I made up the number; what I mean is "the vast majority."

Page 49: *"Ultimately, however, the beast was discovered to possess a beauty so great that it gave rise to musical forms..."* My book *Harmonic Experience* is devoted to the mechanics of how this improbably serendipitous state of affairs could possibly be the outcome of deliberately mistuning our instruments and our ears.

CHAPTER 3: MUSIC AS HEART

Page 68: *"When a strange mode from a strange people resonates with a familiar and perhaps forgotten place in your heart..."* What follows is a more detailed discussion about the affective nature of melodies.

Organization of the Harmonic Realm

By way of reviewing what we have been discussing, remember that the mind seeks the simplest explanation for what it hears. In its quest for simplicity, the mind responds to frequency proportions it can factor by the lowest primes: 2, 3, and 5 (and sometimes 7). It also distinguishes between right-side-up (overtonal) harmony and upside-down (reciprocal) harmony.

Scale-tones sort out into the following categories, or families, which, as we shall soon explain, we will regard as pureblooded families.

The Doubles family: multiples of two of the drone
The Triples family: multiples of three of the drone.
The Quintuples family: multiples of five of the drone.
The Septuples family: multiples of seven of the drone.

Each of the families produces within the listener a characteristic affect. In addition, each of these families has both an overtonal and a reciprocal branch, with complimentary affects to match.

Now here's a truth about pure-blood families: they tend to interbreed. That thickens the plot. The Doubles family interbreeds with *everyone*. Since doubling (or halving) produces the same tone in a higher (or lower) octave, this promiscuous Doubles family interbreeding simply means that any tone can occur in any octave and retain its affect relatively unchanged. Interbreeding between the Triples and the Quintuples families, however, has subtle results. The harmonic qualities of their progeny truly reflect both parents. More than half the tones you hear in music are the result of some such Triples-Quintuples mixing.

One way to sensitize your response to innate harmonic qualities of tones against drones is to recognize a kind of harmonic spectrum that proceeds from simplicity to complexity. I don't want to scare you off with lists and numbers, and you can surely skip this paragraph and the next three with impunity. But for readers interested in the quantification of this gradual and beautiful spectrum from harmonic simplicity to harmonic complexity, you will find listed below the twelve most common tone combinations one hears in music. The simplest harmonies are called "perfect," the most complex are called "dissonant," and the juicy stuff in between is called "consonant." Here are the frequency proportions of the tones, with C as the fundamental tone, listed from simple to complex—that is, as you scan down the page, the ratios increase in complexity.

TWELVE MOST COMMONLY HEARD TONES AGAINST *C* AS THE DRONE

Harmonic Type	Letter-name	Ratio	Family	Branch
Perfect				
	C itself	1:1		
	C the octave	2:1	Doubles family	overtonal
	G	3:2	Triples family	overtonal
	F	4:3	Triples family	reciprocal
Consonant				
	E	5:4	Quintuples family	overtonal
	A♭	8:5	Quintuples family	reciprocal
	A	5:3	Triples-Quintuples family	mixed
	E♭	6:5	Triples-Quintuples family	mixed
Dissonant				
	D	9:8	Triples family	overtonal
	B♭	9:5	Triples-Quintuples family	mixed
	B	15:8	Triples-Quintuples family	overtonal
	D♭	16:15	Triples-Quintuples family	reciprocal
	F♯	45:32	Triples-Quintuples family	overtonal

Generally speaking, the simpler the harmony's ratio, the less work your mind does to understand the harmony, and the more sense we have of safety, relief, openness, resolution, stasis. The more complex the harmony's ratio, the more calories your mind burns to understand it, and the more sense we have of motion, tension, apprehension. The simpler the harmony, the more spacious the feeling; the more complex the harmony the more uptight, and consequently the more need for release. The harmonies in the middle, the so-called "consonances," have aspects of repose mixed with aspects of motion, and these mixtures are where the affective pleasures are the sweetest.

But don't let me tell you how these tones affect you. Each listener hears the mixes of these variables in his or her own way.

There are no Affect Police. The purpose here is to demonstrate the great richness and variety of affective experiences waiting for you to hone in on them with your ears and heart open.

Dee-Yah *Intimacy*

We have considered a variety of tones heard against a fixed drone. Now it's time to consider the relationship of two tones in succession (also against a drone, which for now will be ever present). A dramatic contrast between two successive tones occurs when the first one is harmonically very complex, the following one is very simple, *and* they are distant from each other by the smallest scalar interval, a half step. This sequence sets up a tension and a release, a contraction to an expansion, a narrow squint to a level gaze. I call this ever-recurring harmonic pattern *dee-yah*, the *dee* standing for closed-up tension and the *yah* standing for open release.

For instance, if (against a C drone) you sing a D-flat followed by a C, the two tones are only a half step apart. Even though they are adjacent in the scalar dimension, the harmonic distance between them is great. The frequency proportion between D-flat and the C directly below it is complex (16:15), and the harmony of C to the drone is the simplest possible (1:1). So the harmonic complexity releases into simplicity by a slight melodic descent: a falling *dee-yah*. You can sing this descending move dispassionately, as if merely noting that two lovers are kissing in the park. But what if *you* were the lovers, or the kiss itself? To be truly inside the feeling of these tones as you sing them is to realize "Hey, that's *my* tension and *my* release, *my* grip on things and *my* letting go." An intimacy comes into it. It's not just about you, it's something you're living through.

This is far from an idea, *not* the same as pattern recognition—it is a succession of feeling states. And it is tricky at best to name these states, to try and wrap language around them.

They feel the way they feel, and resist being nailed by words. A good way to increase the affect is to sing the *dee* loud and the *yah* soft. The tension is then directed outward, the relaxation brought inside. The painful little jab is assuaged by calm relief—one of the most expressive and intimate experiences in all of music making.

Just as, in the physical world of objects and gravity, falling is easier than rising, so in the aural world a descending *dee-yah* is especially relaxing. But another highly affective *dee-yah* is from B to C, also a half step but ascending. In this case, the complex 15:16 moves to the simple 1:1. (To be precise: the B listed in the table is seven tones *above* the drone; its ratio is 15:8. The B I want you to sing here is a half step just *below* the drone.) The transition from *dee* to *yah* in each of these cases is so compelling that they are given the name *leading tones.* Harmonically, each leads to C in its own way, D-flat from the reciprocal realm and B from the overtonal realm. Try singing one pair and then the other—D-flat to C, then B to C—over and over again. Comparing their affects is one of the most illuminating of all musical practices.

After C, the next simplest tone in the scale is G, so the falling and rising half steps surrounding G present an equally compelling affect. A-flat to G falls from a reciprocal consonance to a perfect harmony (somewhat like D-flat falling to C), and F-sharp to G rises from an overtonal dissonance to a perfect harmony (much like B rising to C). Each is a classic *dee-yah,* offering maximal contrast between the tension of the *dee* and the relaxation of the *yah.* They are much loved and much used, separately or in combination.

We have mentioned the most starkly contrasting *dee-yah* examples. When there is somewhat less harmonic contrast between the *dee* and the *yah,* there is more subtlety. Feelings get mixed. You can learn a great deal about music (and yourself, not distinct from music) by simply singing or playing two adjacent scale-tones and investigating the relationship between their affects. Sing them (against the keynote drone, always) back and forth, back and forth. Their relationship will gradually unveil itself, and, as your experience deepens, that relationship opens out into free passage between aspects of yourself.

Indeed, *any* two scale-tones bind together to form a kind of affective gestalt—a little emotional package. If two successive tones can do that musical surgery on your insides, imagine the work of three. Three-tone melodies comprising the first three notes of a major scale—C, D, and E in this case—can be put together in so many affective ways that many pop songs begin and go on (and on) that way. Entire songs can easily be made with four tones. Five-tone collections of tones, called pentatonic modes, are responsible for much of the music of the planet, including "Amazing Grace." Western music typically employs seven-tone (heptatonic) modes, from which are constructed most of the melodies you hear around you every day.

An infinite number of affective narratives (my fancy term for tunes) can be created from these modes, but however they are constructed, and however they feel, they are the result of simple moves from tone to tone to tone. To internalize a sequence of tones against a drone, like the *dee-yah* examples given above, is to model in miniature our responses to the great melodies we so cherish. And as you practice them, you will gain insight into why music seems to have its own innate grammar. Music's grammar is based not on logic but on affect, the way things feel, and *dee-yah* is one of its fundamental rules.

Page 74: "*I love that G seven flat thirteen in the middle of 'Stella'!*" This chord in "Stella by Starlight" comes at bar 17, lasts for eight beats (thereby establishing a new harmonic rhythm), accompanies the highest notes in the tune, and gives the improviser a chance to build a chorus with wildly dramatic shape.

Page 74: *"How 'bout the C nine flat thirteen*... This chord in "All the Things You Are" is one of the most perfect moments in American music, or maybe all music. It serves as a way of returning from a long harmonic journey back to its beginning with stunning particularity and beauty. It corresponds to the moment of recapitulation in a classical symphony, but is clothed in the sophisticated tonal language of jazz-influenced popular music. It is not simple to know how to improvise on it, partly because different players have different ways of treating it.

Page 74: *"I'm down with Hindemith's quartal flat-two cadences..."* I think this guy was referring to the following progression of two chords: the first chord, spelling upward, is: D♭–F♯–B; the resolution is: C–G–C. This cadence is modally mixed, mysteriously gorgeous, and sounds faintly medieval but is actually quite modern, like Paul Hindemith.

Page 76: *"Tonal harmony is the language of our hearts, not our tongues."* Quite a bit of neuroscience has addressed the mystery of musical grammar, but what I have seen proceeds from the idea that musical grammar is rule-based and logical. Much more difficult for science to address is the qualitative nature of musical meaning. How could you measure, or get any objective read on feeling-based grammar? An April 23, 2001, *Science Update* posting from *Nature* reports on studies asking subjects to listen to sequences of five chords ordered in familiar and unfamiliar ways. An unexpected chord produced the same mental activity in the listeners as did misplaced words in a sentence. I think such ideas of musical meaning are not misdirected, just missing the main idea, which is that music makes us feel certain ways. The feelings must be the subject. The grammar of music is primarily an affective grammar, and though not disparate from rule-based meaning, is surely not defined by it. Is it even a subject for science? I actually think so, but as in all scientific inquiry, the nature of the investigation needs to fit what is being investigated.

Page 78: *"'This was not just music about desire . . . It was desire itself.'"* The August 25, 2008, issue of the *New Yorker* ran a piece by John Adams, a sort of teaser for his book *Hallelujah Junction*, which was released by Farrar, Straus and Giroux shortly thereafter and reviewed in the *New York Times* on October 8, 2008. What I have written here comes from these sources as well as personal history. I'll be happy to plug his book: it reads well and rings true. (Now, by way of complete disclosure, I should say that John plugged my book *Harmonic Experience* calling it "the handbook of the twenty-first century musician"—but too late for publication. He's written some kind words about this book as well.)

CHAPTER 4: FEELING MIND, THINKING HEART

Page 84: *"Triune brain theory…is no longer part of contemporary neuroscience, though it still seems useful to many psychotherapists."* Check out "Transaction Analysis and the Triune Brain," an essay by Claude Steiner (posted on his Web site, www.claudesteiner.com/triune.htm), for a fascinating account.

Page 84: *"In* The Body Has a Mind of Its Own, *Sandra Blakeslee and Matthew Blakeslee write…"* The full title is *The Body Has a Mind of Its Own: How Body Maps in Your Brain Help You Do (Almost) Everything Better.* The quote is from page 208. I ravenously read this marvelous book after having completed the manuscript for *Bridge of Waves*, but have tried to reflect some of its information, insight, and fine writing in the final draft. Recommended as a compelling update of this branch of neuroscience.

Page 88: *"There's a wonderful set of ten Zen pictures and poems called* The Ten Bulls…*"* My favorite version of *The Ten Bulls,* sometimes called *Ox-Herding Pictures,* is reproduced in the ever-delightful *Zen Flesh, Zen Bones,* complied by Paul Reps, originally published by Charles E. Tuttle, Boston, 1957.

Page 90: *"'Enough talk for the night.'"* The translation is by Daniel Ladinsky, from his 1999 *Love Poems from God* (New York: Penguin, 2002).

Page 91: *"'palpable and mute...'"* The famous opening couplet of the poem *Ars Poetica* by Archibald MacLeish is

> A poem should be palpable and mute
> As a globed fruit ...

Page 96: *"'Art...is an artifice used by humans to harmonize their two brains.'"* The quote is from Dr. Odent's book *Birth and Breastfeeding* (East Sussex, U.K.: Clairview Books, 2007), in a chapter titled "Old and New."

Page 99: *"In a 2008 article in the* New Yorker *titled "The Eureka Hunt..."* The article is written by Jonah Lehrer, and is a great read.

Page 100: *"According to Harvard psychology researcher Shelley Carson, distractibility can even increase the amount of information available to the conscious mind."* The primary source for this paragraph is an article in the *New York Times* from May 20, 2008 (*Science Times* section), "Older Brain May Really Be a Wiser Brain," by Sara Reistad-Long.

Page 100: *"Humanity has . . . connected itself into a collective, modern version of its ancient brain."* Also from the *Science Times* section of the *New York Times,* an article on July 22, 2008, "If You Have a Problem, Ask Everyone," by Cornelia Dean.

You can tell by the number of exciting articles trickling down from research journals to the general reader how central a concern neuroscience has recently become to the culture at large. We really want to know what makes us tick, and we seem to be learning.

Page 103: *"I kept coming back to the fact that the ratios of tonal harmony* feel *so whole-making."* A longtime friend, T. J. Crowe, a musician who teaches college math, has great love for his subject. He has gently pointed out to me that my sense of mathematical rigidity comes more from mathematicians than from mathematics. Fair enough. From his personal, loving, and open-ended viewpoint he comments about my pivotal use of math in teaching music theory, and draws the following analogy: "You happen to use math to quantify and categorize patterns that help you understand human responses to sound, just as a potter uses her feeling of the clay to mold her shapes. Feeling the clay or using the math, these are two among many ways we have of getting what we want. Mathematics is on par with artistic intuition in this pragmatic respect. There's no reason to elevate one over the other." (See also note to pages 188–89 in chapter 8.)

CHAPTER 5: MUSIC AS LIFE

Page 135: *"...my thick, heavy book,* Harmonic Experience...*" Harmonic Experience* was dedicated to my guru, Pandit Pran Nath, and shortly before he died I was able to present him with a copy. He had become quite frail, but on this particular afternoon he was sitting up in a chair, straight and calm. I presented the new book to him by very gingerly placing its considerable bulk on his lap. Guru-ji picked it up slowly, tested its weight, looked up at me with his big, brown eyes and said, "Strong wrists needed." So that is what I say to prospective readers.

CHAPTER 6: MUSIC AS STORY

Page 146: *"Much has been written about the soundscape of Western life..."* *The Tuning of the World* (New York: Random House, 1977). This wonderful book belongs on the shelf (and in the heart) of every proactive listener. "We have split the sound from the maker of the sound," the author points out, in a much-quoted passage. "Vocal sound, for instance, is no longer tied to a hole in the head but is free to issue from anywhere in the landscape." He terms this lamentable condition of modern life *schizophonia*.

Page 161: *"...subsequently, tonal harmony arose as we needed it."* See the illuminating article "Evolution's Ear," by Bruce Bowe, in *Science News*, August 30, 2008.

Page 161: *"Tones remove the barrier between persons and things..."* The Victor Zuckerkandl quote is to be found on page 119 of *Homo Aestheticus: Where Art Comes From and Why* (Seattle: University of Washington Press, 1995), by Ellen Dissanayake. The book is a thoughtful, far-ranging and well-written exploration of how humans are inherently aesthetic and artistic creatures. It makes the case for art as a biologically evolved element in human nature.

Page 163: *"According to Allan Kozinn..."* "Essay in D: The Critic's Cogitation about Titles," *New York Times*, November 6, 2008. The same article recounts a host of capricious titles contemporary composers have drawn from various media and advertisements, including David Lang's "Eating Living Monkeys," a sort of antititle since it evidently has nothing to do with the music. Composer George Crumb says, "People take composers' titles too seriously."

Page 166: "Short-term memory *handles pitches and rhythmic pulses...*" I am again indebted to Bob Snyder's comprehensive *Music and Memory: An Introduction* (cited in the notes to chapter 1), in which see, on page 12, Table 1.1, "Three Levels of Musical Experience."

CHAPTER 7: MUSIC AS MIRROR

Page 168: "*We are the mirror...*" These lines from a quatrain by Jelaluddin Rumi, as translated by John Moyne and Coleman Barks, are to be found in *Open Secret: Versions of Rumi* (Aptos, Calif.: Threshold Books, 1984). The quatrain is number 1652, on page 22. *Open Secret* was the first among many subsequent books bringing Rumi to the Western eye, ear, and heart by way of Coleman Barks's magic English, and whenever I pick up my much-marked copy of it, it is still quivering from my initial thrill. If you haven't yet happened upon his versions of Rumi, you have a whole nother life ahead of you. I've set about sixty of his translations, mostly contained in the song cycles, on three albums to be found at the Web site ColdMountainMusic.com: *Say I Am You; Rumi & Strings;* and *The Indian Parrot.* Coleman Barks's own poetry is alive and moving; it has encouraged me to find my own.

Page 171: "*Music is our creation story...*" I figured out harmony by first simply hearing it, then configuring a theory my hearing could live in. In doing that, I met many kindred minds along the way. The same thing has become true for my metaphysics: I "hear" the nature of life, and the cognitive house it can live in is being written right now. Music showed me how to do this. I'm glad. Stay with me.

Page 173: "*When you look for God...*" The quote is also from *Open Secret* (page 50), and you can hear Devi sing it beautifully in the song cycle "In the Arc of Your Mallet," on the album *Say I Am You*, mentioned in the first note to this chapter.

Page 175: "*Beloved, your way of knowing is amazing…*" This is my version, from Hildegard's Germanic Latin, with Devi's help.

Page 176: "*About forty years ago the idea of a 'holographic paradigm' began to surface in the scientific community.*" For a well-written summary of "the holographic paradigm," with just the right mix of sympathy and objectivity, google "holographic paradigm Joe Kissell" to read his wonderful "Interesting Thing of the Day" post (June 26, 2004).

Pages 176–77: "*With the discovery of superstring theory, musical metaphors take on a startling reality…*" Brian Greene's *The Elegant Universe* (New York: Vintage Books, 2000) is a widely read, often quoted summary of string theory written not only with great love of the subject but also a generous spirit in explicating it for the engaged layman. The quote is from the beginning of chapter 6, "Nothing But Music: The Essentials of Superstring Theory." Later in the book (on page 377, under the subhead "What Are Space and Time, Really, and What Can We Do about Them?"), he points out that a graviton, the smallest bundle of gravitational force, is a "particular pattern of string vibration," and that "we are led to identify the fabric of spacetime itself with a colossal number of strings all undergoing the same, orderly, graviton pattern of vibration….Such an enormous, organized array of similarly vibrating strings is known as a *coherent state* of strings." Now I do believe that fairly describes an excellent symphonic string section at full throttle. However efficacious string theory proves to be in describing whatever it is we seem to be living in the middle of, most of the musicians I know are rooting for it, if only for their resonance with its innate metaphors.

Page 177: *"Just the idea that you have the subatomic world projected on the sky today is mind-boggling."* This expression of astonishment was quoted in an article by Ron Cowen in *Science News* (April 11, 2009), "Planck by Planck: Mapping the earliest moments of time."

CHAPTER 8: MUSIC ON THE ZEN ELEVATOR

Page 185: *"I'm like a bird from another continent, sitting in this aviary."* This fragment of a translation by Coleman Barks is from "The Tavern," in *The Essential Rumi*, trans. John Moyne and Coleman Barks (San Francisco: HarperSanFrancisco, 1995).

Pages 185–86: *"One must become familiar... if never quite comfortable, with phenomena that seem paradoxical."* The quote is from an article in the April 2008 issue about graphene, a newly isolated form of carbon ("Carbon Wonderland," by Andre K. Geim and Philip Kim).

Pages 188–89: *"Then the metaphor of number doesn't work anymore."* My mathematician-musician friend T. J. Crowe, perhaps not yet fully realizing how I was playing the devil's advocate in these descriptions of puzzlement over paradoxes, eloquently voiced his inclusive point of view. Concerning the utility of numbers, he says, "Any time you name something, you point out certain relationships and ignore others. An equation says, 'Here are two things that are obviously different, but for our purposes we'll consider them identical.'" He goes on to say, "It's not like there's something called 'reality' that we're trying to describe. It's more that we're just using language to make things better. We use names and numbers to help us get what we want, like making better music. But every name, like every equation, leaves something out."

T. J. also pointed me in the direction of the philosopher Richard Rorty, a panrelationist (one who appreciates the creative force of relativity on all sides), who asserts that whatever sorts of things have intrinsic natures, numbers do not. "It simply does not pay," he says, "to be an essentialist about numbers." T. J. points out that any given number—"17," for instance—is thus "a good example of something without essence, thereby inextricably linking it to all other numbers in a sudden cognitive gestalt switch to ultimate inclusiveness." In the same spirit, in teaching Zeno to his class, T. J. resolves the paradox simply: "Space ain't numbers." (I wish T. J. Crowe had been my math teacher when I was first grappling with algebra.) And to this discussion, my grandnephew, mathematician Joshua Batson, adds, "Maybe mathematics is to the actual motion of physical bodies as sheet music is to music."

Page 191: *"From there on we have systematically 'alphabetized the goddess'..."* The reference is to the profound book *The Alphabet Versus the Goddess: The Conflict between Word and Image* by Leonard Shlain (New York: Viking Penguin Compass, 1998).

Page 192: *"'One might say that now exists all the time beyond the concept of relativity...'"* From *Meditation in Action* (Boston: Shambhala, 1969), page 56.

Page 192: *"A movie released in 2009 called* Watchmen *features a character named Dr. Manhattan..."* The *New York Times* movie critic A. O. Scott said in his review that if he'd had Dr. Manhattan's powers the movie might not have felt quite so interminable.

Page 195: *"The Hindu poet Tukaram...reported in the seventeenth century that God said to him..."* See Tukaram's poems in *Love Poems from God: Twelve Sacred Voices from the East and West* by Daniel Ladinsky (New York: Compass, 2002)

Page 195: *"'...the dichotomy between forever and emergent might turn out to be as false...as the dichotomy between waves and particles.'"* From an article in the *New York Times*, "Laws of Nature, Source Unknown" (December 18, 2007).

Page 196: *"'Why talk about all...'"* From *Rumi: Fountain of Fire*, translated by Nader Khalili (Hesperia, Calif.: Cal-Earth Press, 1994), ghazal number 2381.

Page 197: *"'Seems like we're just set down here...'"* In Annie Dillard's *Pilgrim at Tinker Creek* (New York: HarperPerennial, 2007).

Page 198: *"Plotinus had experiences of unification..."* A good account of the life and thought of Plotinus is in the *Columbia Encyclopedia*, 6th ed. (New York: Columbia University Press, 2000).

Page 199: *"Music that shakes and shocks the body is earth therapy for minds and souls who seriously need to stay here now."* The musician Ben Vigoda has an abiding interest in improvisational games — their history and their benign effects in musical groups. His book *Musical Games: A Guide for Group Improvisation*, presently being prepared for publication, is a comprehensive survey of an influential movement in contemporary music. Along with clear descriptions of, and instructions for, over 150 games, there is a section called "The Theory and Practice of Musical Games," from which the following passage, germane to the body-planet relationship of our text, is excerpted:

> A pendulum is a weight hanging from a string. If you give the weight a push, it will swing back and forth — slower for a longer string, faster for a shorter string. A pendulum with a 1-meter string will swing back and forth in almost

exactly 2 seconds. If this pendulum hits a drum at each end of its swing it would go boom, boom at 60 beats-per-minute. Your arms and legs are also pendulums. A ¼-meter pendulum, just about the length of your calf or forearm, will hit the drums at either end of its swing at 120 beats-per-minute, which also happens to be pretty close to the frequency of every popular dance tune on the planet. The human body is made of pendulums, and we dance to music at this speed.

Page 202: *"Repeatedly we are reminded... a* glimpse *of the* Absolute." Language evolves just as surely as musical styles evolve, and I view the language presented here to be a snapshot of that evolution. Although I have culled from myriad sources, the single book that has most guided these paragraphs is *A Song for the King: Saraha on Mahamudra Meditation,* by Khenchen Thrangu Rinpoche, edited by Michele Martin with Peter O'Hearn (Somerville, Mass.: Wisdom Publications, 2006). Saraha, a ninth-century Indian master teacher, sang metaphorical songs to bring his listeners to enlightenment. *A Song for the King* presents clear, lyrical translations of the poems along with lucid commentary by a contemporary Tibetan master. Throughout the book, great care is taken with language, from the Tibetan root-sources to the current connotations of words and terms. A fuller definition of *non-minding,* for instance, is found on page 160: "As in the statement 'I don't mind,' there's an indifference to the dramas of the self. In this context, *non-minding* would mean not engaging in ordinary thinking — not being caught by the conceptualizing that binds us to the relative world — which then allows for the realization of the deeper truth, the seeing of mind's empty nature." There is also an excellent glossary.

Page 204: *"'... a silence as comes to all of us in little earfuls...'"*

Mary Oliver's wonderful poem "This World" can be found in *Why I Wake Early: New Poems* (Boston: Beacon Press, 2005).

Page 205: *"A Buddhist term for discernment in the relative world is* cognitive lucidity, *or simply,* lucidity." An alternative word for "lucidity" is *clarity.*

CHAPTER 9: THE ENLIGHTENED LISTENER

Page 214: *"'...unmarked box to unmarked box, as rainwater down into flowerbed, as roses up from ground.'"* See "Unmarked Boxes" in *Open Secret,* cited here at the beginning of chapter 7.

Page 223: *"Hence these questions you might ask."* At the same time I was writing this book, the visionary inventor/musician Jaron Lanier was writing *You Are Not a Gadget: A Manifesto* (New York: Knopf, 2010), an extraordinarily clear call to every last one of us who has ever felt the slightest unease with the "personal reductionism" of a newly technological world. Maybe the book is even more important to those of us who haven't felt such twinges. If you'd like some sympathetic juice in keeping your personhood alive and thriving in a postpersonal world, this book is revelatory in scope, depth, and practicality. Aside from being one of the primary inventors of virtual reality (which term he coined), the author is also an engaging and informed musician; he speaks not only as a technology insider but from inside the heart of music as well.

Page 236: *"Don't be held sound-hostage by anyone—locally, regionally, or globally."* A useful organization to check out is NPC, Noise Pollution Clearinghouse, at www.nonoise.org/.

Page 239: *"...Maureen Hurley likens a poem to a stone thrown in the pond of our collective consciousness...*" Her essay, "I, Poet," was published in the *West Sonoma County* paper, July 3, 1991.

Page 243: *"To what extent, if any, do we need to resist this?"* This is a key question that *You Are Not a Gadget* (see note to page 223 above) addresses.

Page 244: "*'Because it's too close to be recognized...'*" This is an adaptation of a well-known aphorism from the Buddhist Shangpa tradition as transmitted by Kalu Rinpoche.

CHAPTER 10: LIVING THE WAVES

Page 247: *"Some of us even develop into playful people."* The Genesis of Animal Play by Gordon Burghardt (Cambridge, Mass.: MIT Press, 2005), has been a primary guide on this subject.

Page 254: "*'Given the profound interconnectedness of everything in the universe...'*" The Universe in a Single Atom: The Convergence of Science and Spirituality (New York: Morgan Road Books, 2005) is the Dalai Lama's well-told, personal account of his scientific education, and the emerging braid of Buddhism and science.

More Books

There are so many wonderful books. I know this because thousands of them are spread out all over the house. Devi and I tried to organize our library about twenty years ago but, except for a few traces here and there, that configuration has largely melted. I think some of the old travel guides are still in the entry foyer, but the newer ones have likely been lost or left behind. The big photography books are mostly on the center shelf in the living room because it's the only one tall enough for them. But in our house generally, finding a book is like calling a cat: you have to wait until it's hungry.

Nonetheless, there are a number of books within arm's reach of my writing desk, which means that even if they aren't presently hungry they probably have been recently, that is, some time during the writing of *this* book. So, beyond what has already been mentioned in the preceding pages, here is a list of the books that have, during these months of writing, found me delicious.

There are two books by Joachim-Ernst Berendt I'd like to mention. *The Third Ear: On Listening to the World* (Shaftesbury, U.K.: Element Books, 1988), and *The World Is Sound—Nada Brahma:*

Music and the Landscape of Consciousness (Rochester, Vt.: Destiny Books, 1991). Mr. Berendt treats the most liberal, cultural, aesthetic, and spiritual questions in an exhaustive, often didactic style, which is my way of saying that he says good things in a way I wouldn't say them. His sources are literary, historical, and scholarly, and they are brilliantly and relentlessly strung together to drive his points home. Given the experiential nature of his subject matter, however, I miss the presence of the author. The redeeming exception is chapter 7 of *The Third Ear*, a beautifully told epiphany of solitary listening on the shore of a mountain lake. I continue to consult these books because they are sincere, intelligent, and full of useful stuff. Also, they were written early on in the history of cultural attunement to the nature of sound, so for me they have been longtime, informative sources.

An even earlier book, *The Symphony of Life*, by Donald Hatch Andrews (Lee's Summit, Mo: Unity Books, 1966) holds a special place in my heart. The author, a Yale chemist and lover of music, was one of the first modern writers to metaphorically connect musical harmony, rigorous scientific empiricism, and the innate interdependence of all things. He writes with a wide-eyed, innocent lyricism that has inspired and influenced many later writers, including me. I found his book in a used bookstore, and that's where you're going to have to find it too, because the volume is long out of print. I'd advise you to surf for one now before the last trumpet sounds.

Deep Listening: A Composer's Sound Practice by Pauline Oliveros (Kingston, N.Y.: Deep Listening Publications, 2005) is not only for composers and performers, but for everyone interested in how consciousness may be affected by profound attention to the sonic environment. Ms. Oliveros, known for her transcendent improvisational performances and her masterful teaching, guides the reader to "listening beyond hearing," a holistic approach to inner tranquillity.

Allow me to mention two recent books that engage fiercely

with the potential danger of certain defining characteristics of the Western mind. *The Passion of the Western Mind: Understanding the Ideas That Have Shaped Our World View,* by Richard Tarnas (Ballantine Books, 1991), states (in the epilogue, on page 443) that "The driving impulse of the West's masculine consciousness has been its dialectical quest to not only realize itself... but to come to terms with the great feminine principle in life, to reunite with the feminine.... *This* is where the real act of heroism is going to be." He goes on to say, "A civilization cannot become conscious of itself, cannot recognize its own significance, until it is so mature that it is approaching its own death." A more recent book, *Devices of the Soul: Battling for Our Selves in an Age of Machines,* by Steve Talbott (Sebastapol, Calif.: O'Reilly Media, 2007), is a loud voice in a growing choir of discontent with the effect of contemporary technology on the human spirit. To give you the chilling gist, one chapter is titled "Who's Killing Higher Education (Or Is It Suicide?)." And in this category let me mention once again Jaron Lanier's trenchant, declarative, and only too timely *You Are Not a Gadget: A Manifesto.*

I've already referred to a pair of books about the music/brain relationship (see "Sources, Notes, and Comments," page 267 for more), but I'd like to mention them again. *Music, the Brain, and Ecstasy: How Music Captures Our Imagination,* by Robert Jourdain (New York: W. Morrow, 1997), was written in the late '90s and is already slightly hoary in respect to the fast-growing field of music-related neuroscience; but it is well written by a musician with clear insight and a great love of his subject, and that kind of love doesn't age. Although many advanced musicians enjoy the book, it is essentially a generalist's survey cruise through a musical landscape that opens the reader to ecstatic experience. The other title, *This Is Your Brain on Music: The Science of a Human Obsession,* by Daniel J. Levitin (New York: Plume, 2007), is written by a high-profile neuroscientist specializing in music. It has less warmth but clear scientific focus. One might say it is *about* science, in that the passion of the author is to make his field of inquiry transparent, accessible, and useful to the engaged layman. In this reader-friendly book, he succeeds.

A book I wish I'd read a lot earlier in my life is *Nature's Numbers: The Unreal Reality of Mathematics,* by Ian Stewart (New York: Basic Books, 1995). In a well-written, accessible way the author addresses many of the issues I've had to grapple with haphazardly, giving the reader a clear sense of what mathematics can and cannot do. He dreams of a new math, "morphomatics," which proceeds not from nature's numbers, but from nature's synamics through time.

And lastly, I'd like to mention three more books about connectivity written from a scientific viewpoint for the interested general reader. The first, *Uncertainty: Einstein, Heisenberg, Bohr, and the Struggle for the Soul of Science,* by David Lindley (New York: Anchor Books, 2008), is my idea of a page-turner. The author, a PhD in astrophysics and a proficient, clear science writer, shows how the innate tensions between truth and uncertainty have played out historically in the near history of twentieth-century physics. Real people, real battles, real souls. *The View from the Center of the Universe,* by the husband-and-wife team of Joel R. Primack and Nancy Ellen Abrams (New York: Riverhead Books, 2006), is essentially a survey course about the scale of the universe and our place in it. It's a thoughtful, well-ordered essay about human meaning in a vast cosmos, a guided tour from every imaginable angle. The third book is the most mysterious of all, but it may capture you. *The Wholeness of Nature: Goethe's Way toward a Science of Conscious Participation in Nature,* by Henri Bertoft (Hudson, N.Y.: Lindisfarne Press, 1996), is a difficult book to read, much less to describe, but it keeps seeming to want me to read more of it. I will quote a few words (from page 344, in the notes) that may suggest an overall sense: "The analytical mode of consciousness is tuned toward seeing many ones (i.e., discrete things or events)...." In comparison, the holistic mode of consciousness is tuned toward being able to see "the One that is 'hidden' in the many—hidden by our customary mode of consciousness." Bertoft's guiding lights were Goethe and the physicist David Bohm, both of whom recognized the crucial need for scientists to apprehend the world from the point of view of wholeness.

To this list I will add my own books listed not chronologically, but by increasing poundage.

The Listening Book: Discovering Your Own Music (Boston: Shambhala, 1991) is a plea for paying attention to what is already given in everyone's life. Although it has a few musical practices in it, it is meant (to quote Jim Aiken) "for anybody who has ears."

The Musical Life: Reflections on What It Is and How to Live It (Boston: Shambhala, 1994) dovetails with *The Listening Book*, but goes on to investigate wider issues more extensively. Of special interest (as previously noted) is the final section, *Sound Is the Teacher*, about the harmonic series as both a musical tool and a metaphor for connectivity.

The work you have in your hands, *Bridge of Waves*, can be considered the third in this series of books.

Harmonic Experience: Tonal Harmony from Its Natural Origins to Its Modern Expression (Rochester, Vt.: Inner Traditions International, 1997) is for practicing musicians who are willing, for the sake of gaining insight into a cogent reframing of harmonic theory, to reconsider it from the beginning. The path leads from the ancient, pure resonances of just intonation all the way through the brilliance of contemporary harmony in modern tuning, and integrates these into a single view.

My Listening List

Since this is a book about music written by a musician, why is there no list of music recommended for listening? The reason,

END PAPERS

which you already know, is that I want you to discover your own list, to listen underneath the noise of your life to the small voice in your ear, and let it guide you to your loves and your conscience. And there is so very much music to love. And most of it is so readily available, just waiting for you to learn from it, and to know yourself by it. If any of the many words in this book have done anything in your service, Musical Reader, let it be to encourage you to resolutely seek out for yourself the music that most eases your outer life and illumines your inner one.

Acknowledgments

On this day as on every other, thanks to my teachers: Buddy Hiles (at age 13), Bill Russo (at 17), Duke Ellington (who was and is a blessing in all dimensions), Easley Blackwood, Paul Sills, Viola Spolin, Murshid Sam Lewis, Pir-o-Murshid Hazrat Inayat Khan, G. S. Sachdev, Hamza El Din (you've never left), and my guru Pandit Pran Nath, all of whom live in my heart. And to my musical colleagues and collaborators who have shaped my life, I thank you with my open ears: John Adams, Hank Dutt, Michael Ellison, Matthew Goodheart, Joan Jeanrenaud, Ben Johnston, Shira Kammen, Fred Kaz, Art Lande, George Marsh (since Day One), Pauline Oliveros (maven of Deep Listening), Terry Riley (of The Blessing born), Roy Whelden, Kirk Whipple and Marilyn Morales, Jennifer Wilsey, and the many others sounding and resounding through my musical life.

And to my deep friends who have nurtured me and whom I have loved, please accept my thanks: Dan Barrett, Joanna Bull (she's the goddess of my youth, and is still she), Coleman Barks (who gave me his gleam), Saphira Linden, Joseph Raphael (who models the artist's life), Alidra Solday, Lara Summerville (of the level gaze), and Francis Weller (who can read this safely now) and, especially, those whose names I have not written.

Since so much of my life has found its way into this book, it makes sense to thank everyone in my life, and indeed I am wholeheartedly grateful to all those in my purview for the opportunity to bring this work forward. First and foremost, however, I want to thank Dave O'Neal, Shambhala's longtime editor, whose innocent morning call three years ago, and whose subsequent nurturing guidance, has resulted in *Bridge of Waves*. And let me add my gratitude toward Shambhala Publications for feeling like family and for being alive and well in this needy world.

Thank you to the readers of this manuscript in the various stages of its preparation: to Dick Blasband, who steered me toward the limits of my own intuition; to T. J. Crowe, whose responses have softened and enlivened my own; to Larry Hamberlin, who saw the editorial path with his musical eye; to Donna McLaughlin, who flew me straight; to Robert Morris, who remodeled my contextual house; to Ben Ratliff, whose ear is on the street and in the heart of American music; to Bob Snyder, whose clarity gave me places to think from; to Brad Vines, for connecting me to science still aborning; to Ben Vigoda, for his insights into musical play; and especially to my wife Devi for her meticulous eye, spacious guidance, loving hand, and, above all, her forbearance through the white heat of words.

Finally let me thank my fifty years of students for what they have taught me. And let me especially thank those whose voices and spirits have surfaced in these pages: Norman Beede, Matthew Dallman, Carol Eberle, Bonnie Felix, David Fraser, Daniel Hillriegel, Davi Jai, Katarina Konietzko, Jack Leissring, Noam Lemish, Francis Martineau, John Mazzei, Chris Mohr (perennially 53), David Montoya, Peter Moore, Ari Nelson, Alan Tower, Luke Westbrook, Debra White, Sherry Woods, Jane Valencia, and the many I've forgotten to name, or who have forgotten me.

About the Author

Credit: Devi Mathieu

William Allaudin Mathieu is a composer, pianist, teacher, recording artist, and author. He has composed a variety of chamber and choral works; numerous song cycles based on the poetry of Rumi, Hafiz, Kabir, Mary Oliver, and Gary Snyder; and made numerous solo piano recordings.

Allaudin has written three earlier books on music, *The Listening Book* and *The Musical Life*, published by Shambhala, and *Harmonic Experience: Tonal Harmony from Its Natural Origins to Its Modern Expression*, published by Inner Traditions. He currently performs with his wife, the singer Devi Mathieu, and the string player Shira Kammen in Ephemeros, a San Francisco Bay Area trio dedicated to the performance of early and contemporary music.

Allaudin was a disciple of a North Indian vocalist, Pandit Pran Nath, for twenty-five years. He studied African music with Nubian musician Hamza El Din, jazz with William Russo, and European classical music with Easley Blackwood. In 1958

Allaudin received his BA from the University of Chicago. In the 1960s he spent several years as an arranger-composer for Stan Kenton and Duke Ellington, was the musical director for the Second City Theater (which he helped found) in Chicago, and the Committee Theater in San Francisco. In the 1970s he taught theory, composition, and improvisation on the faculties of the San Francisco Conservatory of Music and Mills College. In 1969 he founded the Sufi Choir, which he directed until 1982. The last three decades have been devoted to composition, writing, performance, recording, and teaching from his home in Sebastopol, California.

His Web site is ColdMountainMusic.com.

You can contact Allaudin Mathieu through Shambhala Publications, or by writing to P.O. Box 912, Sebastopol, CA 95473, or by sending an e-mail to info@ColdMountainMusic.com.